Two Summers at the Tests

TWO SUMMERS AT THE TESTS

ENGLAND v SOUTH AFRICA 1947
ENGLAND v AUSTRALIA 1948

JOHN ARLOTT

THE PAVILION LIBRARY

First published in the Pavilion Library in 1986 by
Pavilion Books Limited
196 Shaftesbury Avenue, London WC2H 8JL
in association with Michael Joseph Limited
44 Bedford Square, London WC1B 3DP

British Library Cataloguing in Publication Data
Arlott, John
Two summers at the tests.
1. Test matches (Cricket)—England—History
I. Title
796.35'865   GV928.G7

ISBN 1 85145 018 1
ISBN 1 85145 019 X paperback

Printed and bound in Great Britain by
Billings and Sons Limited, Worcester

INTRODUCTION

To read this book for this Pavilion Library reprint—or resurrection—was like looking down the wrong end of a telescope: everything was distant—yet wholly clear. The naïveté of almost forty years ago is blush-making; but the enthusiasm, the identification with the players, the transcendent enjoyment—almost revelling—in the new post-war euphoria, the hunger for everything the eye can see, is bitterly nostalgic. Even more poignant is the pang at the frequent references—conjuring up warm, sad memories—to old friends, alive in the book, but now dead.

Enough of sentimentality. These were stirring days. Pataudi senior's Indians of 1946 had ushered in post-1945 cricket almost before anyone realized it; before many people had come back to the game; and before many had truly taken in the advent of peace. It had sunk in only slowly; the true post-war cricket awakening came to England in 1947.

The old Cardusian image from the latter part of the nineteenth century rattles in the mind; how, when the news reached the London clubs that W. G. Grace was not out at lunch, St John's Wood Road became a long procession of hansom cabs as the clubmen made their way to watch him. Through their golden summer of 1947 Denis Compton and Bill Edrich exerted a similar attraction, not merely over the clubmen with no work to do, but everyone who could find a dead uncle—or even a sick aunt—as an alibi to escape work and watch those two go their eventful and—lest it be forgotten—record-breaking way which was their, and our, pleasure through that long summer of sunshine.

Rationing was still in force; most drinks were in short supply; there were shortages, disorganization and a thousand petty left-over irritations; but none of them really mattered; it was, indeed, a summer of sun.

There was, too, so much to be relished; perhaps the cricketers were not, Cardus-fashion, larger than life, but from their very freshness and refreshedness, they seemed so. There was Len Hutton, all scholarly care as he bent over his work; Cyril Washbrook, cap a-cock, patrolling the covers as threatening as he was jaunty. Charlie Barnett—too little seen, Jack Young and, above all, Godfrey Evans bursting with the joy of it all; for cricket in that, of all summers, was not a care-worn—nor even a technological—matter, but the enjoyment of men happily back in the game where they belonged. Doug Wright bounded back, most exciting of bowlers; every ball a lottery ticket, but drawn with unique skill; Norman Yardley a companionable, refreshingly old-fashioned—in the best sense—captain. Still, though, it was pre-eminently the summer of Compton and Edrich. Denis Compton reducing batting to the level of human fallibility and then rescuing it by some apparent afterthought which proved to be a stroke of genius; and all performed with a gusto which echoed all round the ground. Bill Edrich, belligerent, competitive, hurling himself in to bowl in a quite prodigal burst of fury; and batting as if life depended upon it, yet still determined to ride his own particular whirlwind.

The South Africans, not yet bedevilled by Apartheid, under a captain—Alan Melville—as stylish a person as a batsman; and with a background of Oxford and Sussex which made him already a familiar figure on English grounds. Dudley Nourse, his vice-captain, four-square, competitive; very much a South African and always a hard nut to crack. Bruce Mitchell, the thoughtful, patient defender; Ossie Dawson, of the languid outswingers and polished batting style; Tony Harris, an arch enjoyer of his cricket. Then their philosopher bowlers; not one of them had a Test average below 40 in that series! Lindsay Tuckett, tall, loose-limbed and unfailingly good-natured, a valuable fast medium swing and cut merchant; Norman—'Tufty'—Mann, so soon and so tragically to die, who wheeled away slow left-arm and spun and planned and never wavered; and Athol Rowan, perhaps the finest of post-war off-spinners; tall, fair, good-looking and quizzical, he was K-legged from a war wound. In 1959–60 he routed Lindsay Hassett's Australians at Johannesburg—9 for 19, 16 for 58 in the match—before that leg wound put him out for the rest of the season and ended his cricket after the following tour of England. The cricket was full of goodwill.

If the 1947 summer left English followers confident, that of 1948 deflated them. It was yet another Bradman season and the crowds rolled up as they had done before the war; and he did not fail them. In Tests he made 508 runs at 72.57; Arthur Morris and Syd Barnes had better averages; but only Morris scored more runs; and, if the Don sometimes started an innings uncertainly, once into action he was as authoritative as ever.

Yet Ray Lindwall and Keith Miller stole the show. As in 1921, when Gregory and MacDonald were the destroyers, English batting after a war was starved of experience against high pace; and these two compared with any pair of fast bowlers we had seen. Lindwall, genuinely fast, was as resourceful as any slow bowler with his changes of pace, yorker, bouncers—and bouncers 'that didn't'—late swing, slower ball; every artifice. Keith Miller most surely captured the public imagination; superbly athletic, he was an immense drawcard with a huge following among the ladies and whole-hearted admiration from the men, too. He commanded high pace, and constant surprise; he would start to walk back to his mark and, after two or three strides, whip round and bowl at full pace; or, off his full run, deliver, at slow pace, not simply a leg-break but a blind length googly. A genuine all-rounder at Test level, he struck the ball splendidly and enjoyed his cricket even when he came straight to the dressing-room in his evening dress from the night before; he lived life and cricket like a millionaire.

The West Indians in recent years have accustomed us to the fast bowling battery; but when Bradman threw in Lindwall, Miller, Bill Johnston (perhaps the most under-rated of modern Test bowlers) and Sam Loxton at Headingley, cricketing England was, to say the least, surprised: though, of course, Jardine had done something similar at Melbourne on the 1932–33—'Bodyline'—tour when he used Larwood, Voce, Allen and Bowes—plus Hammond who was lively when he chose.

These years later, Australia won massively; the book gives the cruel margins; yet England after the war did not resent it as they might—indeed, would—nowadays. There was—and even at this time-range, it is inescapable—a kind of back-handed glory in it all. The Australians captured the imagination of all cricketing England: not only Bradman, Lindwall and Miller but all these other characters like that versatile bowler and gloriously comic tail-end batsman, Bill Johnston; the phlegmatic Ernie Toshack who kept an end going while the fast bowlers rested; the boyish-looking and instantly likeable Neil Harvey; that miniaturist batsman and dry joker, Lindsay Hassett. Their fielding, too, was in the great Australian tradition with Miller spectacularly acrobatic at slip, Harvey fast and sure-handed in the country; Barnes quite dangerously brave at short-leg, and Don Tallon a masterly, prehensile and unobtrusive wicket-keeper.

England, too, had her heroes; and at Headingley at least they had a glimpse—brief but positive—of winning. Denis Compton, especially at Old Trafford, established the position in the public imagination that he had first made in 1947; Len Hutton, thoughtful and reliable—heroic at The Oval—as he and Cyril Washbrook bore the brunt of that great opening attack as promise of the success they were to achieve in South Africa during the following winter there. Neither should we forget those game tail-enders—Godfrey Evans, Jim Laker and Alec Bedser—doing rather more than keeping their ends up. Through all that story, too, runs the thread of Alec Bedser's terrific bowling labours, solid, sweating, never flagging, often almost alone in keeping the English attack sharp, and taking twice as many Australian wickets as the next man.

Looking back from 1985, it seems a different world—as of course it was—a world of great figures—were they not?—or was it but a young(ish) man's enthusiasm that made them seem so? No, it was not; they were.

TWO SUMMERS
AT THE TESTS

ENGLAND *v* SOUTH AFRICA 1947

ENGLAND *v* AUSTRALIA   1948

by

JOHN ARLOTT

THE SPORTSMAN'S BOOK CLUB

(1)

GONE TO THE CRICKET

Being primarily an account of
the Test Series of 1947.

To
MY FATHER
Who knows nothing about cricket
and cares less but who was
wery good to me

CONTENTS

THE STORY OF THE PLAY

'NO, he's not at home; he's gone to the cricket,' my mother used to say. Now my wife uses the same words.

The words are the same, the state of mind is the same; only my destination is different, and that only differs geographically. Then, those years ago, I might be gone, with my cut-down bat, to play in the field of vetches. Later, with my narrow flannels, my uncle's old white shoes, and my single pad, I would be gone to our improvised net on the bumpiest piece of land on which boys ever tried to bowl fast. Or to school cricket, form or house—or to THE NET at school. This was no common net—it was planned by that same John Wilson whom I have only just recognized as my old schoolmaster after working in the same building with him for two years. It was matting stretched over wood; it resented spin, but the ball came off speedily to the delight of those who stepped up to drive. To be allowed upon it was the sign of the school captain's favour. Or my mother might be explaining that one of my long-planned trips to the County Ground at Southampton was taking place: there I would sit absorbed in every ball of the day from 11.30 to 6.30— my eyes not leaving the game even while I ate my cucumber sandwiches impossibly early at half-past twelve —my hand worked automatically until only crumbs were left. After I had left school it could mean that I was on my annual holiday, watching cricket with John on a carefully planned route which granted the shortest journeys between matches consistent with sight of the greatest number of county teams in ten days. It might mean, must mean, on every Saturday afternoon of the season except the holiday Saturday, that I was gone to open the innings with John, scoring one to his ten, but staying as long as he did and batting with the ugliest style ever seen on a cricket field. For a brief period of intoxicating joy it meant that I was away with the Hampshire side, permitted to field as twelfth man—or that I was playing evening and Sunday matches in Worcestershire.

Now, on summer days, my wife will explain to you, with the aid of a scribbled list, that I am in Taunton, that I go from Taunton to Swansea, from Swansea to Birmingham, and from Birmingham to Cheltenham, but that I shall be back the night before the Oval Test—or the day before that if the spinners get to work at Cheltenham. If her list doesn't seem clear, then the office, with a little confirmation from Outside Broadcasting Department, will place me somewhere on the map of England. For more than twenty years now I have been 'gone to the cricket' upon the slightest opportunity. And now, as cold winds indicate that the cricket season is about to commence, I am gone to the cricket again. Tomorrow the South African tour opens on the ground which I can see across the Severn from my bedroom merely by lifting my head.

The cricket season of 1947 is to be, primarily, a year of England versus South Africa. The domestic scene will be chiefly concerned with the question as to whether a re-constituted Yorkshire side can retain the championship against a strong Middlesex eleven: Gloucester, Derbyshire, Somerset, and Lancashire, the four strongest bowling sides, are the outsiders.

For England the season is to show whether a side can

be found to challenge Australia in England in 1948. Of the party to tour Australia during last winter there are a number of certain non-starters for Test cricket. Only eight survivors of that party are to be considered—the first four batsmen—Hutton, Washbrook, Edrich, and Compton (virtual certainties for any England side for probably eight years to come)—two bowlers, Wright and Bedser (the former probably the best bowler in the world and the latter young enough, strong enough, and keen enough to improve with experience)—and a wicket-keeper, in Evans, good enough to serve England for another ten years. Yardley is, apparently, to succeed Hammond as captain; a pleasant personality, a useful bat, a brilliant fieldsman, and a bowler known to take good wickets. Ikin, an all-rounder who now rarely bowls, a world-ranking fieldsman, and a batsman of courage, is, obviously, going to have to produce hundreds instead of fifties, or lose his place. Of the players who did not make the trip, there are plenty of batsmen to demand consideration for places already satisfactorily filled—Brookes, Avery, Robertson, Dollery, Barnett, Simpson, Watson, and Place among them. Martin of Kent, who was successful in the 1946 Test Trial, is the chief challenger for the place of pace bowler. The slow left-arm Young and Cook and the off-breakers Knott and Robinson, leg-spinner Hollies and all-rounder Howorth, have only to produce honest achievement at the right time to command a place in the England side for at least one Test. The way is open for any young cricketer who can show honest achievement to walk into the England side: never since 1921, if even then, has the opportunity been so patent.

For South Africa the situation is different. Their selectors, unlike the English selectors of 1946, have been prepared to give young cricketers a chance, to look to the future; in other words, to *build a team*. Their selected seventeen players for the tour are:

Alan Melville (Transvaal), 36, captain: batsman.
A. D. Nourse (Natal), 36, vice-captain: batsman.
Bruce Mitchell (Transvaal), 38: batsman; bowls occasionally.
K. G. Viljoen (Transvaal), 36: batsman.
A. Rowan (Transvaal), 25: off-break bowler; fair bat.
J. Lindsay (North-eastern Province), 38: wicket-keeper.
N. Mann (Eastern Province), 26: slow left-arm bowler.
J. Plimsoll (Western Province), 29: fast-medium left-arm bowler.
D. Dyer (Natal), 32: batsman.
O. C. Dawson (Natal), 28: medium-pace bowler and batsman.
L. Tuckett (Orange Free State), 27: fast-medium bowler.
G. Fullerton (Transvaal), 24: batsman; can keep wicket.
T. A. Harris (Transvaal), 30: batsman.
D. Begbie (Transvaal), 28: batsman and leg-spin bowler.
V. I. Smith (Natal), 21: leg-spin bowler.
L. Payn (Natal), 32: slow left-arm bowler.
D. Ovenstone (Western Province), 25: wicket-keeper.

It is an interesting and well-balanced side; the fielding is bound to be good; there is, in Fullerton, a possible third wicket-keeper, lest the side have the same misfortune as the Indian party of the previous year, which, at one period, had both its wicket-keepers injured and was using its opening bowler to keep wicket. Of this team Dyer, Rowan, Mann, Dawson, Fullerton, Begbie, Smith, and

Ovenstone, eight of the seventeen, have been picked with an eye to the future.

The only worry is the weather. The season of 1946 showed that gates will be near to capacity everywhere and that only weather can mar the tour. April the 29th—nets-in-the-rain and the Worcester floods have receded into old history and the season starts tomorrow.

A summer of touring last year taught me to pack the essentials for a four-day match into a brief-case—those 'essentials' did not include an overcoat—and, as the wind howls across the hills and reaches me here, sharp-edged as a Wright googly, I regret the omission, but I am warmed by the fact that I am gone to the cricket once more.

JOHN ARLOTT.

WORCESTERSHIRE *v.* SOUTH AFRICA

Played at Worcester on April 30th, May 1st and 2nd, 1947

THE touring side's first match—now established as taking place at Worcester—has become the formal and fashionable opening of the English season. In the first post-war season, Worcester beat the Indian touring side after a very close game. For 1947, however, they lacked A. P. Singleton, now tobacco-planting in Rhodesia, who had captained them in the previous year. Singleton was probably the best captain in England in 1946, and in the first match of that season had opened each innings successfully, taken a vital wicket, fielded brilliantly, and captained his side thoughtfully. Alan White, for all his courage and the attractiveness of his batting, could hardly hope at once to replace so good an all-rounder. Also missing as compared with the 1946 side against India was 'Doc' Gibbons—for so many years the neat and painstaking backbone of the Worcester batting—and Buller, the old-hand wicket-keeper, now replaced by young Hugo Yarnold. R. E. S. Wyatt, however, added experience and a suggestion of mellow distinction to this year's team.

The South Africans fielded what must have been roughly—roughly because at such long range and without local tests—the combination envisaged by the selectors as the first-choice eleven for the Tests. Melville, its most experienced batsman, had with him four solid batsmen, the senior wicket-keeper, two pacers (one right-arm, one left-), a slow off-breaker, a slow left-armer, and an all-rounder who bowled the leg-break and googly.

15

Alan White won the toss and orthodoxly decided to bat in the grey light.

The Severn water had receded from its invasion of the ground and from its ten-foot mark high on the pavilion bar, to its normal charted channel, leaving only a white ghost's robe on trees and walls and buildings to tell of its record-breaking rise of only a few weeks before, but traces of it were expected to be found still lurking in the wicket.

Tuckett, fast-medium right-arm with ease and power, opened the South African bowling with Plimsoll, less fast than Tuckett, left-arm, bringing the ball into the batsman and persuading it off the pitch to the limit of hope on the deadish wicket. The first two Worcester batsmen were the brothers Cooper—Eddie, an established county batsman who threatens to become more than ordinary, and Fred, formerly on the Lancashire ground-staff and playing his first game for the county. There was only the forbidding weather to show that the early stages of the game did not belong to June rather than April. The ball was landing regularly 'there or thereabouts,' the batsmen leant upon it unhurriedly and with certainty, if not with aggression. The first twenty minutes passed in the time-honoured method of mutual inspection. The shine spent itself on the off-mud of the wicket and the spectators settled back into their overcoats, pulled collars and mufflers about their ears, and prepared to 'enjoy the cricket.'

The first South African bowling change brought on Rowan. The sight of an off-spinner after the 1946 successes of every off-break bowler in England arrested attention—and then retained it. Rowan bowled the two Coopers at once; Tuckett had Kenyon caught at the wicket before that batsman had time to discover whether or not he liked his bat, and then Rowan bowled R. E. S. Wyatt. Tuckett retired for Norman Mann, slow left-arm, who at once clean bowled Howorth. Worcester were now 37 for 5, and there were enquiries at the secretary's office regarding return trains on Thursday—and the caterers wondered.

Alan White lacks the resources of more experienced batsmen in defence, but he puts a strong and usually straight bat to the ball in attack and is not visibly afraid of the turning ball—nor, apparently, disconcerted when he plays it off the edge. He and Bird remained in occupation despite Rowan, Mann, rain, sleet, and the Novemberish light. Bird blended courage, a sharp eye, and not undeserved luck—he was abetted by White, a surprisingly correct Yarnold, and by Jenkins, who gave his now celebrated imitation of a veteran batsman playing himself in in a Test Match. In the end Bird had 79, Worcester 202, and the spectators some hope of a three-day match. Rowan, with four of the first five Worcester wickets, and, in all, 5 for 39, had a good first day: he bowled his off-breaks just below medium pace to a good length with varied flight and appreciable spin.

When South Africa batted the perennial Perks bowled high, hostilely, and vigorously from the road end to Dyer and Mitchell until Mitchell played too late to a sharp inswinger; but the monumental Dyer and Viljoen batted successfully for Thursday morning and South Africa seemed to be starting to bat their way into the 1947 season.

Score at end of first day:
    Worcestershire (*first innings*) 202.
    South Africa (*first innings*) 50 *for* 1 *wicket.*

Thursday, May 1

The electric light over the pavilion bar shone like a beacon across the dark ground when Dyer and Viljoen

went out to start the second day on a wicket damp
enough to encourage and transmit spin. While the spectators were still experimenting in elementary draught-
exclusion, Viljoen followed an outswinger from Jackson
as if hypnotized, for Wyatt to give another of his object-
lessons in slip-catching—advanced course 'One-handed
with ease.' Dyer was majestic, playing slowly, but with a
confidence and correctness which promised many runs
indeed when experience and warming-up should lead
him to more profitable strokes. In the cold morning
Perks and Jackson, aided by a light several candle-power
below questionable, bowled down wickets right and left.
There was little to remark of the South African batsmen.
Only Rowan (nervously), Lindsay (anxiously), and
Mann (riotously) gave numerical significance to the
death-throes of the South African innings, which was
punctuated by rain and ended for 165, leaving Worcester
a windfall lead of 37 runs.

During the lunch interval the sun appeared, as if to dispel current rumour, but also for sinister purpose. The
Cooper brothers followed the roller to the wicket and
met the initial seam-employment of Tuckett and Plimsoll
with considerable assurance and some indication of their
Lancashire origins. They played down the line of the ball,
pushed to leg, dabbed to third man, and never seemed
hurried in stroke while, with slight assistance from extras,
they put on 44 for the first wicket. But then sun superseded roller in influence over the wicket. Rowan dismissed both Coopers once more, and Kenyon, without
assistance from his fieldsmen. Then he caught Wyatt off
Mann, who went on to take the wickets of White,
Howorth, and Yarnold. With 7 wickets down for 83,
Worcester had lost their advantage.

Neither side had batted well against steady spin bowling on a turning wicket. The South African batsmen might be excused on the grounds that some of them had never before encountered such a wicket, and that the remainder had to attempt to recall their experience from a distance of twelve years. The Worcester batsmen, however, on a wicket of a type prevalent throughout 1946, had failed completely to bat in the manner which ought to be within the command of every regular English county player. South Africa seemed now to be in a winning position.

Score at end of second day:
   Worcestershire 202 and 83 for 7 wickets.
   South Africa 167.

Friday, May 2

Bird and Jenkins held up Rowan and Mann for a few overs and tarnished their bowling figures to a slight degree before the Worcester innings ended for 111. South Africa wanted 147 to win and had all the time in the world in which to make them. Perks and Jackson swung the shine off the ball: then Jackson switched to off-breaks. He was joined by Howorth, who moved sleepily up to the wicket and seemed to turn his arm barely strongly enough to propel the ball the length of the wicket to the length spot where his break-away occurred. Jenkins crept closer and closer to the batsman at silly mid-off, until it seemed that a good swing, even if it missed the ball, would decapitate the fieldsman. Dyer had looked so permanent that it was surprising to find that he had scored only 12 when he was out.

Nourse and Melville carried their responsibilities carefully. Nourse dropped his bat very late on the turning ball and watched it savagely as it rolled slowly back to the bowler. Melville produced an off-drive which we recognized with delight. But Jenkins caught Nourse, and crept still nearer to the bat. Begbie played a shot worth four runs towards extra cover, only to see that Jenkins had caught it at inception and was moving still closer. Rowan struggled, but the spinners were on top all the time. A hitter might have saved South Africa—Mann made a gesture in that direction, but fell, playing back— and Worcester had again beaten a touring side. They had been favoured by the light and the pitch, but their work in the field had been excellent. Even thus early in the tour, on the evidence of Tuckett, Rowan, and Mann, it seemed that the South African bowling would win most of the side's matches provided only that the batting did not throw them away.

WORCESTERSHIRE *v*. SOUTH AFRICA

Worcester, April 30, May 1 and 2

Worcestershire

Cooper (E.), b Rowan	.	12	lbw b Rowan	.	22
Cooper (F.), b Rowan	.	3	b Rowan	.	20
Kenyon, c Lindsay b Tuckett	2	b Rowan	.	3
R. E. S. Wyatt, b Rowan	2	c Rowan b Mann	.	1
A. F. T. White, lbw b Rowan	25	c Melville b Mann	.	2
Howorth, b Mann	.	0	c Dyer b Mann	.	9
R. E. Bird, b Tuckett	.	79	c Nourse b Rowan	.	13
Yarnold, c Dyer b Mann	.	25	c Melville b Mann	.	4
Jenkins, b Rowan	.	27	b Mann	.	17
Perks, c Begbie b Mann	.	3	st Lindsay b Rowan	0
Jackson, not out	.	6	not out	.	5
Extras	.	18	Extras	.	15
Total	.	202	Total	.	111

Bowling Analysis

	O	M	R	W		O	M	R	W
Tuckett	20	8	38	2	...	7	1	13	0
Plimsoll	7	2	29	0	...	10	5	13	0
Rowan	30	11	59	5	...	20.5	6	34	5
Mann	21	6	40	3	...	24	10	36	5
Begbie	4	0	18	0					

South Africa

B. Mitchell, b Perks	3	c Jackson b Howorth	9
D. Dyer, c Bird b Perks	26	c Yarnold b Jackson	12
K. G. Viljoen, c Wyatt b Jackson	26	lbw b Jackson	2
D. Nourse, b Jackson	0	c Jenkins b Howorth	16
A. Melville, b Perks	8	b Jackson	14
D. Begbie, c Perks b Jackson	0	c Jenkins b Howorth	8
A. Rowan, lbw b Parks	28	b Howorth	14
L. Tuckett, st Yarnold b Howorth	8	lbw b Jackson	9
J. Lindsay, not out	15	not out	7
N. Mann, b Perks	19	b Howorth	6
J. Plimsoll, b Jackson	8	b Howorth	0
Extras	26	Extras	10
Total	167	Total	107

Bowling Analysis

	O	M	R	W		O	M	R	W
Perks	30	8	66	5	...	3	1	6	0
Jackson	32	12	63	4	...	29	9	53	4
Howorth	15	9	7	1	...	27.2	11	38	6
Jenkins	7	4	5	0					

Worcestershire won by 39 runs.

THE FIRST TEST MATCH

Played at Nottingham, June 7th, 9th, 10th and 11th, 1947

NEITHER side can have faced the first Test Match with a great amount of confidence. The South Africans had frequently batted so unhappily that their bowling had needed to be magnificent to save them. They had lost to Worcestershire and the M.C.C., but had achieved some good wins against opponents just short of first class. Melville had scored several hundreds, Viljoen, Nourse, and Mitchell (2) had also made centuries. Dawson and Harris had hit hard to the sixties, but the batting had rarely seemed solid against keen bowling. The previous match, against Northamptonshire, had settled one problem for them—the selection of the wicket-keeper. The Northampton wicket was of a 'greenness' to make the injured and resting Northants seam bowlers Clark and Partridge shake their heads and rue their inability to bowl on it. Plimsoll and Dawson came awkwardly off the pitch, but Lindsay 'took' them magnificently and with the stamp of a class wicket-keeper, to make his place for the first Test certain. Despite Plimsoll's good figures in that match, the state of the team's batting did not allow him to be included: Dawson, a batsman and a magnificent fieldsman, would open with the new ball. Tuckett, Rowan, and Mann had bowled their way into any Test Match, and Smith spun the leg-break so hard that it would turn on anything, so he also went into the side.

England selected twelve men for the match. Yardley was appointed captain; Washbrook, Hutton Compton, and Edrich, all in form, were automatic batting selections; Evans is the established England wicket-keeper,

despite the good form of Haydn Davies; and Bedser and
Wright, like the four batsmen, deservedly held their
places from the Australian tour. Hollies, the Warwick
leg-spinner, was also chosen. Cook, the Gloucestershire
slow left-arm bowler, had won his place by his good
bowling for the M.C.C. at Lord's. Dollery was the one of
the six possible batsmen eventually chosen for No. 5, and
J. W. Martin came in as an opening bowler *faute de mieux*
and for old times' sake. Wright was the player of the
England twelve to be omitted. Comment here should be
restricted to pointing out that the only justification for his
omission would be that the selectors, confident of being
able to win the match easily, were giving Hollies a chance
to show whether he could replace the best leg-break and
googly bowler in the world against the possibility of
Wright being unfit to play in a match against Australia in
1948.

First Day—Saturday, June 7

I like to go to Trent Bridge. It is a clean, business-like
ground, the arrangements are tidy and have no edge of
officiousness. Perhaps it is so easy to feel at home there
because it is a ground where the old players come back to
the pavilion as by right and are welcomed. At this game
there was Tom Wass, legendary bowler of fast leg-breaks
(with C. B. Fry there to vouch for the fact) with his two
spinning fingers wedged in the palm of his hand beyond
the strength to extract. There too, was George Gunn,
savouring some profound joke, Tich Richmond, round
and jolly as ever, Jack Moss, surely the oldest living umpire, Bill Voce, relaxed at last, Sam and Arthur Staples,
Bill Flint—and Arthur Carr always expected but not arriv-
ing. Such a team of pavilion oracles any critic might desire.

Melville won the toss and smiled at the wicket—which

seemed to smile back. Melville, graciously interpreting this as an invitation, chose to bat. Umpires Smart and Coleman came priest-like down the pavilion steps, to be greeted by a shower of rain: to preserve the Test Match whiteness of their coats they returned to the pavilion for twenty minutes before starting play.

J. W. Martin, precise and military, hair parted dead centre and brushed at right-angles, his trousers just short and narrow of normal, with squared shoulders and the gait of at least a major, commenced the bowling from the Ratcliffe Road end. Knees up and elbows out, he advanced to the wicket, increasing his speed, to the yard before the crease; there he checked, and then delivered the first ball of the match to Mitchell, who stood rather timidly at the opposite crease. Mitchell promptly smote it between cover point and third man for four runs and then turned his back on the scene as if ashamed to admit such an act at so solemn a time. Martin's next ball decided, only inches before pitching outside the off stump, to be an inswinger; it darted across the wicket, beat Mitchell, the leg stump, Evans standing back, and long leg, to continue to the boundary for four byes. A gentleman enquired whether *Wisden* contained 'records' like eight off the first two balls of a Test. Martin's next ball decided, equally late, to be an outswinger and snarled away outside the off stump. In the remaining four-days-all-but-twenty-five minutes, Mr. Martin was not observed to attain anything further startling in the way of deviation from straight. Bedser at the other end showed a greater sense of the fitness of things in a Test Match. With an arm seeming better lubricated in the shoulder-joint than before his tour of Australia, he began with three maiden overs of irritation. Martin continued to check his run at the vital moment, but to wheel his arm furiously: he was pushed for singles to deprive him of the consoling symmetry of maiden overs.

Mitchell went about the whole business of opening with the practised formality of a head-waiter at the start of a banquet. Melville, however, wore a slightly unnatural donnish air of concentration as compared with the gaiety of his Sussex days. Absentmindedly he edged a ball fine and sharp to Evans and Evans did not catch it. In place of Martin, Edrich now ran fast and on a low centre of gravity to the wicket and propelled the ball even faster and lower to commence with two maiden overs of sheer fury. Twenty-three runs had come, decorously, unhurriedly, and solemnly earned, before Bedser, departing from his habit and the current fashion of the inswinger, made one go the other way, to the surprise of Mitchell, who was bowled by it. Viljoen, who always looks worried, may have been less worried than he looked as he concentrated on taking lunch not out. Forty-four for one wicket ruined no appetites at lunch, which was a most pleasant meal. Immediately after that ceremony Viljoen was lbw to Edrich—which also *hurts*. Nourse had with him, for the opening stages of his innings, a bat made entirely of edge: for ten minutes he reflexed violently, lastminuted, scratched and scraped, but he stayed.

The Trent Bridge wicket, ever since the day of Shrewsbury, has been known as one on which only patient cricketers should play. The patient batsman may be sure that runs will come, the patient bowler will feel less temptation to suicide than one more anxious in temper. The wicket prepared for the first Test might have been regarded by batsmen as a form of superannuation—providing an income of runs without anxiety. Nourse and Melville spent a sheltered time upon it after the slight shocks of their settling down. In their contrasted styles they went down the sunny afternoon. Melville seems to feel warmly towards a cricket ball. This day he stroked it, persuaded it, or, even at his most violent, did little more than guide it gently. Nourse, on the other hand, obviously regards a 'Match Special' with a certain degree of hostility. After his early narrow escapes from its machinations he watched it with a grim suspicion. He would glare at it and bolt the door of his defence against it, or he would suddenly, sharply, as if with intent to take it by surprise, deal it a terrific blow with the full strength of his mighty forearms. Once when Bedser sent the ball to him he hit it back to him with such forceful dislike that it went racing on to the pavilion rails. This occurrence caused a number of elderly gentlemen to recall Maclaren and Fry forcing pace-bowlers to post fieldsmen for the drive; but Nourse was obviously thinking solely of the present. Hollies bowled with a round, rolling manner and leg-break and googly spins, which were, on this wicket, suggested rather than exhibited.

'Sam' Cook of Gloucester did not bowl in his first Test Match until Melville and Nourse saw hundreds clearly before them. Cook, brought up as a cricketer on wickets where the ball turns in the direction of spin applied, found this wicket as responsive as a slab of marble. As he bowled, the conviction must have grown upon him that more than usual was required of him. So he bowled a little faster, tried to make a ball or two go with his arm, once tried to bowl the inswinger. He became barely recognizable as the man who had spun so accurately at Lord's. He bowled a full-pitch to Melville, who waved his bat gently and dispatched the ball into the crowd sitting in the region of the square leg, where, on less formal occasions than a Test Match, there is a car park. Tea came and went. Time seemed to be marked only by the lengthening shadows and the climbing South African total. Then Melville mistimed a drive, but by the time Martin had moved off his heels and set off in pursuit of it, it was barely a chance.

The steady procession of the England bowlers went on —Martin with a fury blandly purloined by the pitch, Bedser with that patience in face of adversity which the Australian tour taught him, Edrich with the belief that he was about to take a wicket implicit in his every action, Hollies with a gentle arc of flight, Cook with a worried frown, and even Yardley, with memories of having bowled Bradman—but giving no indication of how he achieved that feat. Then Nourse, with the idea of hitting Hollies in the general direction of the Trent, moved across his wicket and was bowled round his legs. All the critics-by-the-grace-of-*Wisden* told one another that 319 was the record for the wicket in Test cricket—and several other things. Before the day ended at seven o'clock, Dawson had a few minutes left in which to identify himself in South Africa's 376 for 3 wickets—which could hardly be anything but happy for them. The English bowling had rarely looked more than steady, sometimes less; the fielding was rarely more than tidy, sometimes less; the wicket-keeping of Evans was good, but he might have taken two difficult chances.

South Africa—First Innings

A. Melville, not out	. . . .	183
B. Mitchell, b Bedser	. . .	14
K. G. Viljoen, lbw b Edrich	. .	10
D. Nourse, b Hollies	. . .	149
O. C. Dawson, not out	. . .	3
Extras (b 6 l-b 10, w 1)	.	17
Total (for 3 wkts)	.	376

Fall of Wickets

1	2	3
23	44	363

Second Day—Monday, June 9

The day had hardly started when Melville leant forward to a ball from Martin and played a stroke which lacked his concentration of Saturday. He was bowled, to make way for the intrepid Tony Harris, who prefers fielding to the cares of Test Match batting. But with four hundred up and Dawson playing on his best level of elegance, Harris looked for delights and found them. Dawson played the off-drive in most handsome fashion, Harris preferred the cover-drive, but also produced some cuts of a sound vintage. There was a very strong breeze blowing across the ground towards the nearest stretch of the Trent when Hollies was put on to bowl at the pavilion end. Now, Hollies tosses the ball fairly high, and he found that the breeze would carry the ball beginning on the off stump across to the leg. Once arrived there, the spin would tend (no more than tend on this still bedlike wicket) to take it back again towards the off stump. At 450 he had Dawson stumped: at 505 Harris hit out at him to give Hutton a comparatively easy catch, and Tuckett was immediately lbw. Bedser took Mann and Lindsay, and Hollies got Smith. Rowan was left high and dry with 34, and South Africa were all out 533. Only 157 runs added for the 7 Monday wickets, but a heartening total. And, screamed the man with *Wisden*—a record. It had cost the English bowlers five hundred runs to cut their way through to the South African tail. Never before in the tour had the consciously unreliable South African batting seemed so steady.

The South African fielders who followed the umpires

at the start of the English innings wore a happy and certain look with better reason than in any earlier match of the tour. Hutton and Washbrook, opening the batting, wore a humbler air, but went about the opening minutes with an air of experience. Tuckett looked a good opening bowler on a batsman's wicket, and Dawson, slower and less penetrative, compelled respect because he bowled the now almost obsolete outswinger, and interest because he bowled it with an action pleasing to the eye.

Hutton batted as if with the certain knowledge that the first possible slice of ill-fortune would cut him off. Washbrook played a number of balls deliberately with his body —preferring to allow the inswinger to hit him rather than hit it. They were still together when Melville, deciding that the amount of shine needed by Dawson no longer remained on the ball, accordingly brought on Rowan. The first stage of the task of opening batsmen is to see the new-ball bowlers off, and this had been accomplished. Did this lead to some degree of relaxation on the part of the batsmen? Washbrook clouted Rowan's first ball for four, looked at the next, pushed the third away for one, and gave the bowling to Hutton. Now, Hutton's batting had been that of a master batsman struggling against something which is not vulnerable to his weapons. His first ball from Rowan swung out just a little, suggested a dip, and then straightened—and Hutton was lbw. Washbrook hit another four off Rowan before he died the death of a true Lancashire man—both pads in front to Tuckett's inswinger.

Forty-eight for two in face of 533 caused Edrich to frown even more seriously than usual as he went to tea with Compton. After tea Mann came on to bowl: slow left, with no man in the deep. His first eight overs were maidens and his fieldsmen ventured close indeed to the

usually punitive bats of Edrich and Compton. With
Rowan also bowling a couple of maidens, the atmosphere
seemed to be warmer and closer than the thermometer
showed. Then Compton hit Rowan for three fierce fours
in an over and the tension slackened. This problem of
Edrich and Compton had been recognized by Melville
after Compton's innings for the M.C.C. and their dual
efforts in the game with Middlesex. Melville had plans at
least for keeping them quiet. Mann's field in particular
was placed with meticulous accuracy, and he, blandly, at
times impudently, bowled to it. At seven o'clock Compton and Edrich were still there after a subdued spell of
batting in which responsibility was borne with conscious
gravity.

This was South Africa's day once again. They had
made their morning runs, through Harris, Dawson, and
Rowan, gaily and, with an impregnable total behind
them, had bowled with thought. Tuckett, on a pitch
which gave him no help, always bowled a length and at
the wicket. Mann and Rowan used subtle flight and a
provocative length to keep the English batsmen always
fighting to prevent a poor position from deteriorating
further. The Springbok fieldsmen had inherited the
initiative from their batsmen and retained it because they
remained on their toes in carefully estimated positions.
Compton and Edrich together at the end of the day was
the only warming thought for the English supporters.
The placid wicket remained slightly bored, showing no
disposition towards haste.

South Africa—First Innings

A. Melville, b Martin	189
B. Mitchell, b Bedser	14
K. G. Viljoen, lbw b Edrich . . .	10
D. Nourse, b Hollies	149
O. C. Dawson, st Evans b Hollies . .	48
T. A. Harris, c Hutton b Hollies . .	60
A. Rowan, not out	34
L. Tuckett, lbw b Hollies . . .	0
N. Mann, b Bedser	8
J. Lindsay, b Bedser	0
V. I. Smith, c Yardley b Hollies . .	1
Extras (b 7, l-b 12, w 1) .	20
Total .	533

Bowling Analysis—First Innings

	O	M	R	W
Martin . . .	36	4	111	1
Bedser . . .	58	14	106	3
Edrich . . .	20	8	56	1
Hollies . . .	55.2	16	123	5
Cook . . .	21	4	87	0
Yardley . .	5	0	24	0
Compton . .	2	1	6	0

Fall of Wickets

1	2	3	4	5	6	7	8	9	10
23	44	363	384	450	505	505	528	530	533

England—First Innings

Hutton, lbw b Rowan	17
Washbrook, lbw b Tuckett . . .	25
W. J. Edrich, not out	44
Compton, not out	65
Extras (l-b 2, w 1) .	3

Total (for 2 wkts) . 154

Fall of Wickets

1	2
40	48

Third Day—Tuesday, June 10

Here, said those critics early enough on the ground to take their seats or drinks before play commenced, is a batsman's wicket on which our batsmen may play their way slowly to safety. Before those seats were warm under them, or, alternatively, before their glasses empty to the Plimsoll line, disaster was upon England. Tuckett began again where he left off the night before—bowling by faith and length and his strong right arm. Compton, apparently failing to realize that play had officially begun, played at him one of those charming flourishes with which batsmen are apt to amuse themselves on their walk out to the wicket or while handling a bat in the dressing-room. Mitchell took the resultant slip catch with eager confidence.

Dollery made sufficient strokes to show that he was not going to be overawed by the occasion or his side's situation. A boundary almost at once looked like Dollery well on the way to a hundred at Edgbaston. Then Dawson, who was doing his twice-daily duty of propelling a few outswingers the length of the Test Match wicket, bowled him, and Yardley inherited a peck of troubles. He and Edrich stayed to show that the wicket was guileless as ever. Sir Julien Cahn's former groundsman, now at Trent Bridge, does not construct wickets to be death-traps before the captain's last innings. Yardley even hit Mann against the spin on the leg side. Edrich conveyed the impression that the last hair of his intense eyebrows was concentrating on the game: he would not relax, but played Tuckett in particular with immense care.

Then Ian Smith came on with his wilful leg-breaks. By now Yardley and Edrich, although they had only put on 36 runs, wore the air of batsmen settled to their task. Perhaps Smith bowls less 'tight' than the other South African bowlers; at least Edrich seemed in less difficulty with him than with, for instance, Mann. Smith occasionally bowled a full-toss, and that Edrich was more willing to hit. But the leg-breaker is the most likely of all bowlers to bowl the ball with overspin so acute as to make it dip sharply. It was such a ball, apparently a full toss, but dipping sharply, which yorked Edrich with England's score a mere 198. At precisely the same total Tuckett had Yardley lbw. Bedser struck a mighty blow for six off Smith—and swinging on arrival by No. 8 indicates little to follow. Melville caught Bedser off Smith.

Then came England's Nos. 9, 10, and 11—looking like Nos. 11, 12, and 13. Cook was bowled by Tuckett while his bat was still only half-way down. Martin's stroke was only just good enough to edge Tucket to Lindsay, who pouched the catch neatly and then stumped Evans like lightning off Ian Smith. England were all out for 208 on a batsman's wicket.

At twenty-five minutes past twelve Edrich and Yardley

were batting together for the fifth wicket; before one o'clock England were batting again, following-on 325 runs behind. Before lunch Hutton was out in the second innings, bowled by the best ball of the match, which came from Tuckett: after suggesting that it might be going with the bowler's arm, it came back very late, and hurried off the pitch.

After lunch Washbrook and Edrich looked like a well-established, if not enterprising, pair. This was no time for Edrich's more defiant strokes, and Washbrook continued to play the inswinger most inelegantly with pads, thigh, or rump rather than with his bat. Neither seemed to be wielding the mastery which Melville and Nourse had shown on Saturday, but they were without initiative, fighting even to gain a foothold. They looked two competent batsmen playing carefully on a good batsman's wicket, and tension fell lower than it had been since the first-innings departure of Hutton and Washbrook.

Edrich reached his fifty, and then, before the fact-gatherers had verified his 'number of minutes,' Smith bowled him exactly as in the first innings. Melville had used Smith wisely. He is a bowler who may be hit hard and who may allow the batsman to get on top. Therefore he could not be allowed to bowl long spells at this moment of dramatic issue. Melville brought him on for five overs and whisked him away, back for three more overs, and off again. In his third spell he dismissed Edrich. Compton curbed his normal boyish mischief, even to the extent of patient respect to Smith, and when Rowan made one go with his arm so that Washbrook's bat barely edged it to Lindsay, England were 133 for 3. Dollery started slowly, and he and Compton were most unlike their county selves. Just after tea, Dollery whipped out a walking-stick four and the thought occurred that England might not only be saved, but saved gallantly. Then the persistent Dawson bowled him a half-volley which he hit hard and straight for the pavilion rails. The ball was bare inches off the ground and Dawson in the middle of his follow-through, but he swept down, put one hand under the ball to catch it miraculously at full forward stretch and regain his balance with the ease of an acrobat —a barely Christian caught-and-bowled. England, 170 for 4, were 155 runs behind, and Compton and Yardley alone stood between the South African bowlers and a pitiful England tail only too fresh in the memory. An hour and three-quarters left for play—and five of these same six wickets had gone in twenty-five minutes on this very day. England supporters contemplated the possibility of a three-day finish. The Trent Bridge wicket, only too conscious of its perfection, seemed to leer at its critics of Saturday.

Tuckett and Mann persisted in accuracy and direction and waited for the England wickets to go on falling. Compton and Yardley moved carefully within the line between wicket and wicket. Melville, at silly mid-off, might once or twice have breathed down Yardley's neck. The time until seven must have stretched before them both like an eternity: Wednesday was no more than a nightmare occurring to J. W. Dunne. The confident single was the height of any English supporter's ambition; South Africans were jubilant. Only for a moment or two before the close of play had they any reason to feel doubtful—five of the last seven scoring shots were fours. Still, England needed 48 to escape being beaten by an innings, with six wickets to fall (and one contemplated their worth grimly and without optimism).

South Africa—First Innings

A. Melville, b Martin	189
B. Mitchell, b Bedser	14
K. G. Viljoen, lbw b Edrich . . .	10
D. Nourse, b Hollies	149
O. C. Dawson, st Evans b Hollies . .	48
T. A. Harris, c Hutton b Hollies . .	60
A. Rowan, not out	34
L. Tuckett, lbw b Hollies . . .	0
N. Mann, b Bedser	8
J. Lindsay, b Bedser	0
V. I. Smith, c Yardley b Hollies . .	1
Extras (b 7, l-b 12, w 1) .	20
Total .	533

Bowling Analysis—First Innings

	O	M	R	W
Martin . . .	36	4	111	1
Bedser . . .	58	14	106	3
Edrich . . .	20	8	56	1
Hollies . . .	55.2	16	123	5
Cook . . .	21	4	87	0
Yardley . .	5	0	24	0
Compton . .	2	1	6	0

Fall of Wickets

1	2	3	4	5	6	7	8	9	10
23	44	363	384	450	505	505	528	530	533

England

Hutton, lbw b Rowan	.	17	b Tuckett	. .	9
Washbrook, lbw b Tuckett		25	c Lindsay b Rowan .		59
W. J. Edrich, b Smith	.	57	b Smith	. .	50
Compton, c Mitchell b Tuckett	. . .	65	not out .	. .	83
Dollery, b Dawson .	.	9	c and b Dawson	.	17
N. W. D. Yardley, lbw b Tuckett	. . .	22	not out .	. .	45
Evans, st Lindsay b Smith .		2			
Bedser, c Melville b Smith		7			
Cook, b Tuckett	. .	0			
J. W. Martin, c Lindsay b Tuckett	. . .	0			
Hollies, not out	. .	0			
Extras (b 1, l-b 2, w 1)	.	4	Extras (b 7, l-b 8)	.	15
	Total .	208	Total (4 wkts) .		278

Bowling Analysis—First Innings

		O	M	R	W
Tuckett	. . .	37	9	68	5
Dawson	. . .	30	2	35	1
Rowan	. . .	16	6	45	1
Mann	. . .	20	13	10	0
Smith	. . .	29.1	9	46	3

Fall of Wickets—First Innings

1	2	3	4	5	6	7	8	9	10
40	48	154	165	198	198	207	208	208	208

Fall of Wickets—Second Innings

1	2	3	4
20	116	133	170

Fourth Day—**Wed**nesday, June 11

Compton and Yardley each had a net before the last day's play began, and each opened confidently. This by current standards was almost an innovation. Yet some of the greatest batsmen of the past always had a net before batting in a Test Match, and it seems a most logical step to take. It is easy to recall some vital early dismissals which might well have been avoided by preliminary practice.

The whole pre-lunch play was different. Compton and Yardley took no foolish risks, but Compton in particular looked for runs all the time. The solitary chance was offered by Yardley, to first slip, off the long-suffering Tuckett, when the score was 298 for 4 after a quarter of an hour's play. The catch was not taken, but at that time it did not seem particularly relevant. Yardley forced well on the on side, making some of his strokes very late. Compton exerted a mastery only possible in a natural batsman—he hit Mann on the off side and Tuckett to third man by strokes made with the lazy confidence of a painter's preliminary pencil study for a painting. There was time for him to shape to play one shot, change his mind and play another, and yet play the second one lazily. Rarely has greatness in batting so stamped itself upon a game of dramatic development or flourished in its highest form under such acute responsibility. They were still together at lunch, notwithstanding every switch of the South African bowling.

Directly after lunch Mann made a ball, attractively pitched outside the off stump, leave Compton's bat and fly off the edge to Mitchell at slip for a safe catch. Now, with Compton gone, England were only 82 ahead and four and a half hours remained for play. Evans came briskly to the wicket with the air of a man about to enjoy himself. It is difficult indeed to rate his innings. One knows that Evans is not a great batsman—yet this was a great innings. He was as high as No. 7 for England largely because the side carried three number elevens. His strokes were made forcefully, off the full meat of the bat, and, if some of them were audacious, none of them was in violation of the canons of batsmanship. The hook, the square cut, the cover-drive were swept away for fours with the speed only attained through perfect timing. Yardley's patient craft lost some of its bloom neighboured by these more vivid plants of Compton and the secret Evans. But at a quarter to three Yardley's score was 99 when he yielded to his inborn craving for the on side and shaped to play Dawson there—Dawson whose only ball deviating from the straight is the outswinger. The stroke Yardley had in mind must have been the pushed single between short leg and mid-on—a most tempting stroke for a man who is 99 not out. He was 99 out, bowled Dawson, and returned to the pavilion with his head down. Did he not, I wonder, have the comforting realization that he was receiving more applause for 99 than he would have had for a hundred—that he was receiving both sympathy and admiration? And, on a more enduring level, surely he must have appreciated that ninety-nines are much rarer and more memorable in Test cricket than centuries. I recall the Australian Chipperfield as the man who made ninety-nine in a Test at Nottingham. I have to consult *Wisden*— one moment, I have to consult *Wisden*—to find that he did make a hundred also in a Test Match, but I had forgotten it. Yardley and Compton had added 237 runs, and England had put up a fight; they might feel that their defeat was less disgraceful than threatened.

Evans went on hotfoot and bursting with impudence expressed in grace. Bedser, not this time with reason for despair, followed his desperate 7 in seven minutes of the first innings with 2 in half an hour in the second innings, while he kept up an end for Evans. Cook stayed for a quarter of an hour, during which Evans took the bowling to himself. When Cook had to play a ball he was applauded for stopping it, and he brought the crowd's heart to stopping-point when he hit a four on his own account. Evans's innings was exciting in its brazen handsomeness—74 runs in seventy-seven minutes, 56 of them in boundaries, before Smith, his return well timed by Melville, caught and bowled him.

When Smith had Cook caught, Martin and Hollies, the last pair, came together at 3.38 with England 500 for 9. With rolling and sweeping coming in the tea interval, three hours and seven minutes remained for play, and England were 175 runs on. Thus, if the last wicket fell now, South Africa were asked to score at the rate of fifty-seven runs an hour to win—a task to be accomplished with ease and relish on this wicket. The two batsmen in hazard were both of poor quality, not even remembered for feats of allowing the ball to hit the bat against time. Any county bowler would expect to account for either in an over. One man in the pavilion suggested that he had seen Martin score double figures, but admitted that this was not in a first-class fixture: he could remember no similar instance in the case of Hollies. But Tuckett was too tired to sweep Hollies and Martin away; and they did not bat well enough to get themselves out against the other bowlers. Nourse, captaining South Africa while Melville was off the field with a pulled muscle, hardly dared, especially as a deputy, to follow the old recipe of using the worst bowler in the side. These two batted together for forty-nine minutes and added 51 runs. Martin hit two sixes high to the score-board stand. When Rowan clean bowled Martin for 26, Hollies had scored 13: his highest score in his forty-one innings in county cricket of 1946 was 5 not out.

South Africa now needed 227 runs in two hours and eighteen minutes—and a hundred runs an hour was not practicable, even on this still peaceful wicket, against the new ball bowled by Martin, Bedser and Edrich. After Bedser had taken Mitchell's wicket Melville and Viljoen, disguising the sadness they must have felt, decorated the end of the day with pleasant runs. Melville, for all his limp, played a mellow innings, with a second hundred of the match (a Record! said the man with the *Wisden*) to give flavour to an epilogue whose light notes were like chamber music coming after Beethoven's Ninth.

It may be said that a dropped catch at slip lost the match for South Africa. I prefer the judgment that a pre-play net for Compton and Yardley saved the game for England. The match had emphasized several points for the English selectors at the low cost of an unfavourable draw. Martin was obviously not sufficiently experienced, or, alternatively, not sufficiently a thunderbolt to retain his place, and his fielding had been below Test Match standard. Cook was not yet long-headed enough to bowl on dead wickets. Dollery might well be given another chance. Most certain of all, England could not afford again to go into a Test Match without Wright, the best bowler of any type in England.

Always I shall remember the first Test of 1947 for the agony of every South African well-wisher as a certain win leaked slowly away through the tiny hole of a dropped catch and the inability of Martin and Hollies to get out. It was a drama, not of a single event, but of almost two hours, runs and time ebbing away, the clock being pushed ahead by odd runs, until the game that had been so thoroughly and deservedly theirs was lost by an hour.

South Africa

A. Melville, b Martin .	189	not out . . .	104
B. Mitchell, b Bedser .	14	c Evans b Bedser .	4
K. G. Viljoen, lbw b Edrich	10	not out . . .	51
D. Nourse, b Hollies .	149		
O. C. Dawson, st Evans b Hollies . .	48		
T. A. Harris, c Hutton b Hollies . . .	60		
A. Rowan, not out . .	34		
L. Tuckett, lbw b Hollies .	0		
N. Mann, b Bedser . .	8		
J. Lindsay, b Bedser . .	0		
V. I. Smith, c Yardley b Hollies . . .	1		
Extras (b 7, l-b 12, w 1) .	20	Extras (b 1, w 5, n-b 1)	7
Total .	533	Total (1 wkt) .	166

Fall of Wickets

1	2	3	4	5	6	7	8	9	10
23	44	363	384	450	505	505	528	530	533
21	—	—	—	—	—	—	—	—	—

Bowling Analysis

	O	M	R	W		O	M	R	W
Martin . .	36	4	111	1	....	9	2	18	0
Bedser . .	58	14	106	3	....	14	3	31	1
Edrich . .	20	8	56	1	....	4	1	8	0
Hollies . .	55.2	16	123	5	....	9	1	33	0
Cook . .	21	4	87	0	....	9	0	40	0
Yardley . .	5	0	24	0	....	—	—	—	—
Compton . .	2	1	6	0	....	4	0	14	0
Hutton . .	—	—	—	—	....	2	0	15	0

England

Hutton, lbw b Rowan	.	17	b Tuckett . .	9
Washbrook, lbw b Tuckett		25	c Lindsay b Rowan .	59
W. J. Edrich, b Smith	.	57	b Smith . .	50
Compton (D.), c Mitchell b Tuckett	. . .	65	c Mitchell b Mann .	163
Dollery, b Dawson	. .	9	c and b Dawson .	17
N. W. D. Yardley, lbw b Tuckett	. . .	22	c Tuckett b Dawson	99
Evans, st Lindsay b Smith	.	2	c and b Smith . .	74
Bedser (A.), c Melville b Smith	. . .	7	c Harris b Smith .	2
Cook, b Tuckett	. .	0	c Dawson b Smith .	4
J. W. Martin, c Lindsay b Tuckett	. . .	0	b Rowan . .	26
Hollies, not out	. .	0	not out . . .	18
Extras (b 1, l-b 2, w 1).		4	Extras (b 15, l-b 13, w 2) . . .	30

Total . 208   Total . 551

Fall of Wickets

1	2	3	4	5	6	7	8	9	10
40	48	154	165	198	198	207	208	208	208
20	116	133	170	408	434	472	499	500	551

Bowling Analysis

	O	M	R	W		O	M	R	W
Tuckett .	37	9	68	5	....	47	12	127	1
Dawson .	30	2	35	1	....	25	7	57	2
Rowan .	16	6	45	1	....	63.2	8	100	2
Mann .	20	13	10	0	....	60	22	94	1
Smith .	29.1	9	46	3	....	51	15	143	4

Match drawn.

THE SECOND TEST MATCH

Played at Lord's on June 21st, 23rd, 24th and 25th, 1947

THE English selectors had a fright at Nottingham which ensured a strong England side at Lord's. Martin and Cook, who had failed in the first Test, were dropped. Dollery, who might conceivably have been given the benefit of the doubt and a further trial, was also left out. George Pope became the pace bowler, Wright took his proper place in any England side of today, and Barnett of Gloucestershire came in. The selection of Barnett once more was less a retrograde step than it seemed to some who looked upon him as an old player. He was not yet thirty-seven; his batting was still as audacious and successful as that of any opening batsman in England and his bowling, used more than for many years, had been so successful as to take him into the first five in the bowling table; moreover, unlike some players of his age, he did not need to be hidden in the field. His selection argued some degree of confidence in that it represented the choice of a forcing No. 5 in anticipation of a solid batting foundation to his position. The South Africans made no change from their team at Nottingham.

First Day—Saturday, June 21

Lord's with thirty thousand people crammed into it— the early weather just uncertain enough to add a spice of gamble even to the payment of gate-money, and the South Africans, who had so nearly won at Nottingham, to play the second Test Match—that was scene and setting on this June Saturday.

Yardley took a considerable amount of the initiative in

the match by winning the toss. The qualification to his advantage lay in the morning dew-life in the wicket, so that much depended upon the ability of Hutton and Washbrook to see the pace bowlers off. The normal opening gambits of Tuckett and Dawson against Hutton and Washbrook were made. Tuckett made an occasional ball lift, and both he and Dawson moved the ball late in the early damp atmosphere. Three runs off the first seven overs meant that the noose was tight indeed. Washbrook continued to play the inswinger with his rump and Hutton was making stroke after stroke direct to the fieldsmen. The South Africans were keen and well placed in the field, and there was obviously no intent on the part of Hutton and Washbrook to look for runs or trouble at this juncture. In the hour and a half of play before lunch Hutton and Washbrook scored 58 runs: the only boundary was a straight drive from Washbrook. Smith did not bowl, the noose was too tight for relaxation to be risked. Tuckett, Dawson, Mann, and Rowan bowled to a field discussed and arranged in advance. But Hutton and Washbrook have played this game before. They consented to be besieged, and regarded the sortie as beyond their immediate province. After lunch Hutton had no opportunity to show whether he proposed to impose himself rather than be imposed upon. In his second over after lunch Rowan bowled the ball he seems to bowl so well at Lord's, where he bowls perhaps in the air-cushion made by the Grandstand—it floated out and then turned back to bowl Hutton for a monumentally patient 18.

Eighteen out of the 75 runs scored for the first wicket will look ordinary enough in the records of Test Matches, but, once again, Hutton and Washbrook had seen the initial edge off the attack and the morning dew from the wicket. So solid, so experienced, are these two batsmen that it is a great pity that they are not, in the full sense of the expression, an opening *pair*—their running between the wickets is slow and based apparently on a cautious determination that lack of understanding shall not lead to complete misunderstanding. They have lost runs between the wickets too consistently for any more charitable conclusion.

With Edrich poring over the bowling like a student over a book before an examination, Washbrook was moved to parade some more attacking shots and threatened to adopt his more punitive county-match style. Then the new ball was taken, with the England score still short of 100. Dawson bowled his outswinger starting nearer the middle stump than usual to compel a stroke from Washbrook, who edged it to Tuckett at slip. For heartrending seconds Tuckett alternately held and lost the ball, but eventually gripped it and stayed bent for the second while relief overcame anxiety. Ninety-six for 2. Compton and Edrich were together, a state which, continuing, meant much—ending, possible disaster for England. Slowly they settled into the day.

Smith was thrown at Edrich for two overs; Mann urged the merit of length. The South African fielding was now obviously being handled according to a careful plan. But neither batsman was disturbed from the normal course of his innings' development. Edrich's initial care is familiar, it is the product of concentration and determination backed by a knowledge of the relative danger of his strokes. Compton was again and again checking the attacking shot which comes unprompted to his batting mind in favour of the safe and negative stroke. Then, with light, pace, and temper of wicket established, they revealed the extent of their armouries before playing calmly through the last few minutes before tea. One six from Edrich, played on the forearms and twist of body, thundered to the Tavern. They put on 111 runs at rather more than one a minute, and England had averted the threat of the struggle which would have materialized if either of them had gone out closely after Washbrook.

After tea there was an air of doom for South Africa about the methods of the two Middlesex batsmen. As they settled eye and hand again after the interval, Melville was powerless. Each rigidly abstained from the rising ball of Dawson or the spinner of Mann outside the off-stump. Neither made any attempt to take a liberty until they were again comfortable. Then came the spate. The South African fielding was heroic; Mann bowled over after over of precise length, but no one else could check the battery of strokes. Melville's field was a remarkable index of the strokes of the two batsmen. For Denis Compton no one was used between wide mid-off and wide mid-on. Yet Compton made no attempt to play the straight drive into the gap. Indeed, there was little need for him to do so while he could place the ball with force and certainty through the gaps, narrow as they were, in the cover-field. When he hooked, he hooked rather earlier than, for instance, Sutcliffe, playing the ball away in a spin-curve all along the ground through an arc running towards long leg. For Edrich there was a man on the long-on boundary, yet, again and again, he played his characteristic pull-drive to the boundary between clock-tower and pavilion. The field retreated from its former tight position in a well-mustered attempt to cut off boundaries. Indeed, against a field anything short of first-class, both Edrich and Compton might well have had another 60 runs that day. Harris was gay as a cricket and fast as a rabbit in the field; Dawson ran and threw with the speed and elegance of a Greek athlete; Melville was often quicker than the eye at silly mid-off or silly mid-on or in his retreat position at extra cover.

Rain robbed them of half an hour's batting, yet, between three and seven—less than three-and-a-half hours of play —Compton and Edrich put on 216 runs against what was certainly the steadiest bowling combination to be seen on English cricket fields in 1947 and probably the strongest fielding combination. Again, Lindsay was an admirable wicket-keeper: the only two possible catches to him came off the under-edge of the bat, going almost straight downwards. The greatest compliment one can pay him, and that an accurate one, is that one hardly ever noticed him. The difficult ball on the leg side, the long or short throw-in, went into his gloves with a complete negation of flourish or strain: he was never more completely stamped as a natural wicket-keeper in the entire tour. It was this background of first-class outcricket that showed to the full the stature of Edrich and Compton. Edrich, moving in a blur of feet to watch the ball on to a bat bent upon punishing, was paired with Compton placing the ball to an inch with strokes which appeared casual only to the casual glance. There was a naturalness about Compton's strokes which argued beyond doubt the born ball-player.

England's 312 for 2 at close of play saw them in the position which South Africa had occupied at the end of the first day at Nottingham—safe from defeat unless a cricket miracle occurred.

England—First Innings

Hutton, b Rowan	18
Washbrook, c Tuckett b Dawson . .	65
W. J. Edrich, not out	109
Compton (D.), not out . . .	110
Extras (b 2, l-b 8) .	10
Total (for 2 wkts) .	312

Fall of Wickets

1	2
75	96

Second Day—Monday, June 23

With England 312 for 2 when the day started, Melville was bound to direct his strategy towards avoiding being swamped. Tuckett and Dawson on the slightly dewy wicket were obviously to be treated with respect. But Melville must have been a little disheartened by the friendly assurance of the respect paid by Edrich and Compton. The wicket at Lord's for this match had obviously been constructed to last four days of cricket. It was, pre-lunch life excepted—and that was not appreciable—quite as comfortable a batsmen's wicket as that at Nottingham. Rowan and Mann, relieving the faster bowlers, bowled defensively. Mann, in particular, low in flight, fastidious as to length and direction, was spinning the ball hard. If neither moved the ball off the wicket with the snap which compels the false stroke, that was not because they did not spin. Rowan once made Edrich edge the ball when attempting to force him, and Mann made a leg-break defeat Compton's positive stroke. Otherwise the two batsmen played like master batsmen—more—they played like master batsmen who know that their cricketing luck is in—a distinction upon which Hutton could undoubtedly be illuminating. Ian Smith, who had twice bowled Edrich at Nottingham, came on at the pavilion end after Rowan and Mann had successfully resisted attempts at demoralization. Edrich at once struck him four times for four off consecutive balls. Smith's spell was restricted to three overs, and he bowled no more in the innings. Again Melville's fielding plan and the alertness of his fieldsmen reduced the batsmen's scores to as low a figure as was possible by human cricketers. England were 443 for 2 at lunch, Edrich 173, Compton 177. It was an awe-inspiring morning's performance.

Five minutes after lunch the two were scoring at almost two runs a minute, batting as if they had never left the crease. Then Edrich, in trying to force Mann, committed a fault so rare in him as to be remarkable—he lifted his head—and was bowled. They had added 370 for the third wicket, and I did not need the man with *Wisden* to tell me that it was a record: I had acquired a sixpenny book of my own which told me so. Barnett, obviously under orders, and certainly, being Barnett, fuming, after being seven hours in his pads, rather than fearful of anti-climax, attacked from his first ball. Compton and Edrich had scored fast while respecting the good ball. Barnett's proportion of respect-worthy balls was smaller than theirs. He swished the ball into the covers and he and Compton scored 49 runs at two a minute. Rowan's catch to end Compton's innings was worthy of the batsman and a reward which Tuckett had earned. Now Tuckett bowled Barnett, Rowan caught Yardley off him, and he bowled Evans and Bedser. George Pope, who refused to be affected by the prevailing fever of hitting, was not out 8 when Yardley declared with England in an impregnable position—554 for 8 wickets at half-past three on the second day. Tuckett had so ravaged the tail as to prevent the massacre which threatened. Yardley lost few runs by declaring—Tuckett would certainly have swept away Wright and Hollies, and so rapid a complete dismissal of the entire England team would certainly have given South Africa a moral fillip. This was an unsatisfactory gamble against the number of runs likely to be made by Wright and Hollies, with runs in any case of no great importance.

With the wicket still absolutely perfect, Yardley must have been thankful for a total 'in the bank' which enabled him to juggle a little in the hope of striking early blows to unsettle the South African batting. Edrich and Bedser opened, and Pope, Wright, and Hollies also bowled in the first twenty overs of the innings. Melville played with the assurance of a batsman in form and the mellow ease of stroke of a man to whom batting is a fine art. Mitchell turned upon his problems a cold, detached brain. Each solved his problems, and the England bowling was not better than the wicket allowed it to be. Wright bowled balls which beat each batsman without bowling him. The England fielding was sound, but not quite so good as the South Africans'. The South African innings was two hours old and worth 95 runs, tea had come and gone without unsettling either batsman, when Compton, the sixth England bowler, had Mitchell quickly and narrowly stumped. Viljoen, whose second innings at Nottingham had had a solidity and power in the drive which seemed to promise many runs against the English bowling, scored only 1. He looked so uncomfortable against Wright that the surprising thing about his innings was that it lasted ten minutes. Viljoen might, however, have regarded himself as unfortunate in that he was bowled by Wright's faster ball—and hardly in human recollection had Wright's 'quickie' been straight.

Again Nourse bore a burden of responsibility which was communicated to the spectators through his initial unease. Melville, however, is a calming partner, and Nourse's courage is his own and not excelled by that of any other cricketer. They had made the South African total at Nottingham with less assistance from Mitchell than they had received in this innings, and they were both still in at the close of play and had put on 63 runs. English supporters slept less soundly for the fact that they were still together, while South Africans had anxiety for Melville's not out 96 overnight, with a third consecutive century in sight. The English bowlers, except Wright, had done nothing to suggest that they could force a victory. Bedser, without the inspiration of an early wicket, had showed less enthusiasm than usual and had bowled a number of balls looser than Yardley could afford. He looked a little tired. Pope was more accurate and Hollies turned a little, but only in Wright could Yardley find hope for wickets.

England—First Innings

Hutton, b Rowan	18
Washbrook, c Tuckett b Dawson . .	65
W. J. Edrich, b Mann	189
Compton (D.), c Rowan b Tuckett . .	208
Barnett, b Tuckett	33
N. W. D. Yardley, c Rowan b Tuckett .	5
Evans, b Tuckett	16
Pope (G. H.) not out	8
Bedser (A. V.), b Tuckett . . .	0
Extras (b 2, l-b 10) .	12

Total (for 8 wkts dec) . 554

Wright and Hollies did not bat.

Bowling Analysis

	O	M	R	W
Tuckett . . .	47	7	115	5
Dawson . . .	33	11	81	1
Mann . . .	53	16	99	1
Rowan . . .	65	11	174	1
Smith . . .	17	2	73	0

Fall of Wickets

1	2	3	4	5	6	7	8	9	10
75	96	466	515	526	541	554	554	—	—

South Africa—First Innings

A. Melville, not out	96
B. Mitchell, st Evans b Compton . .	46
K. G. Viljoen, b Wright. . . .	1
D. Nourse, not out	24
Extras .	0
Total (for 2 wkts) .	167

Fall of Wickets

1	2
95	104

Third Day—Tuesday, June 24

Melville, in the first over of the day, hit a four to make his score 100 and to allow his followers to buy a score-card. Yardley realized that this was one of the days when Wright was happy about bowling and used him consistently. Pope was steady and almost impossible to hit. Melville and Nourse seemed less at their ease than on the previous evening. A series of fierce appeals prevented their settling down and Melville had to dive on his face to ground his bat when Pope fielded a stroke into slips and returned it with remarkable speed. Pope's speed in the field is considerable when one takes into consideration the construction of the man. His body seems unduly long, and its length is exaggerated by the fact that he *never* bends at any point between neck and hips. When he bends to pick up a ball from the ground, his back is completely straight. When he bowls, approaching the wicket with strides which land heel first, his bowed-arm delivery is accelerated by a body swing which is from the hips alone—the trunk is inflexible. He overcomes this awkwardness by considerable length of arm and speed of movement in the close-fielding positions. From the ring, at which range his grimly amused twinkle and weather-beaten wryness of expression are not visible, his appearance, when his shining bald dome moves forward on a sinewy neck, is, above the shoulders, reminiscent of a tortoise pushing its head out of its shell. Yet the watcher would be foolish who failed to recognize in George Pope immense strength, drive and a determination which urges him on beyond the bounds of exhaustion to the end of remarkably sustained spells of bowling. There was little greenness for him in the Lord's wicket, and he had to share the new ball with both Bedser and Edrich. Nevertheless, he almost compensated for the lack of essential body-swing in his bowling and for the unsympathetic state of the wicket by an accurate length, a sharp and late inswing, and a direction which barely wavered.

Melville and Nourse had batted for more than an hour before Hollies came on and bowled a maiden over; then, in his next over, he pitched his leg-spinner outside Melville's leg stump. Melville swept at it with a suggestion of carelessness and hit it straight at Bedser standing at short leg for that particular stroke, which, however, can hardly have been expected from Melville. Melville's three centuries in succession were a record—I saw the man with *Wisden* before he saw me, and told him it was a record; he informed me coldly that he knew very well that it was.

Nourse's method with Wright was to hook him with a forearm jerk when he pitched short and to play back very late indeed to his good-length balls. It was in going back to him that he was lbw for 61 and South Africa were 230 for 4. With Bedser, Edrich, and Pope obviously unhappy on a wicket which had no goodness in it for them, Yardley now employed Compton as a slow left-arm stock bowler. Compton bowled orthodox, round-the-wicket break-aways. If his action was lackadaisical, he was pitching steadily on or outside the off stump just short of half-volley length, and turning. Dawson and Harris stayed together until lunch, but looked much less happy than at lunch. A side which carries forcing batsmen at Nos. 5 and 6 must either back them in attack by a large score for the first three wickets or one of the first four batsmen must bat with them in turn. Neither Dawson nor Harris is suited to that policy of waiting for the bad ball which circumstances now dictated as necessary for South Africa. Neither, on the other hand, is of the purely attacking type with allied technique which gives an even chance of success in an attempt to take the bowling by the scruff of the neck and beat a way to dominance. Uneasily, but bravely, these two stayed together until lunch and for half an hour afterwards, when Evans stumped Harris as he reached forward to Compton—Harris regrounding his bat so quickly as to make the decision extremely close. Dawson and Harris had added 60 runs, but in eighty-five minutes, which is the measure both of their anxiety and their divorce from their natural styles and rates of scoring. Hollies had Dawson brilliantly caught by Barnett at 300, and then the South African tail reverted to the form it had shown throughout the tour, except at Nottingham.

Wright took three quick wickets and Pope one and South Africa were all out for 327. The last seven batsmen had put on barely a hundred runs on a perfect wicket, and Yardley asked them to follow on 227 behind with less than three hours of play remaining on the third day. The Royal visit cut down that time and heralded Edrich clean bowling Melville—whose luck had to change, one felt —for 8. When he clean bowled Viljoen also in his third over (Pope and Bedser had opened the bowling), Edrich had taken two wickets for one run and South Africa were in considerable trouble. Nourse brought a truculent temper to his difficulties and took three fours off Edrich's next over. Then, equally grim, he relapsed into defence. Hollies, as fourth change, bowled a sequence of maiden overs. Mitchell batted like a man husbanding his strength and, with Nourse, saw the day out. South Africa were in a bad position, but, so long as Nourse and Mitchell could stay, it was not desperate.

England—First Innings

Hutton, b Rowan	18
Washbrook, c Tuckett b Dawson . .	65
W. J. Edrich, b Mann	189
Compton (D.), c Rowan b Tuckett .	208
Barnett, b Tuckett	33
N. W. D. Yardley, c Rowan b Tuckett .	5
Evans, b Tuckett	16
Pope (G. H.) not out	8
Bedser (A. V.), b Tuckett . . .	0
Extras (b 2, l-b 10) .	12
Total (for 8 wkts dec)	554

Wright and Hollies did not bat.

Bowling Analysis

	O	M	R	W
Tuckett . . .	47	7	115	5
Dawson . . .	33	11	81	1
Mann . . .	53	16	99	1
Rowan . . .	65	11	174	1
Smith . . .	17	2	73	0

Fall of Wickets

1	2	3	4	5	6	7	8	9	10
75	96	466	515	526	541	554	554	—	—

South Africa

A. Melville, c Bedser b Hollies . . . 117	b Edrich . . 8
B. Mitchell, st Evans b Compton . . . 46	not out . . . 47
K. G. Viljoen, b Wright . 1	b Edrich . . 6
A. D. Nourse, lbw b Wright 61	not out . . . 58
O. C. Dawson, c Barnett b Hollies . . . 36	
T. A. Harris, st Evans b Compton . . . 30	
A. Rowan, b Wright . 8	
L. Tuckett, b Wright . 5	
N. Mann, b Wright . . 4	
J. Lindsay, not out . . 7	
V. I. Smith, c Edrich b Pope 11	
Extras (l-b 1) . 1	Extra (l-b 1) . 1
Total . 327	Total (for 2 wkts). 120

Bowling Analysis—First Innings

	O	M	R	W
Edrich . . .	9	1	22	0
Bedser . . .	26	1	76	0
Pope . . .	19.2	5	49	1
Wright . . .	39	10	95	5
Hollies . . .	28	10	52	2
Compton . . .	21	11	32	2

Fall of Wickets

1	2	3	4	5	6	7	8	9	10
95	104	222	230	290	300	302	308	309	327
16	28	—	—	—	—	—	—	—	—

Fourth Day—Wednesday, June 25

Again the cricket tricked those who took their seats late. Edrich bowled Nourse with the first ball of the day. Edrich has little in his bowling except pace and skilful use of the bowling crease: had Nourse had a pre-match net he might have altered the entire complexion of the game. Dawson followed him and, with Mitchell as his partner, looked altogether happier than on the previous day. Yardley was soon bowling Wright and Compton as stock bowlers. Each was turning, albeit slowly, on a wicket which still denied the pace bowlers life or even promise of life. Barnett, who stood higher in the first-class bowling averages than any member of the team except Pope (but with only 32 wickets), was never asked to bowl. Edrich, having bowled out the three first batsmen, now caught Mitchell brilliantly bare inches off the ground when a ball from Wright flew off the edge of his bat, touched his pad, and was dropping short in slips: Dawson and Mitchell had been South Africa's last hope of resistance. Next Edrich caught Dawson off Compton. Harris, patently unhappy, played a turning ball from Compton, which pitched outside his off stump, straight to the middle of George Pope's chest. As it bounced off, and the crowd strained its ears for the resultant drum-like thump, Yardley snatched it out of no-man's air.

Rowan and Tuckett were brave in saving the innings defeat, but Wright bowling a length was too much for the South African tail, as Tuckett had been for the later English batsmen.

Washbrook and Hutton had only 26 to make to win. They made them firmly and in business-like fashion. Their view, one felt, was reasonable enough—that it would be foolish to get out, thus causing the hard-working Mr. Edrich the inconvenience of coming to the wicket in so small a matter. Accordingly they did not hesitate to play two maiden overs from Dawson and one from Mann and to average only two runs per over—after all, that way no one could feel foolish. But for the fact that conscience or a sense of mischief prompted another player to inform the umpire, a ball would have been bowled in a Test Match while one bail was in mid-off's pocket—a feat for which even *Wisden* records no precedent.

England had won a Test Match, but with less final satisfaction than South Africa had in failing to win the previous game. The English weaknesses were glaring. How much of the win was due to Edrich and Compton may be gathered not only from the batting, but also from the bowling figures and the catches made. Edrich was the only one of the three pace bowlers to have any success whatever, and he produced match-winning bowling in the South African second innings. His performance tended, perhaps not quite fairly, to acquit the wicket of blame in respect of the comparative failure of Pope and Bedser. Hollies had bowled steadily, but Compton hardly looked a slow bowler likely to trouble Australian batsmen. The fielding of the English team was appreciably better than at Nottingham, largely because Barnett, Wright, and Pope were better fieldsmen than their predecessors. Both Wright and Compton, however, had been called to bowl for considerable spells, yet spend the alternate overs as deep fielders. Evans missed two sharp chances, but no wicket-keeper in the world could have been guaranteed to have done better.

For South Africa the position was altogether different. The batting form of the tail had been that normal in county matches. This had been partly obscured in the first Test by the initiative created by winning the toss and the performances of the earlier batsmen. Melville needed a de-

fensive batsman at No. 5 or 6, or both, plus one tail-ender
capable of steady, even if runless, defence. His bowlers
were good—capable of dismissing for a relatively low
score by Test Match standards any English batsmen except Edrich and Compton. It was the very excellence of
the South African fielding and bowling which convinced
the more knowledgeable critics that, given corresponding
general form and luck (a factor always present in cricket
and essential to any success), these two are perfectly
capable of producing much the same batting results
against Australia. Once again the initiative had gone with
the winning of the toss. At Nottingham the English tail
had saved the game; the South African tail, faced with
almost the same task, had failed to do so.

England

Hutton, b Rowan . . 18	not out . . . 13
Washbrook, c Tuckett b	
Dawson . . . 65	not out . . . 13
W. J. Edrich, b Mann . 189	
Compton (D.), c Rowan b	
Tuckett . . 208	
Barnett, b Tuckett . . 33	
N. W. D. Yardley, c Rowan	
b Tuckett . . . 5	
Evans, b Tuckett . . 16	
Pope (G. H.), not out . 8	
Bedser (A. V.), b Tuckett . 0	
Extras (b 2, l-b 10) . 12	

Total (8 wkts dec) . 554   Total (no wkt) . 26

Wright and Hollies did not bat.

Bowling Analysis

	O	M	R	W	....	O	M	R	W
Tuckett .	47	7	115	5	....	3	0	4	0
Dawson .	33	11	81	1	....	6	2	6	0
Mann . .	53	16	99	1	....	3.1	1	16	0
Rowan .	65	11	174	1					
Smith . .	17	2	73	0					

Fall of Wickets

1	2	3	4	5	6	7	8	9	10
75	96	466	515	526	541	554	554	—	—

South Africa

A. Melville, c Bedser b Hollies . . .	117	b Edrich . .	8
B. Mitchell, st Evans b Compton . . .	46	c Edrich b Wright .	80
K. G. Viljoen, b Wright .	1	b Edrich . .	6
A. D. Nourse, lbw b Wright . . .	61	b Edrich . .	58
O. C. Dawson, c Barnett b Hollies . . .	36	c Edrich b Compton	33
T. A. Harris, st Evans b Compton . . .	30	c Yardley b Compton	3
A. Rowan, b Wright .	8	not out . . .	38
L. Tuckett, b Wright .	5	lbw b Wright .	9
N. Mann, b Wright . .	4	b Wright . .	5
J. Lindsay, not out . .	7	c Yardley b Wright .	5
V. I. Smith, c Edrich b Pope	11	c Edrich b Wright .	0
Extras (l-b 1) .	1	Extras (b 3, l-b 4)	7
Total .	327	Total .	252

Bowling Analysis

		O	M	R	W		O	M	R	W
Edrich	.	9	1	22	0	. . . .	13	5	31	3
Bedser	.	29	1	76	0	. . . .	14	6	20	0
Pope	.	19.2	5	49	1	. . . .	17	7	36	0
Wright	.	39	10	95	5	. . . .	32.2	6	80	5
Hollies	.	28	10	52	2	. . . .	20	7	32	0
Compton	.	21	11	32	2	. . . .	31	10	46	2

Fall of Wickets

1	2	3	4	5	6	7	8	9	10
95	104	222	230	290	300	302	308	309	327
16	28	120	192	192	201	224	236	252	252

England won by 10 wickets.

THE THIRD TEST MATCH

Played at Old Trafford, Manchester, on July 5th, 7th, 8th and 9th, 1947

AFTER the amiable perfection of the Test wickets at Trent Bridge and Lord's, reports on the pitch at Old Trafford promised excitement. County players told almost hair-raising stories of the 'green' wickets there: Gover, in his declining years the fastest bowler in England, was the villain of most of the stories. The Lancashire club, in taking the M.C.C. recommendations on the preparation of wickets more seriously than (on the evidence of the Lord's Test wicket) the Lord's groundsman had done, had produced a series of 'green' wickets. On the 'green' wicket the close, thick grass aids the seam bowler, who, as well as coming off steeply, produces the effect of a 'cut' break merely by the use of a normal swing grip and action.

Bedser and Pope, who in the Lord's Test had taken one wicket—that of the South African No. 11—between them, were dropped from the English team. Bedser was obviously tired after his Australian tour—or, more to the point, after fourteen almost unbroken months of cricket immediately upon beginning first-class cricket. In their places were chosen Gladwin of Derbyshire and Cranston of Lancashire, each playing in his first Test. This meant that Edrich, successful as a pace bowler at Lord's, was to open the bowling. The other opening bowler, presumably, was to be Gladwin, who does not open the bowling for Derbyshire (Copson and Pope do so). Gladwin was in the top three in the first-class bowling averages. Cranston, in his first season of county cricket, had played well for

Lancashire against strong opposition and at critical stages of matches: he had made no long scores, produced no impressive bowling figures, but his runs had invariably been useful and his wickets decisive. The changes in the side strengthened the batting, but left the bowling weaker and promised to throw an increased strain of bowling upon Edrich and Compton.

Melville left out Harris and Smith for Dyer and Plimsoll. Dyer, a purely defensive batsman, was brought in to give more solidity to the batting, which had collapsed at Lord's. Plimsoll had bowled well in lesser matches, and the Old Trafford wicket seemed likely to help him; although he was not an outstanding batsman or fieldsman, he was probably better as either than Ian Smith, who had not bowled well at Lord's.

First Day—Saturday, July 5

When Melville won the toss, he must have thought for a few moments before he decided to bat. The wicket was 'green', the early morning dew was still upon it, with little heat in the air to dry it rapidly, and a very strong wind was blowing down the wicket from the Stretford end. This wind, although distressing to fieldsmen and to batsmen, was likely to give help to the bowler canny enough to use it thoughtfully. But in these days, when Press criticism can make a captain a failure in all but actual fact, it is always wise to bat on winning the toss. The captain who puts his opponents in and does not skittle them out receives far more blame for his 'gamble' than he would if he decided to bat and his side were put out easily.

So South Africa batted. Melville took Dyer in with him, and Edrich—with the gale behind him—and Gladwin opened the bowling. Yardley used these two bowlers and the other two seamers in the side, Cranston and Barnett, from the start, at twelve o'clock, until 2.45, before he brought on either of his spin bowlers, Wright and Hollies. In this time the four bowlers took only one wicket between them, although they bowled steadily enough for South Africa to make only 84 runs in the two hours. These figures bear little relation to what might have happened if Melville had put England in. On the 'green' wicket it is the two-shouldered bowler who recruits the full aid of the wicket—the bowler who bowls the ball *down* on to the pitch. Edrich, with his low, slingy delivery, and Gladwin, who employs much of a horizontal push, do not bowl the ball which will come sharply off a wicket such as this Test wicket at Old Trafford. Barnett is barely of medium pace and, like Gladwin, he had taken most of his wickets during the season because of the mistakes of county batsmen rather than because he genuinely *beat* them. Gladwin, by virtue of his action, which gives the ball very little lift, tends, especially on the Chesterfield wicket, to bowl frequent balls which are practically shooters. Now, presented with a seam bowler's wicket, he was unable to make full use of it. Cranston, whose action definitely sends the ball down into the green, was limited by his lack of experience—after less than three months of county cricket he was not yet 'doing' enough with the ball: he appeared to be bowling purely straight. Barnett's pace was just too slight to serve against watchful batsmen in a Test Match. Tate would have rubbed his hands with delight and done great destruction on such a pitch—but, where it might have conquered, this England attack was monumentally steady. Again and again Gladwin's inswinger smacked Melville's pads, but never, in the umpire's view, fatally. It was an almost elementary stroke that gave Hutton a catch at short leg, and South Africa were 32 for 1 wicket after fifty minutes with Melville gone.

Mitchell and Dyer was hardly a combination for forcing cricket, but it was a partnership which denied hope to the bowlers. Dyer twice rolled out a majestic off-drive, but, in the main, he was obviously preoccupied with the fact that South Africa had lost the previous Test Match and that he was now playing his first Test. Mitchell allowed a considerable amount of the English bowling to hit his bat until lunch-time. When Wright came on in the early afternoon he bowled one ball to Mitchell which beat him completely. But the hundred went up with both Mitchell and Dyer playing solidly and hitting the bad ball for certain runs. Dyer's fifty in his first Test Match was a slow business, but he had that strength which the South African batting had frequently needed. Just when it seemed that the English bowlers had completely shot their attacking bolt, Edrich gathered up his energies in one great burst—as he can do more often and to a greater extent than any other man now playing county cricket—and hurled down a ball which beat Dyer for sheer speed, well set as he was, and bowled him violently.

Nourse now came in to make his most determined start of the series—and to make English well-wishers wonder if it would not have been better to allow Dyer to remain. He struck ten determined runs from an over by Edrich to look firm at once. For the first time in the innings the runs were coming at one a minute, when Nourse went as suddenly as he had come—Yardley caught him brilliantly off Cranston. Viljoen's care seemed to cramp the spectators' eyes as he watched away the minutes to tea—a meal to which Mitchell seemed to go almost reluctantly as one unwillingly dragged from innings-building. There was the savour of veteran technique now with Mitchell and Viljoen going warily against bowling which resumed the steadiness from which Nourse had briefly threatened to disturb it. Gladwin was always dropping the ball in the right place, compelling care, but never the hasty stroke. Wright had a poisoned foot and was obviously not happy to be bowling. Once again Hollies employed the wind—bowling against it, so that there seemed an upwards check to his highest-thrown deliveries—and Viljoen several times played too soon at him, but hastily checked, and almost re-played his stroke.

The very smoothness of the partnership made Mitchell's run-out a shock to everyone watching the game: there was a complete misunderstanding between the two batsmen, and Hutton, from long-on, threw the ball in fast, straight, and with the coolness of the complete cricket brain. Mitchell had made 80, and, with the exception of one ball from Wright, nothing all day had looked likely to get him out. When Cranston bowled Dawson for 1, the game had once again turned in England's favour and 5 wickets were down for 215—a score which flattered the bowling. Rowan had to some extent overcome his tendency to play the half-cock stroke at forearm's length from the body and set about being junior partner to Viljoen. Viljoen, appreciating the responsibility thrust upon him by Mitchell's run-out, retired into his shell, only being lured out of it by invitations to the hook. Rowan at length went down the wicket to Hollies; the wind checked the ball, and he played his stroke too soon—his bat was on the upstroke of the follow-through when the ball hit his pad farther down the wicket than most umpires care for when lbw is in demand. Rowan was given out just after half-past six, so that Tuckett slouched out to the wicket with the air of a man just awakened from sleep in the pavilion, to stay with Viljoen until the end of the day. 278 for 6 was by no means a good score; but then, it was by no means a good day. The batsmen were obviously cold, and the very strong wind was unsettling to everyone on the field. The English attack had never been so good as the final score suggested. With the forcing batsmen, Melville, Nourse, and Dyer, all out fairly cheaply and the runs made by the more sedate Dyer, Mitchell, and Viljoen, South Africa had gone too slowly on a wicket which the bowlers had quite clearly failed to use to the full.

South Africa—First Innings

A. Melville, c Hutton b Gladwin	17
D. Dyer, b Edrich	62
B. Mitchell, run out	80
A. D. Nourse, c Yardley b Cranston	23
K. G. Viljoen, not out	66
O. C. Dawson, b Cranston	1
A. Rowan, lbw b Hollies	13
L. Tuckett, not out	6
Extras (b 1, l-b 9)	10
	—
Total (for 6 wkts)	278

Fall of Wickets

1	2	3	4	5	6
32	125	163	214	215	260

Second Day—Monday, July 7

Once again, on Monday, the wind howled hate at the cricket from a grey sky that remained uncertainly poised between the shades of smoke and storm. Edrich had not played cricket for a whole day, and he came to Old Trafford on this Monday with an immense credit balance of energy, which he proceeded to invest in his bowling. One delivery which flew over Tuckett's head full toss to the wicket-keeper standing back would, observed in isolation, have been credited rather to a siege engine than to human bowler. Using the crease thoughtfully, he bowled several balls to Viljoen which only the hastiest of strokes, produced by desperate reflexes, kept out of the wicket. Once again Edrich split open the morning's cricket by clean bowling Tuckett explosively. Viljoen was now looking anxiously for the loose ball and hitting it hard, but loose balls were scarce. Both Gladwin and Cranston were bowling on the wicket and to a good length, but, after Gladwin had had Mann caught by Hollies, Lindsay worked very hard indeed against the morning's new ball and showed more ability to play the pace bowlers than any of the other batsmen low in the order. He stayed with Viljoen for forty minutes until it seemed certain that he would be with him until he made his hundred. But when Viljoen had made 93 he played a ball from Edrich—or rather Edrich made him play at a ball—which he edged high to Compton at third slip as a catch more difficult than the catcher made it look. Then Edrich took Plimsoll's wicket to become quite the most successful bowler of the innings. Wright's poisoned foot allowed him to spend his day far from the cold wind of the cricket match.

If the South African 339 was low as compared with the opening innings of the previous Tests, it was a total which could easily have proved a winning one on this wicket which reacted to pace, seam, and spin. South Africa had scored their sixty runs of the day at only thirty an hour—and the state of the wicket was a considerable factor in their comparative slowness.

Hutton and Washbrook started the English innings determinedly—particularly Washbrook, who hit several fours off Tuckett. This may well have been because they thought it wise to make as many runs as possible before the effect of the roller wore off. Tuckett enforced less purely defensive play than usual, but neither batsmen had seen Plimsoll before. When Tuckett dropped a little short of a length, the ball rose steeply and quickly, but he appeared deliberately to pitch the ball up, particularly immediately after one had reared high. Plimsoll has the advantage of being a bowler—fast-medium left-arm, round-the-wicket—unusual in English cricket now. He used the wicket perhaps better than Tuckett, but was that degree slower, which made him relatively less dangerous. He had bowled six overs for seven runs when he had Hutton caught at the wicket—a heartening opening spell for his first Test Match. Hutton had scored only 16 of the 40 for the first wicket, and had not looked particularly happy, but whether this was due to the wicket or his current lack of success it was difficult to tell. Within ten minutes Washbrook, who had hit the ball very hard indeed on several occasions, was caught by Nourse off Tuckett and England were 48 for 2—a worse position than South Africa's had been: the innings was only fifty minutes old and the two opening bowlers were still on, with a little shine still on the ball and the wicket helping them.

But Edrich and Compton were together, and that was a circumstance which by now had become something of a nightmare to the South Africans. Edrich and Compton played their usual careful opening strokes against some good bowling from both the pacers. Several balls got up, one or two from Plimsoll came in late and sharply, and he made one go away from Edrich's bat. But the two batsmen had scored barely double figures when Melville brought on Mann and Rowan—no doubt to give them also a chance of moving one of the two batsmen before he settled. Edrich's care after his normal period of playing-in argued very good bowling (Mann was bowling as steadily as ever) or a bowler's wicket—probably both. Compton played some very quick and attractive shots to the turning ball—some of them almost, it seemed, as afterthoughts—he soon caught and passed Edrich and went to tea with 55 to Edrich's 36.

England were 143 for 2 when the new ball was taken at five o'clock. This was one of the crises of the game, almost certainly the turning-point. The light was not good, the pitch was still helping the seam, and both Tuckett and Plimsoll are men of considerable stamina. Plimsoll at once bowled Edrich at least two balls with the new ball which might have dismissed any batsman. Edrich promptly hit him, with quick-footed, fast, daring shots, for four, six, four, six, four, in two overs and again for six a few overs later—all three sixes played into the swing to long-on. Plimsoll had had thirty runs scored off his first fifteen overs, forty were taken off these five with the second new ball. In the first thirty minutes of the new ball Edrich scored 42 runs, catching right up to Compton again. Tuckett was only a little less expensive, and the game had been turned decisively. The danger had been attacked and driven off. This was so vital a piece of cricket that it is amazing that it seems to have provoked no discussion at all. It is certain that Plimsoll might, against any less determined batting, have won the Test Match for South Africa. Edrich, even more perhaps than Compton, brought to the problem both the mind and the temperament of a great cricketer. Any batsman, as Hutton could so well testify, who is scoring runs in great profusion is having some luck—whatever the extent of his gifts. This was Edrich's lucky season, and there is no doubt he knew it. He backed his attack upon this danger, not only with his skill, fitness, and knowledge of the opposing bowling, but he threw in also his luck—and he turned the scale. There was nothing that Plimsoll could do except to go on bowling and hope for the mistake—which against such bowling would inevitably have come from many batsmen less capable or for whom the luck was running at less full flood. There was nothing that Melville could do except keep Plimsoll on—as he did—until the gamble had gone one way or the other. But when Edrich was away from the bowling, there was Compton. There was no escape for the bowlers, no relief for the fieldsmen, until these two had ridden out the storm with a power and fluency which almost obscured their difficulties.

Edrich and Compton now hit runs with such certainty that the ball which flew, the ball which turned—and many did—seemed less a thing of danger than a fresh adornment to their batting. So much were they on top of the attack that it was difficult to believe that Compton had hit a catch to Tuckett off Dawson, who was undertaking only relief duty as a bowler. But so it was. The two Middlesex men had put on 228 in three and a quarter hours.

Barnett had only been three and a half hours in his pads on this occasion: once again he had no alternative, with the score at 276 for 3, except to hit. As soon as Barnett came in, there was indication of the difficulties Edrich and Compton had been mastering when a ball from Dawson struck him in the chest. Mann, wisely, though possibly desperate at the possibility of a Barnett onslaught immediately after Edrich and Compton, bowled him a full-toss which Barnett, eagerly, hit straight down mid-on's throat. England ended the day with 311 for 4 wickets: the three best opening batsmen in England could only make 46 between them, but Edrich and Compton had made 256. It was another example of Edrich and Compton rising to great heights of batting on a pitch which was never kind to them and against bowling which, bowled to other batsmen, looked very good indeed and which was backed by keen fielding. The South African bowlers faced the night's sleep with the knowledge that Edrich was not out and would be waiting for them in the morning.

South Africa—First Innings

A. Melville, c Hutton b Gladwin . .	17
B. Dyer, b Edrich	62
B. Mitchell, run out	80
A. D. Nourse, c Yardley b Cranston .	23
K. G. Viljoen, c Compton b Edrich .	93
O. C. Dawson, b Cranston . . .	1
A. Rowan, lbw b Hollies . . .	13
L. Tuckett, b Edrich	13
N. Mann, c Hollies b Gladwin . .	8
J. Lindsay, not out	9
J. Plimsoll, c Evans b Edrich . . .	8
Extras (b 3, l-b 9) .	12
	—
Total .	339

Bowling Analysis

	O	M	R	W
Edrich . . .	35.1	9	95	4
Gladwin . .	50	24	58	2
Cranston . .	34	12	64	2
Barnett . . .	5	3	11	0
Wright . . .	9	1	30	0
Hollies . . .	23	8	42	1
Compton . .	7	1	27	0

Fall of Wickets

1	2	3	4	5	6	7	8	9	10
32	125	163	214	215	260	287	298	327	339

England—First Innings

Hutton, c Lindsay b Plimsoll . . .	12
Washbrook, c Nourse b Tuckett . .	29
W. J. Edrich, not out . . .	141
Compton (D.), c Tuckett b Dawson .	115
Barnett, c sub b Mann	5
N. W. D. Yardley, not out . . .	1
Extras (b 2, l-b 5, n-b 1) .	8

Total (for 4 wkts) . 311

Fall of Wickets

1	2	3	4
40	48	276	289

Third Day—Tuesday, July 8

On Tuesday the sun shone on Old Trafford and the price of the visit was three and a half hours of play lost to the rain which heralded and escorted the sun. After morning rain the ball several times rose head-high. Yardley worked hard, playing the rising ball with courage, his bat close to his body, and his normal on-side bias. Edrich went on batting with a command of the awkward ball remarkable in one so short—however steep the angle of ball from pitch, he was right over it as he played it; again he was hard on Plimsoll upon the slightest opportunity. Yardley, who found Rowan bringing the ball on to him in the way which suits his stroke between square leg and mid-on, made two-thirds of his runs in fours. After Yardley had gone, Cranston played the forward defensive stroke earnestly, carefully, and with courage, as junior partner to Edrich. Tuckett's ball to bowl Edrich did so completely on its merits: it bit and turned back off the wicket at pace from a blind length. Cranston, Evans, and Gladwin each batted well enough to arouse hopes of a long stand, but Tuckett hit the stumps with two more inswingers and the English innings was worth 478, 139 more than South Africa's. There was the awkward period of thirty-five minutes for the South African innings on Tuesday night —too long for a 'night-watchman' from the tail, long enough to lose a good batsman for few runs. Melville could not keep grace nor attack out of his batting as he and Dyer concentrated on staying in, but Gladwin bowled Dyer and then worried Mitchell. At the end of the rain-punctuated day South Africa were 125 runs behind with nine wickets to fall, and a draw seemed the likeliest result on Wednesday.

South Africa

A. Melville, c Hutton b Gladwin	17	not out	12
D. Dyer, b Edrich	62	b Gladwin	1
B. Mitchell, run out	80	not out	0
A. D. Nourse, c Yardley b Cranston	23		
K. G. Viljoen, c Compton b Edrich	93		
O. C. Dawson, b Cranston	1		
A. Rowan, lbw b Hollies	13		
L. Tuckett, b Edrich	13		
N. Mann, c Hollies b Gladwin	8		
J. Lindsay, not out	9		
J. Plimsoll, c Evans b Edrich	8		
Extras (b 3, l-b 9)	12	Extras (l-b 1)	1
Total	339	Total (for 1 wkt)	14

Bowling Analysis—First Innings

	O	M	R	W
Edrich	35.1	9	95	4
Gladwin	50	24	58	2
Cranston	34	12	64	2
Barnett	5	3	11	0
Wright	9	1	30	0
Hollies	23	8	42	1
Compton	7	1	27	0

Fall of Wickets

1	2	3	4	5	6	7	8	9	10
32	125	163	214	215	260	287	298	327	339
12	—	—	—	—	—	—	—	—	—

England—First Innings

Hutton, c Lindsay b Plimsoll . . .	12
Washbrook, c Nourse b Tuckett . .	29
W. J. Edrich, b Tuckett	191
Compton (D.), c Tuckett b Dawson .	115
Barnett, c sub b Mann	5
N. W. D. Yardley, c Melville b Plimsoll .	41
K. Cranston, c Dawson b Rowan . .	23
Evans, b Tuckett	27
Gladwin, b Tuckett	16
Wright, not out	4
Hollies, c Nourse b Plimsoll . . .	5
Extras (b 2, l-b 7, n-b 1) .	10
	——
Total .	478
	——

Bowling Analysis

	O	M	R	W
Tuckett . . .	50	5	148	4
Plimsoll . . .	35.3	9	128	3
Rowan . . .	17	1	63	1
Mann . . .	35	12	85	1
Dawson . . .	14	2	44	1

Fall of Wickets

1	2	3	4	5	6	7	8	9	10
40	48	276	289	363	415	439	466	471	478

Fourth Day—Wednesday, July 9

Morning sun, strong enough to pierce the local smoke-ceiling, made the wicket at Old Trafford perfect for spin-bowlers on the fourth day. Parker or Verity—or, to look nearer today, Goddard or Clay—would have walked through any side in the world in two hours on this wicket. England, without a natural spinner, watched go by an opportunity which should always be anticipated by selectors. A wet wicket, and hence on some occasions a drying wicket, is so usual at Old Trafford that no side should go into a game there without either a slow left-arm break-away bowler or a right-arm off-breaker. Within a few minutes of the start of play Denis Compton was bowling slow left-arm, turning his leg-breaks eighteen inches and often lifting to the level of lifted eyebrows. The ball from Compton off which Mitchell was caught by Hutton at slip rose higher than Kortright could have made a long-hop fly on the Trent Bridge or Lord's Test wickets of this year.

A magnificent cover-drive by Melville which tore over the slow outfield was the first sign of South Africa's ability to take advantage of England's lack of a bowler capable of using the wicket. Wright, fit again from his poisoned foot, was bowling well, and so was Hollies, each of them turning sharply, but Compton ought to have been the bowler of the day. He was turning too much, often lifting too much, and, above all, was bowling too many balls wide of the off stump and turning away. No good slow left-hander would bowl, on such a wicket, this ball, which allows the batsman to play no stroke at all. Compton, who, within the bounds of his scanty bowling experience, varies his flight and speed, did better than there was right to demand he should do.

In a desperate situation Nourse used his strength of

approach and stroke. When Edrich once again bowled
Melville, tearing a stump out of the ground, and South
Africa were 96 for 3, there was such a burden of runs and
time upon both Nourse and the newly arrived Viljoen
that most batsmen in their places would have gone
slowly. But Nourse had obviously decided that Compton
must be hit off, and accordingly hit him, with a brutal
crash, into the crowd at long-on; he sent a four whistling
past third man, while Viljoen went quietly and ran when
called. In the face of Nourse's fierce hitting only Gladwin
could keep runs down to the two-an-over rate of steadiness, but he never appeared likely to beat the batsman;
rather he challenged him to attempt to force and thereby
get himself out. In face of Nourse's painstaking defence
to the good ball, only Edrich or Wright seemed likely to
beat him completely.

With South Africa behind, there were only two courses
open to the side. The first was to play for time on a wicket
on which England lacked a suitable bowler for the pro-
ceeding of destruction. The second was to go for runs in
the hope of setting England a score to make in short time,
and then to hope that the natural spinners Rowan and
Mann would get England out. Nourse made his hundred
at only just under a run a minute. Yardley brought on
Compton again, but Nourse hit him for six and he was
finally driven off. Then, when Nourse and Viljoen had
scored 121, Wright, who could usually make Viljoen go
the wrong way to his googly, had him caught by Hutton.
South Africa were now 78 runs on, and with six wickets
to fall, there was only three and a half hours left for play.
A stalemate draw seemed certain. Then Edrich bowled a
ball which came so fast off the pitch that even Nourse
with his tense, late stab in defence could only turn it on to
his wicket. It was hard that day not to admire Nourse:

his was memorable among all Test innings; its quality
enhanced by its setting. He might easily have put his head
down and played for a draw or for honour in resistance,
but he attacked bowling which ought to have been on
top, smashed the major danger (in Compton), and scored
himself a hundred at a speed not far short of Macartney's.
There was about his innings less than Macartney's grace,
but much of the fierce, short-armed power of Nourse—
for Nourse bats more like *himself* than many batsmen
have the power to do. It was not Compton, the batsman
employed as a spin bowler, but Edrich, the batsman employed as a fast bowler, who won the match for England
—when he took the wickets of Nourse and Dawson and
then of Tuckett. And he had struck the first blow when
he bowled Melville in the morning. Three batsmen,
Melville, Nourse, and Viljoen, scored 206 of South
Africa's 267. The turning ball on a soft English wicket
was again, in a summer of harder wickets than usual,
too much for the less experienced South African
batsmen.

England wanted 129 to win and had two hours and
three-quarters in which to score them. Although the
wicket was now too soft to help Tuckett and Plimsoll,
they bowled steadily enough at Washbrook and Hutton,
who played them for competent runs, pushing the ball
away at calculated angles until Mann and Dawson came
on. Dawson inherited what remained of the shine from
Plimsoll and bowled more steadily than either of the
opening bowlers. Mann and Dawson bowled five consecutive maiden overs. But there was no real fight; England
had batsmen and time to spare, as was expected. Yet, had
Rowan been in his form of the M.C.C. *v.* South Africa
match, South Africa might have won this Test. Certainly
on a wicket such as this at Old Trafford the England side

would not have scored a hundred runs against any two of Goddard, Clay, Hazell, Howorth, or Young. Dawson was used because Rowan had completely lost his form. Mann bowled 14 overs for 19 runs, and he took the wickets of Hutton and Compton. With little experience of such wickets, he was developing under the very eyes of the spectators. Mann is a less attacking bowler than Rowan. But he, who had always been able to keep the English batsmen quiet, was, on this day, attacking them. But his attack was robbed of much of its edge by the fact that there were runs at the other end—he had no adequate partner. When Rowan was put on, he bowled four extremely ordinary overs of irregular length—he, like Mann, was completely unused to such a wicket. Once again, with Hutton, Washbrook, and Compton out, Barnett came out to bat with every reason to feel that his place in the side was at stake in an innings that was relatively unimportant. At once he started to put bat firmly and defiantly at ball and, with four fours, ended the match.

Melville's problem of subsequent selection was the more difficult because it was not clear-cut. He might reasonably claim that England without Edrich and Compton would have lost the first three Test Matches. His batsmen at Nos. 1, 2, and 5 had done as well as their opposite numbers; his bowlers were at least as good as the English bowlers, and he had the better fielding side. The play of Edrich and Compton had been more than life-size, and therein lay a South African problem not to be solved, only to be prayed over.

Plimsoll had neither established himself nor put himself out of future reckoning. Choice between him and Smith would have to depend on the wicket in the next Test. There was a possibility that Begbie, a leg-spinner less dangerous than Smith, but, on South African form, a good batsman, might be brought in—but he had yet to produce runs or wickets in convincing numbers. The problem of the tail was one which seemed impossible of solution: Melville's need was a sound all-rounder.

The England attack had consisted largely of Edrich, Compton, and Wright. On a wicket for which almost any other pace bowler in the country would have thanked the god of cricketers and, on it, have bowled his way into the England Test team, Gladwin had signally failed. He looked, as he is, a steady county bowler, enslaved by the current cult of the inswinger, which, if bowled to a length, will persuade all but the first three batsmen of most post-war counties to get themselves out. That such a negative policy should have taken a man into a Test Match instead of being recognized as a symptom of the post-war weakness of middle-order batsmen was tragic. It is difficult to believe that Bedser could have failed on this wicket, and Perks of Worcester or any other two-shouldered bowler could have destroyed the South African batting, for all the courage of Nourse. The fault lay with current tendency, and not with Gladwin. Conscientious and humble service should not be confused with Test Match potentialities even when backed by the tables of averages. Neither Barnett nor Cranston could be certain of a place again, yet each deserved a further opportunity. Rarely can a side have won two consecutive Test Matches with so many problems unresolved.

South Africa

A. Melville, c Hutton b Gladwin	17	b Edrich	59
D. Dyer, b Edrich	62	b Gladwin	1
B. Mitchell, run out	80	c Hutton b Compton	6
A. D. Nourse, c Yardley b Cranston	23	b Edrich	115
K. G. Viljoen, c Compton b Edrich	93	c Hutton b Wright	32
O. C. Dawson, b Cranston	1	b Edrich	9
A. Rowan, lbw b Hollies	13	c Evans b Wright	0
L. Tuckett, b Edrich	13	lbw b Edrich	17
N. Mann, c Hollies b Gladwin	8	c Barnett b Wright	9
J. Lindsay, not out	9	b Hollies	0
J. Plimsoll, c Evans b Edrich	8	not out	8
Extras (b 3, l-b 9)	12	Extras (b 5, l-b 5, n-b 1)	11
Total	339	Total	267

Bowling Analysis

	O	M	R	W		O	M	R	W
Edrich	35.1	9	95	4		22.4	4	77	4
Gladwin	50	24	58	2		16	6	28	1
Cranston	34	12	64	2		—	—	—	—
Barnett	5	3	11	0		5	1	12	0
Wright	9	1	30	0		10	2	32	3
Hollies	23	8	42	1		14	4	49	1
Compton	7	1	27	0		17	2	58	1

Fall of Wickets

1	2	3	4	5	6	7	8	9	10
32	125	163	214	215	260	287	298	327	339
12	42	96	217	225	228	232	244	244	267

England

Hutton, c Lindsay b Plimsoll	. . . 12	c Dawson b Mann .	24
Washbrook, c Nourse b Tuckett	. . . 29	c Lindsay b Dawson	40
W. J. Edrich, b Tuckett	. 191	not out . . .	22
Compton (D.), c Tuckett b Dawson	. . . 115	hit wkt b Mann .	6
Barnett, c sub b Mann	. 5	not out . . .	19
N. W. D. Yardley, c Melville b Plimsoll	. . 41		
K. Cranston, c Dawson b Rowan	. . . 23		
Evans, b Tuckett	. . 27		
Gladwin, b Tuckett .	. 16		
Wright, not out .	. 4		
Hollies, c Nourse b Plimsoll	 5		
Extras (b 2, l-b 7, n-b 1)	10	Extras (b 9, l-b 8, b 2)	19
Total .	478	Total (for 3 wkts) .	130

Bowling Analysis

	O	M	R	W		O	M	R	W
Tuckett	. 50	5	148	4	....	5	0	26	0
Plimsoll	. 35.3	9	128	3	....	4	0	15	0
Rowan	. 17	1	63	1	....	4	0	13	0
Mann .	. 35	12	85	1	....	14	8	19	2
Dawson	. 14	2	44	1	....	9.5	2	38	1

Fall of Wickets

1	2	3	4	5	6	7	8	9	10
40	48	276	289	363	415	439	466	471	478
63	80	103	—	—	—	—	—	—	—

England won by 7 wickets.

GLAMORGANSHIRE *v.* WORCESTERSHIRE

Played at Ebbw Vale, July 12th, 14th and 15th

IT is truly happy for any man who loves cricket to go
away from the hub of cricket, the Tests and tourists
and trials and the great grounds, to the less imposing
centres where the play may be less 'important' (whatever
that means in cricket), but has the character of the people
who play it and the places where it is played. So down to
Glamorgan, to Wales, to see the match with Worcester
—only it was not in Glamorgan—not even in Wales, and
the poor ignorant Englishman hangs his head in shame.
Two of my favourite counties, several of my best friends,
and a whole week-end in a piece of England I had never
visited before, was holiday.

At Ebbw Vale the ground is no ordinary cricket
ground—no mere patch of green surrounded by seats.
From the pavilion, which is set back from the pitch on
flowered terraces, the bank on the left runs up high and
sheer for almost sixty feet. Whether this hill is natural or
of very old slag, I cannot be sure; I imagine it is something
of each. The bank is cut in terraces so that the spectators
can sit one above the other, and each is seen from feet to
head before the feet of the man above come into the pic-
ture. Straight ahead is the rugby ground and its grandstand—and nothing is so fadedly nostalgic as a football
stand during the cricket season. On the right, within encouraging range of the wicket, is the River Ebbwfawr,
here no more than a few inches deep, bustling busily over
its brown stones. Then, behind the river, the stone wall runs
high up to the road, where passers-by leaned against their
bicycles, some of them almost day-long, to watch the play.

Soot, slag, and coal-dust have won their place in this soil as part of the life and the spirit of the place; the earth is dark beneath the grass. Ebbw Vale has had little first-class cricket: only one county game had been seen there before. I wonder if they think that all first-class games are as full of incident as this one? Here, for three days, while the weather allowed, was cricket full of incident and gaiety and speed. It was accepted as drama. Wooller won the toss and batted on a damp wicket, slowish, but responding to both spin and seam. Solemnly the crowd, sober in its greys and blacks and browns against the dark wall of earth, settled to watch those old hands Emrys Davies and Arnold Dyson open the Glamorgan innings. As solemnly the two short figures walked to the wicket, Emrys Davies jaunty in his uptilt of shoulder and with his cap at an angle, Dyson quiet and silent at his side. Perks bowled the first ball to Davies, and a roar of applause, which would have signalled a fifty at least on any other ground, greeted Emrys Davies having played the ball away on the off side wide of the immediate fieldsman. The batsmen ran two, and the drama was on—' *Come, for the third, Laertes; you do but dally*'—they started on a third, and *Hamlet*-Davies was run out. Glamorgan 2 for 1 wicket.

Perks was characteristically accurate and dangerous even on a wicket too slow to be ideal for a bowler of his pace. He had Dyson caught at the wicket by little Hugo Yarnold when Glamorgan had made 12. Wooller, how-ever, is not a batsman to be overawed by the opposing attack, and with Porter dubious and careful at the other end, he investigated the bowling—and scored 42 in half an hour as he did so. Then he too was caught by Yarnold off Perks, Porter was lbw, and Perks went to lunch with 3 wickets for 20 and having had three catches dropped.

Glamorgan might have been 50 for 7 if these catches had been held—by county standards they were not difficult.

After lunch the two left-handers, Willy Jones and Allan (not Alun, I fear) Watkins, had a sympathetically left-handed partnership for Glamorgan. Willy Jones, possibly the finest outfield in England, is a batsman who is always taking risks. Hence he blends off-side strokes of pace and grace and excitement with 'iffers' which horrify the soberer judge. Upon his day, when he rides his luck without being thrown, he is thrilling to watch. This day he alternated between adventure, which looked unsafe, and defence, which irks him but can be effective. His partner, Watkins of Usk, is probably the most interesting young left-hand bat now in English first-class cricket. Short, grey-faced and quiet, he has immense possibilities. His play is built upon an almost impregnable defence: primarily and basically his wicket is safe. His run-scoring strokes are built on to, not tacked upon, his defence. He balances those strokes, playing on either side of the wicket. Hence he has no 'characteristic' shot, in the sense of a stroke which he might be tempted to employ against the ball not absolutely suitable for it. Two more seasons of county cricket should see him so versed in the tricks of the trade—for he is a shrewd and perceptive man, with his heart and brain in cricket—that his selection for England is automatic. He will make many runs against the best bowling because he has a calm cricketing temperament, a cricketing brain, and a technique of batsmanship which is sound to the last detail. He is also a brilliant short leg, frequently catching the uncatchable.

Howorth, who, that very Saturday morning, had awakened to his morning paper to find himself at the head of the first-class bowling averages, bowled, on and off, for best part of the day. It was difficult, Dick explained, to be top of the bowling: people expected you to take wickets —and cheaply; life was so hard, such a strain to a man inclined to rest and contemplation. He had the wickets of Muncer, Jones, and Pleass, the diminutive Cardiff batsman, before rain came to fit like a glove upon that dark and lowering landscape, with the clouds falling round the beacon like smoke and the air merging with the land in colour. Pleass looks a deft batsman, he helped Watkins to put on 82 runs for the seventh wicket, but his life might have been shorter than it was. Many of his strokes look handsome, but, particularly when playing forward defensively, he 'leaves the gate open' a foot—a huge gap between bat and pad which is to a spin bowler as a carrot before the nose is to a donkey. Lavis, far, far too good to be at No. 9 in any side in the country, saw the day out with Watkins, who was 88 not out and as sound as a bell to the end. Glamorgan's 211 for 7 was surprisingly satisfactory after the early collapse saved by Wooller and two later ones saved by Watkins.

Score at end of first day: Glamorgan 211 for 7 wickets. (Wooller 42, Watkins 88 not out.)

Sunday was the day of a Perks benefit match at Much Marcle. This was a day of sunshine and enjoyment. In the course of it, George Dews, the Middlesbrough footballer and twelfth man for Worcester in this match, produced the finest piece of deep-fielding I have ever seen. On a short boundary he ran twelve yards, and, his body horizontal in a dive, and one hand at full stretch, fielded a mighty drive skimming off the first bounce at immense speed. Landing on the points of his toes and the other hand, he swept to his feet, his body no more than brushing the ground and, the ball leaving his hand before he had reached an upright position, threw the ball full-toss straight into the wicket-keeper's hands.

The Worcester team already contains one fieldsman who is in world class: Laddie Outschoorn, a Burgher from Ceylon, is a promising batsman—a quick eye and deft control of limb being a heartening basis upon which to work. But it is doubtful if he is worth his place in the side purely as a batsman. As a slip-fieldsman, however, particularly to slow bowling, he is in a class alone, reminiscent, at times, of Constantine in the way he pounces forward to catch the ball dropping at the batsman's feet from the dead-bat stroke. He has neat and sensitive hands and takes the ball with a sinuous action indicating an Oriental quality in seeing the ball clearly, early and late, as Ranji and Duleep did.

The subject of Worcester's fielding automatically brings to mind Roland Jenkins, who has not always been successful as a spin bowler—largely his original qualification for selection—because, for many years, Perks, Crisp, Martin, Howorth, and Jackson were getting most of the Worcester bowling. No one needs constant bowling more than the leg-breaker if he is to be successful, and Jenkins has never had that regular employment which gives the spinner confidence in himself—but it may yet come. Since the war he has batted with some success and in a pawky style, stamped by a mock muscle-bound movement of limb, suggestive, deliberately suggestive, I suspect, of age and shrewdness. He is another brilliant fieldsman, either in the silly positions or at cover. He catches, chases, and throws the ball with delight and a humorous exaggeration of all his physical characteristics. He cannot bear to be left out of a cricket match; let him, he seems to beg, bowl or bat or catch or chase, or, at worst, please let him talk unendingly to all and sundry. A likeable little

man and cricketer is 'Our Jenky,' and a good man to play
with. At Much Marcle, by sheer dumb show, depending
upon a clenched right hand which purported to contain
the ball—which was plainly to be seen trickling to the
long-on boundary with no fieldsman near it—he made
two batsmen run up and down the wicket *side by side* in
complete panic three times, but magnanimously allowed
one of them to return alone and make his ground before
he threw the wicket out of the ground. Four runs might
well have been run off that stroke, yet no runs were made
—the batsmen never crossed!—never crossed in almost a
minute of mirth and panic created and dominated by
Jenkins. By this stage wicket-keeper, both umpires, and
most of the field were sitting or rolling on the ground
with laughter, and the spectators were convulsed.

Even after Outschoorn, Dews, and Jenkins there is,
rarely obtaining his place in the county side, Martin
Young of Worcester, another brilliant field. A Worcestershire side which one day includes these four players
will be well worth the spectator's visit for its fielding
alone.

Second Day

Pit and factory shift-work left the male population of
Ebbw Vale largely free to watch at least half of the play
on Monday. They saw Watkins complete a century of
much accomplishment: he pushes the ball away with the
left-handed solidity and broad-seeming bat of a Leyland.
But he is not an easy batsman to label in terms of others,
for the very good reason that he is so essentially himself
and his batting is so definitely built by, and around, himself. He and Lavis put on 75 for the eighth wicket, Lavis
batting elegantly and soundly with that trace of imaginative interest which makes him a cricketer of surprises and
worth. Then Watkins, speeding up, was beaten by

Jenkins' leg-break and Yarnold stumped him with immense gusto. Haydn Davies then scored six, four, six, one, six, six, in fourteen minutes; one of the sixes was a most remarkable stroke, played off the back foot to a ball a foot outside the off stump and clearing the boundary at long-on. I doubt if anyone in first-class cricket today, even Wellard, hits the ball so hard as Davies—who adds to the amazing effect of his strokes upon the spectators by his completely lackadaisical attitude at the wicket. A Glamorgan total of 314 filled the spectators with delight and surprised less biased observers.

The Worcester innings was not a happy one. Cooper has not shown in 1947 his form of 1946, nor approached in figures the standard of his obvious powers. Kenyon is a young batsman who will become at least a first-class county batsman. It is unfortunate for him and for Worcestershire that the side has now so many young players all in need of experience and short of veteran batsmen to give them solidity, now that R. E. S. Wyatt is out of practice, confidence, and, quite often, out of the team as well. Outschoorn, Horton, Yarnold, to some extent Jenkins, and even Alan White, stand in need of a regular model, batting at the opposite end, if their play is to reach the standard of which they are capable.

The Glamorgan bowling was begun by Wooller and Marsh. What a very good cricketer this Wooller is. He is a batsman who hits hard and scores fast runs against good bowling as high as No. 3 in the order. He is a brilliant fieldsman close to the wicket. His bowling, now that Austin Mathews is rarely available and Judge has been a season off the active list, is more than merely useful. He definitely moves the ball both ways—and that, which was once a qualification demanded of any good county pace bowler, is now sufficiently rare to need specific mention.

His action is high more by virtue of his natural height than any remarkable straightness of arm, but he delivers without hitch and with fair speed off the ground. He can bowl for long spells without losing his sting. Wooller ought never to be omitted from a Gentlemen's side nowadays.

Marsh is a bowler of occasional fair pace, but he tires quickly: his first few overs of outswingers are dangerous, but his action is slightly stiff, which restricts his pace off the wicket. After Kenyon and Cooper had scored 43 slow and rather fussy runs for the first wicket there was a steady flow of Worcester batsmen to and from the wicket to a point of 101 for 6. No. 7 was Howorth, whose batting form until now had been appreciably below that of 1946, when he opened the innings with Singleton and early made his thousand runs. Howorth, after a steady start, played some strokes of considerable power: when the bad ball comes to him he can be positively agricultural in his determination to hit it far away. Perks, who partnered him, hit five fours and a six in 35, and the partnership—landing the ball several times in the river, to the annoyance and handicap of the bowler—put on 74 runs at two a minute. Then the innings went down like a punctured balloon and Worcester, with 215, were 99 behind on the first innings.

There was time that night for Emrys Davies and Arnold Dyson to make 25 runs without disturbance: they did not hurry: they might have made more had they taken risks, but there for the morning papers was, Glamorgan 25 for no wicket. It did not look important to those who, far away, read the scores over their synthetic sausage or the toast of dyspepsia. In fact, many of the people on the ground were dissatisfied that Glamorgan had not made many more runs in the hour available with a view to an early declaration on Tuesday. Yet the partnership made a pleasant vignette, delightful to the palate of the cricket-taster. Davies played exquisitely his stroke that sends the quickish delivery to third man. He plays it quickly; no sooner is the actual contact of bat on ball complete than he tends to snatch the bat away like a boy who has been forbidden to do it, and would pretend that 'It wasn't me, mister.' There was reason, too, for their care. The firm of Dyson and Davies had been doing less well than usual, and this was the pair working to put the concern back into steady running order. A few weeks later they were reeling off hundred partnerships, and this was the beginning of their recovery—and recovery, for two men grown old in the service of cricket, can be a harassing business in the face of the new ball and the fine enthusiasm of morning bowling. Dyson puts the ball away on the leg side to the inch and will not be disturbed into demonstration; he merely grows more silent.

Score to the end of the second day: Glamorgan 314 (*Watkins* 111, *Lavis* 52 ; *Howorth* 5 *for* 76, *Perks* 3 *for* 72) *and* 25 *for no wicket. Worcester* 213 (*Howorth* 75 ; *Wooller* 3 *for* 62, *Marsh* 3 *for* 70).

Tuesday was to be a short day, with play ending at 4— or 4.30 for a finish, so that Wooller's need that morning was quick runs for an easy declaration. When Dyson was out to Perks, and with Emrys Davies to give him a stable end and run obligingly, Wooller made a rapid fifty, again bending a keen eye to hard but correct hitting. Then Jenkins was turned loose! Spinning the ball with fierce contortions, urging it on by word and gesture, Jenkins served up to the Glamorgan batsmen deliveries between slow and dead slow. But, they spun like tops. Wooller and Emrys Davies took the score to 106 before

Wooller was out. Then seven wickets fell for 51 runs because the batsmen tried to swipe Jenkins—who was in his element. Even the steady presence of Emrys Davies at the other end could not help them. Haydn Davies placidly went in at No. 4 and hit six, six, six, one, before Darks caught him on the edge of the field by the river, to prevent another six. Then, at ten minutes to one, Wooller declared: there was no great promise that Glamorgan could make any more runs if the remaining batsmen came in, so he retained some slight psychological advantage by declaring than he would have done if his side had been dismissed. His declaration allowed Worcester, after rolling and sweeping and the lunch interval were taken out, two and three-quarter hours in which to score 259—over ninety runs an hour on a wicket which took spin slowly and looked likely to hold together until Judgment Day. Cooper was out at once in trying to force. Alan White wisely told his younger batsmen, in whom he had to place confidence or deny them confidence in themselves, to make no attempt to strike the required eighty-ninety an hour at once, but to play themselves in first. This policy was a good one in respect of Kenyon and Outschoorn, both of whom are natural stroke-players. Well set, they are automatically fast scorers. Both, however, are at their best on fast wickets against quickish bowling.

Wooller and Marsh kept them quiet with the new ball and then Wooller brought on Muncer. Muncer came into first-class cricket far too late. His many years on the Lord's ground-staff while he was not able to win his place in the Middlesex team were years of waste of a very good cricketer. An admirable forcing bat, a bowler of resource and accuracy, and naturally safe catch, Muncer should have been a regular member of a county side long ago. He bowled his off-breaks from round, or over, the wicket according to the varying response of wicket or batsman. He varied his amount of spin, but was usually content to pitch on the middle stump and straighten or come across to the leg stump; his pace was just on the slow side of medium. Kenyon and Jenkins struggled against bowling which turned and, when they tried to increase their rate of scoring, were out. Worcester fell behind the clock, fatally so, it seemed. At ten past three, when White came in at No. 5 to join Outschoorn, they were 98 for 3, wanting 161 in only eighty minutes even if extra time were taken. For twenty minutes they struggled and made 15 runs before Outschoorn was out, hitting at Muncer. 3.30: Worcester 113 for 4, an hour to go and 146 wanted. The game seemed a certain draw. Howorth came in to join White, and Howorth was in no mood to truckle to bowlers—had he not been hit for 42 runs by the disrespectful Wooller? In twenty-four minutes they put on 55 for the fifth wicket, Howorth perpetrating some pulls of no little width before White hit a ball from Willy Jones—a most unusual bowler—into the hands of Muncer.

Then—Perks and Howorth together: Worcester wanting 91 in thirty-six minutes. They hit furiously, and their speed justified their claiming the extra half-hour, to which the umpires assented. The ball flew all over the Ebbw Vale ground—very frequently into the Ebbw, the Glamorgan bowlers hastily half-drying it before they bowled again. Twenty-one runs in six minutes before Howorth hit too soon at a ball from Muncer and was bowled. Horton came next—a Blackburn Rovers footballer and younger brother of Joe Horton, a pre-war Worcester batsman of great promise, who has left big cricket. Young Horton's job was to play second batting fiddle to Perks and to run between the wickets as and when required. Horton is a young man with handsome strokes but not the player for this position; but then neither was any other of the remaining batsmen. Seventy-six runs had come in thirty minutes; Perks now set about getting 70 in the next thirty minutes. Lamming the ball into the river three times, he made a desperate 21 in nine minutes before Willy Jones, safe as the Bank, caught him off Muncer. Now, with seven Worcester wickets down and twenty minutes left, Glamorgan had their chance. But Horton and Darks played it out of their hands and the game was left drawn—mainly by the margin of time lost to the rain on Saturday.

The play was never that of a drawn match. Indeed, it would be difficult to pick upon a game in which so much was to be seen of the best of cricket—decorated, for good measure, with twenty-one sixes. The bowling of Wooller, Perks, Muncer, Jenkins, Howorth, the batting of Wooller, Watkins, Lavis, Howorth, Perks, were all-absorbing and of strong quality; the fielding of both sides, with Outschoorn, Jenkins, Watkins, Wooller, Muncer, and Willy Jones outstanding, was very fine—except when Worcester dropped those fatal catches on Saturday morning. It would be ungenerous to forget the promise of little Hugo Yarnold, who will yet settle into a neat wicket-keeper and a good bat. And the wicket-keeping of Haydn Davies.

I would place Haydn Davies high indeed among contemporary wicket-keepers. With the full knowledge that such a statement is rank heresy to all the fashionable who watch their cricket from high places in the centre of England, I would rank him above Godfrey Evans, England's wicket-keeper. I have great admiration for Evans, but, without having seen his performances in

Australia, I would place him second to Davies. Evans
makes some spectacular leg-side stops, but these tend to
be one-handed or at arm's stretch, and often seem to me
to look more spectacular because he starts a fraction late.
I have frequently seen Davies make perfect stops off similar balls, but they never look quite so spectacular as
Evans's efforts. Davies is, as must be admitted, not so
pleasant to look at as Evans. He is dumpy, almost fat in
build, and inclined to slouch, but he moves, still unpre-
possessingly, at immense speed in a shuffle which maintains balance, and whether standing up or back, makes
stops very wide of the stumps with hands and body both
behind the ball. Watch him at opportunity and, forget-
ting his clumsy shape, observe the give of hands to ball,
the anticipation which carries him to positions from
which hasty late movement is rarely necessary. Or watch
him stump, calmly, lazily, yet with amazing speed.
Davies is an extraordinarily good wicket-keeper. What
ordinary wicket-keeper could, as he did, keep wicket for
six weeks with a broken finger? He did this, merely by
changing the point of contact of the ball in respect of one
hand—merely! This argues a degree of precision which
amazes.

As a batsman, Davies is not to be compared with Evans
except upon a very bad wicket, when his huge hitting,
which he can play late, might turn a match: he hits with
immense power and, proportionally, great frequency. It
is yet possible that he will receive the honours to which
his excellence entitles him, and that will be a recognition
of Welsh cricket which has been too long deferred.

GLAMORGAN *v.* WORCESTER

Glamorgan

Dyson, c Yarnold b Perks	4	lbw b Perks	.	. 16
Davies (E.), run out .	0	not out .	.	. 53
W. Wooller, c Yarnold				
b Perks . . .	42	b Jenkins .	.	. 50
A. Porter, lbw b Perks .	11			
Watkins, st Yarnold b				
Jenkins . . .	111	c and b Jenkins .	.	1 (8)
Jones, b Howorth .	27	b Jenkins .	.	. 2 (6)
Muncer, lbw b Howorth	0	run out .	.	. 6 (7)
J. Pleass, c Jenkins b				
Howorth . .	26	st Yarnold b Jenkins .		0 (9)
Lavis, b Howorth .	52	c Howorth b Jenkins .		6 (5)
Davies (H.), c White b				
Howorth . .	29	c Darks b Jenkins .		19 (4)
W. Marsh, not out .	3			
Extras (b 8, l-b 1) .	9	Extras (b 2, l-b 2) .		4

Total . 314   Total (for 8 wkts dec) 157

(Figures in parentheses denote second innings batting order
where changed.)

Bowling Analysis

	O	M	R	W		O	M	R	W
Perks . .	37	10	72	3	....	23	5	47	1
Darks . .	23	1	54	0	....	8	2	9	0
Jackson	36	9	74	0	....	3	0	3	0
Howorth	36.3	13	76	5	....	9	2	42	0
Jenkins .	4	0	29	1	....	10	0	52	6

Fall of Wickets

1	2	3	4	5	6	7	8	9	10
2	12	61	64	113	115	197	272	305	314
36	106	128	142	146	154	155	157	—	—

Worcester

Kenyon, b Wooller	.	19	lbw b Muncer .	32
Cooper (E.), c Davies (H.) b Marsh	. . .	12	c Lavis b Marsh .	4
Jenkins, c Muncer b Marsh		0	b Lavis. . .	20
Outschoorn, c Porter b Muncer	. . .	18	c Jones b Muncer .	38
Horton, run out	. .	3	not out . .	5 (8)
A. F. T. White, run out	.	14	c Muncer b Jones .	28 (5)
Howorth, b Wooller	.	75	b Muncer . .	46 (6)
Perks, b Marsh	. .	35	c Jones b Muncer .	36 (7)
G. Darks, lbw b Muncer	.	7	not out . .	0 (9)
Yarnold, not out	.	4		
Jackson, c Muncer b Wooller	. . .	0		
Extras (b 15, l-b 7, w 1, n-b 3) .	.	26	Extras (l-b 6) .	6
	Total .	213	Total (for 7 wkts)	215

Bowling Analysis

		O	M	R	W		O	M	R	W
Wooller	.	21.2	5	62	3	....	11	6	16	0
Marsh	.	17	2	70	3	....	3	0	17	1
Lavis	.	7	3	8	0	....	6	1	22	1
Muncer	.	15	2	41	2	....	17	5	47	4
Davies (E.)	.	1	0	1	0	....	12	1	58	0
Porter	.	3	0	5	0	....	1	0	6	0
Jones	.	—	—	—	—	....	4	0	43	1

Fall of Wickets

1	2	3	4	5	6	7	8	9	10
43	43	43	47	70	101	175	202	213	213
8	42	98	113	168	189	210	—	—	—

Match drawn.

THE FOURTH TEST MATCH

Played at Headingley, Leeds, on July 26th, 28th, 29th and
30th, 1947

LEEDS and Manchester are so vastly different as
Test wickets that the selectors of each side could have
been expected to examine their men closely even had
complete success been at their backs. After the Manchester
Test the English selectors, despite the English win, may
well have been more ill at ease than the South Africans,
because the shortcomings of the English team at Manchester had been fundamental. In the third Test the entire
balance of the England side had been wrong—it was not a
case of the failure of men to do the job for which they
had been picked, but failure to pick men for places which
must be filled in any Test team. The major South African
worry was the weakness of the tail, and this problem *had*
to be attacked, even though its solution, or attempted
solution, was, obviously and inevitably, to lead to some
reluctant decisions.

The English selectors decided to include a genuine pace
bowler—Butler—and a natural spinner—Young—in
place of Gladwin and Hollies. This meant that Edrich was
still to be used as an opening bowler, but that the wild
experiment with Compton as a stock spinner was to be
postponed until he had had some practice in the part.
The side looked more nearly a functional unit for the
changes.

South Africa dropped wicket-keeper Lindsay and
Plimsoll for Fullerton and Ian Smith. Originally the South
African party had been picked containing two wicket-
keepers, Lindsay and Ovenstone. Fullerton had subse-

quently been picked purely as the most promising young batsman in South Africa—the fact that he kept wicket for his province being no more than incidental. It was not planned that he should keep wicket on the tour. As a batsman, he had shown more of handsome stroke-play than of disposition to make long scores, but so far as batting was concerned he was obviously infinitely better than Lindsay. He had by no means Lindsay's style as a wicket-keeper, but he had shown that he could keep wicket competently. His selection was dictated by the collapse of the tail at Manchester. Smith for Plimsoll substituted a young man for an older one, leg-spinner for pacer: Plimsoll was a slightly better bat and field, though neither was to be regarded as a considerable asset in those departments.

First Day—Saturday, July 26

There was rain at Leeds overnight: the pitch showed grey-black mud through the grass. Melville won the toss, less a reason for congratulation than usual. His alternatives were neither of them pleasant, his choice was one which was almost certain to seem unhappy. He might bat, sending his side in on a typically damp and slow English wicket where his batsmen's normal timings and judgments would be useless. Otherwise he must put England in on a wicket of a sort to which the English batsmen were well accustomed, but which would give his bowlers little assistance—the ball would turn on it, but at miserably unhurried speed.

Melville batted: his decision could not be called reckless. The South African side was not one confident of winning. They had had the best of the first Test, but had been fought to a draw; they had lost the second and third to a team whose flaws must have been very obvious to them. The English power of recovery seemed to press them back just as Australian defensive actions have so often beaten England in the past thirty years.

There were sawdust piles on the pitch when Butler and Edrich began the English bowling to Melville and Dyer. Butler hardly looks a pace bowler. He carries a lot of weight, not all of it, one would guess, solid. His shoulders drop steeply, his chest seems to merge with his solar plexus, his hips are heavy, and his run-up is sag-kneed. His approach to the wicket is completely uninspiring, but the delivery itself is difficult to fault. He commences with a long diagonal arm-point strongly reminiscent of Tate, then, as he pounds his left foot, arm and shoulders heave right over and his body is swung from side- to full-on. His bowling gains all possible pace off any wicket. A man who bowls half his cricket at Trent Bridge must be able to extract life from a suggestion of dew, a mere flirt of rain, or hint of greenness—or else pound his heart into nought for plenty. Every possibly relevant muscle is employed to the full, and if Butler sometimes bowls a little short, he makes the ball kick enough never to be easy to play so long as he is along the line of the wicket.

He opened this South African innings by bowling too many balls off the wicket. The batsmen did not play a stroke at him at this juncture for fear of the easy and unnecessary chance; but those watching behind the bowler's arm knew that they were settling their eyes in at a remove from the danger which early bowling should always produce. From the other end Edrich bowled furiously and single-mindedly, but his low action tended to skid the ball through rather than to produce the rear—slight but definite—which Butler's action gave to his bowling. Before the day was a quarter of an hour old, in Edrich's second over, the major crisis of the match occurred. From that point onward there was never any real doubt of the course of the game. Melville, whose knowledge of English wickets and brilliant centuries at Trent Bridge had made him a symbol of South African batting, was bowled coming down too late on a ball from Edrich which came in to him a little more sharply off the pitch than even the bowler's edge-of-the-crease delivery promised. The first wicket fell with the South African total at 1, and their batting never recovered. After ten overs had been bowled for four runs and with his own figures 1 wicket for 3 runs, Edrich put on his sweater for Young to bowl in his place. Butler, his first four overs maidens and his first, eight-over, spell in a Test yielding only four runs, followed him, and Wright came on. The tension did not relax: Dyer is a man of patience, addicted to singles in the early stages of his innings. Mitchell moved warily and with minute care. Twenty-three runs came from the first twenty-four overs in an hour and a quarter, and then Dyer touched Wright's leg-spinner to Evans and was out—23—2—9. Nourse came in and thundered his first ball for four. But Cranston and Butler bowled grudgingly tight until lunch, when the unhappy South African batting had extorted only 34 for 2 wickets. Mitchell and Nourse after lunch were grim. Nourse doled runs like slowly thought-out insults; Mitchell was almost detached by contrast, but he too smelt disaster and shuttered his bat against it. He was bowled by Wright with a no-ball, but went on his solemn way unchanged.

Coming on a few minutes after lunch, Butler bowled at the wicket and was a better bowler than he had been at the start. He bowled a ball which moved away off

the ground, and Nourse edged it to Cranston at slip, and
Cranston did not hold it. Almost at once Nourse played
two typical shots to square leg for four runs each. The
sun was now making the wicket livelier, but it was by no
means sticky: there was still time for the late stroke to be
played with the middle of the bat. When the new ball
was taken, after fifty-five overs, South Africa had scored
82. The batting was that of men guarding against disaster.
The crowd was silent and intent, missing little. Mitchell
passed his fifty and was then late for Butler's inswinger
and was bowled. Wright was brought on to bowl to
Viljoen, who came in next. Wright is the only bowler
whom I have observed regularly to baffle Viljoen, who
never seems able to spot his googly. Again he picked
wrongly after paring a few runs, and Wright bowled him.
Nourse scored only 10 runs in half an hour after Mitchell
left: Butler bowled him with a ball which made pace off
the ground, and South Africa, their five chief batsmen
out for 125, were struggling. Dawson was unhappy, the
ball never seemed far enough up to him for him to drive
or, when it was, on this slow pitch, the drive must have
seemed to him a stroke he had still to learn. He was caught
by Young, also off Butler. Fullerton came in just in time
to see Rowan out to Edrich, bowling from the grandstand end, where there is no sight-screen. The light was
grey, the pitch sluggish, Butler and Edrich were bowling
more quickly and penetratively than any pair of English
bowlers had done in the entire series.

The Yorkshire crowd quietly and grimly relished the
position; here was a hostility after their own hearts. The
field was tight, there was no appreciable weak spot in it:
Wright, Compton, and Barnett ran fast and threw straight
in the deep: Edrich, Yardley, Hutton, Cranston made
quick, almost unfairly quick, stops. And South Africa

were 131 for 7. Fullerton, short and slight and fair, looked
dwarfed and timid, but he resolutely stuck a straight if
anxious bat to the ball and the situation did not deteriorate.
At the other end Mann either hit resolutely or allowed the
ball to strike his bat: the basis of his selection of balls for
these alternative forms of treatment was not always apparent. Cranston caught Fullerton in the slips off Edrich,
Butler was too fast for Tuckett, and Mann, hitting desperately in the company of Smith, was a gift to Cranston.
So the dismal South African innings ended for 175 runs.
Caught on a wicket which was the direct negation of the
foundations of their batting, with Melville out at once
and even Nourse struggling in chains, they had little
stomach to the keen warfare waged by Edrich and Butler.
Butler's final figures showed him as a success, and those
figures, allowing for the handicaps under which South
Africa's batting laboured, were fair. He kept the ball on
the wicket after his opening spell, and he moved the ball
both ways. In such a time of slavish adherence to the inswinger it was heartening to see the ball move late to the
slips with all the venom the wicket could give. And he
was always steady: as he slumped off the field he must
have been a happy man. Wright bowled happily—
he turned the ball a little and had two well-gained
wickets—but Edrich, who struck the first and fiercest
blow, and Butler were the sharp edge of the English
attack.

Hutton and Washbrook had an hour's batting on
Saturday evening. In that time, while they took 53 runs
off twenty-four overs, they revealed this wicket as a perfectly well-chosen place for the jobbing batsman to go
about his craft. Hutton had never played in a Test Match
in Yorkshire before, and the crowd reminded him of their
favour when he came out. He moved with certainty and

W. J. Edrich and Denis Compton coming out to bat at Lord's

Alan Melville and Bruce Mitchell walking to the wicket at Trent Bridge

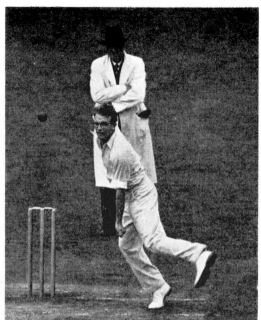

left: *Athol Rowan* (*South Africa*)   Top right: *N. B. F. Mann* (*South Africa*)
Below: *Melville plays Edrich to leg, Third Test Match*
The fieldsmen, left to right, are Compton, Cranston, Washbrook, Yardley

Top left: *R. T. D. Perks (Worcestershire)*   Top right: *H. T. F. Buse (Som*
Below: *The Bedser twins of Surrey, A. V. on the left, E. A. on the right—or is*

Top: *Haydn Davies (Glamorgan) keeping wicket at Lord's. Nourse is the batsman (M.C.C. v. South Africa)*

Centre: *Edrich hits Rowan for six in the Second Test at Lord's. The other batsman is Compton. Lindsay is the wicket-keeper*

Below: *C. Cook (Gloucestershire)*

Evans attempts to stump Mitchell, First Test Match. The other players, left to right, are Bedser, Yardley, Melville, Hollies, Hutton, Edrich

Hutton in play against Dawson. The fieldsmen, left to right, are Tuckett, Mitchell and Lindsay

The remarkable field set by R. J. O. Meyer for Buse (medium-pace) Somerset v. Gloucestershire, Whit-Monday, 1947. The players, left to right, are Gimblett, Lawrence, Crapp (batsman), Buse (bowling), Hill, Emmett (batting), Wellard, Luckes (wicket-keeper), Meyer, Tremlett, Woodhouse, Lee, Coope

one off-drive, played to perfection, brought a great roll of applause. Washbrook further developed his habit of allowing the inswinger to hit his pads or thighs while he held his bat well away from any possible course it might take. This is as effective as it is ungraceful and is done by Washbrook with an air of a man who knows exactly what he is doing. It plainly tells the man not on the spot to realize that the man-who-is has a plan of his own. The practice, too, is disheartening to the bowler, which will not be a factor in persuading Washbrook to discontinue it. England ended the day only 122 behind South Africa with the whole strength of their batting still to be got out.

During the afternoon a decision and instruction by umpire Frank Chester had considerable interest. At certain periods when the light was bad, he appears, from the evidence available, to have instructed Yardley not to bowl Edrich or Butler and Melville not to bowl Tuckett. If the decision was indicated to the captains in precisely this manner, it appears that a justifiable restriction was imposed in the wrong form.

The light was certainly bad, and when the bowling was from the grandstand end, where there is no sight-screen, it must have been difficult for the batsman to follow the course of the ball and he may well have been in some danger. The whole matter was referred to the M.C.C.

Pending their decision, it may not be impertinent to attempt to assess the position. It certainly seems that, at a certain point of bad light, a stage may be reached where fast bowling is dangerous, but slow bowling is not. There, it seems, the umpire should be empowered to say that, *if* a captain uses a certain bowler or bowlers, or *if* he uses a certain bowler or bowlers from one specific end, then he (the umpire) will declare the light too bad for play. Now, under some conditions, as on a 'green' wicket or against well-set batsmen on a plumb wicket, it may be an essential part of a captain's policy to use his fast bowler. If this is the case, he must be in a position to order that bowler to bowl a token ball from the forbidden end in order to have the umpire stop play for bad light. Alternatively, if he can, without prejudicing the chances of his team, use other bowlers, then he is in a position to provide cricket for that public which maintains first-class cricket by its admission money. The captain should, however, and obviously, be given this opportunity of making his decision —he cannot be penalized and his chance of winning taken from him by the *order* of an umpire.

South Africa—First Innings

A. Melville, b Edrich	0
D. Dyer, c Evans b Wright	9
B. Mitchell, b Butler	53
A. D. Nourse, b Butler	51
K. G. Viljoen, b Wright	5
O. C. Dawson, c Young b Butler	5
G. Fullerton, c Cranston b Edrich	13
A. Rowan, c Yardley b Edrich	0
N. Mann, c Edrich b Cranston	29
L. Tuckett, c Evans b Butler	3
V. I. Smith, not out	0
Extras (l-b 5, n-b 2)	7
Total .	175

Bowling Analysis

	O	M	R	W
Butler . . .	28	15	34	4
Edrich . . .	17	4	46	3
Young . . .	17	5	31	0
Wright . . .	20	9	24	2
Cranston . .	11.1	3	24	1
Compton . .	4	0	9	0

Fall of Wickets

1	2	3	4	5	6	7	8	9	10
1	23	113	121	125	130	131	158	175	175

England—First Innings

Hutton, not out	32
Washbrook, not out	21
Total (for no wkt) .	53

Second Day—Monday, July 28

Not long before Monday's play was due to start at Leeds, a mighty thunderstorm fell upon the ground. At this time I was about to travel from Bradford to Leeds and, unconscious of the nearness of rain, was studying what must be the most remarkable skyline in England. Undercliffe at Bradford is a district where some of the wealthier mill-owners resided in the days before motor-cars, and where they have left the delightfully Victorian baroque chalets as their enduring memorial—and endure they will, for the Victorian brickmaker and bricklayer built, at their best, to last. From the Undercliffe, looking towards the centre of the city, the eye refuses to believe its own story. It is as if the entire skyline of Constanti-

nople were concentrated into four hundred yards. A
cemetery occupies a brow of land to the exclusion of all
beyond it except the sky. The ground rises from left to
right to a peak swept up high above the chimney and
mountain-ridge roof of Lister's Mill. Within the cemetery
poorer men have been buried on the lower reaches of the
slope, their dumpy headstones or sinking green mounds
dotting the face of the hill that looks towards Undercliffe.
But, upon the very brow, the wealthy of Bradford were
laid to rest with due masonic reminders of their emi-
nence. A tenable theory is that the interments were begun
at the left, or lower, end of the brow. Thence, as the gate-
ways to eternity were cut out of the hill's edge, the
memorial stones march to the peak. The ground rises
with the march, but the tombstones rise, not only by
virtue of the rise of the ground, but also by the apparent
desire of each burier to install a memorial taller, irrespective
of gradient, than that above the previous entrant. In shape,
too, stone after stone outdoes its neighbour in extravagance, and a good funeral has been had by all—with
shock to the eye of him who looks upon the burying-
place unwarned and through the unreliable eye of early
morning.

But all this, as Charles Reade's publisher might have
said, all this is not cricket. At Headingley the crowds
stood six, eight, even twelve deep in great queues to the
turnstiles—for was not 'Lenoott'n' not out and threatening a century in a Test in Yorkshire? Despite the recent
storm, its waters still deep in gutter and hollow, 30,000
were inside the gates and almost as many more were
turned away. Inside the ground the first-comers had sat
out the storm upon the terrace seats they had won by
their early rising. Now they shouted in unison 'sit down'
to those who sought to stand up in front of them, and

spoil their view. So the standers folded papers or mackintoshes or groundsheets, put them down into the puddles and sat squelching to watch the game fairly.

After an inspection of the wicket at 12, play started at 12.30. The atmosphere was like that of a Turkish bath—the heat, weighed down by cloud, pressed upon the brow, the ball seemed to move sluggishly through it. The crowd steamed in silence. Mann and Tuckett bowled. Almost at once Washbrook swept the ball sharply but straight into the hands of short leg, who dropped it and turned away as if in agony of soul. Hutton and Washbrook went steadily along at their own pace, which was 27 runs in the forty-five minutes to 1.15. At this point Rowan took over from Tuckett at the Kirkstall end. On a wicket which took spin, but repaid it at no great height or speed, he bowled steadily for the fifteen minutes before lunch, by which time England were 94 for no wicket and Washbrook and Hutton had revealed adroitness in dropping the wrist before the rising ball and hitting the short ball hard indeed.

After lunch Rowan continued to bowl, causing a prolonged lapse in play when he went round the wicket, since the wheels of the sight-screen, which had to be moved to accommodate the change, were enmeshed in some old nets. A number of spectators who had taken up that best of all positions for the cricket watcher—beside the screen—left it slowly and with reluctance. There were many people in the ground only too pleased thus to move into the newly created space on the other side of the screen. The ground was not uncomfortably full so far as standing space was concerned, but it was definitely too full for many who had paid to watch cricket to be able to do so. There has been ample indication during the past two years that every seat that is installed at a Test Match

ground is worth at least fourteen shillings a year—a rate
of interest which should not be neglected by county
authorities, who may remember the less frequent occasions on which the huge Australian grounds are completely
full—roughly once in four years, on the occasion of the
M.C.C. visit for a Test.

Washbrook was 43 to Hutton's 53 when the hundred
went up. On a pitch never friendly they had not hurried,
but they had scored whenever reasonable opportunity
offered itself. Now, by taking some quick runs off Smith's
leg-breaks, Washbrook passed speedily ahead of Hutton,
mainly by dexterous strokes on the leg side. Mann came
on for Smith. Rowan, at the other end, bowled steadily
on, the atmosphere wringing sweat from him. He had not
been in form for some weeks, which was due to loss of
confidence rather than to any flaw in his technical equipment as a bowler. Even now, his switch to round-the-
wicket brought full tosses, but soon, so long as no silly
fieldsman stood close, he bowled to the fine point of
length and direction, moving the ball away from the batsman with his arm and bringing it back with sharp off-
break spin. More than once Hutton and Washbrook
evaded dismissal by a hasty and not-too-certain grope
forward which sent the ball spinning off the edge to the
point where short leg would have been—had Melville
dared, for Rowan's confidence, to station short-leg
fieldsmen. Then Mann made a ball leave the ground
sharply to bowl Washbrook, who had scored 75 of the
141 for the first wicket.

Edrich was less certain than he can be, groping at times
in playing Rowan, who was wearing a black trail of foot-
marks to the wicket at the Kirkstall end. Mann and Rowan
drew the net tightly about the batsmen. Hutton was making a century as certainly as I ever saw a batsman do. His

strokes were controlled to the last degree of watchfulness and deep technique. Edrich fretted against the restraint, but fought on, his quick, concentration-bent figure exuding tense care. Rowan bowled for the whole two and a quarter hours between lunch and tea, with Mann at the other end for the last hour and twenty minutes of that time. Now the fieldsmen crept up to the batsmen's legs as Rowan bowled. He wavered once, and then returned to length, direction, and spin. He floated the ball away in the air, he threw in the leg cutter, which is 'spottable' from his hand, but nevertheless difficult to play. But usually he sent the ball away with his arm and tugged it back on the string of spin. Hutton was 89 at tea and Edrich 28, the total 202.

After tea Smith bowled opposite Rowan, who remained unchanged at the Kirkstall end. Hutton made his certain century, four and three-quarter hours long, without a mistake or a suggestion of a mistake, without a ball lifted or a risk taken. The Yorkshire crowd had waited for this, had faced the storm, had sat watchful all day when any other crowd would have howled its disapproval of slow defence, and now it rose and cheered Hutton like an emperor. At once he hit a ball to cover, where Rowan was a tired man, his sweat-sodden shirt clinging to him. Hutton started to run, Rowan moved fast, crab-like, upon the ball, picked up and flipped in with a single action, and Fullerton ran Hutton out. Now came Compton, and the day weighed heavily even upon him. Mann came on for Smith—Rowan still at the Kirkstall end—and the batsmen struggled against bowling which could not be robbed of its sting by heat or length or weight of day. Edrich flung his bat at a ball from Mann which was of too good a length for any treatment but the respectful bat of defence, and Melville took the catch. Barnett was next,

and if Barnett could not hit this bowling, no true batsman in England could do so. He hit a four at once, a
great roaring four with the smack of the country about it;
another stroke was saved from the boundary and counted
only two. Then he tried to hit Rowan against the spin,
and Tuckett lumbered comfortably across from deepish
mid-off to extra cover to pouch a catch that was never so
easy as he made it look. Soon afterwards Rowan came
off. He had bowled from a quarter-past one until a
quarter-past six—lunch and tea took away an hour—he
had bowled for four hours, 46 overs, unrelieved, for 89
runs, against the five best batsmen in England. The bad
balls he bowled could be counted upon the fingers of one
hand, yet the day was so humid as to distress any but the
fittest of men. I know of no other instance of a man
bowling 46 consecutive overs in a Test Match—more
overs have been bowled, but not, I think, consecutively.
Moreover, this was a performance by a bowler who,
until he took up the ball, had been accounted utterly out
of form for a month.

Compton, a new, hard-working, careful Compton,
gave Mitchell a slip catch when a ball from Mann lifted.
With Yardley determined to push the score along and
doing so with considerable competence, Cranston tried to
follow his example, only to give Melville a catch, also off
Mann. Yardley seemed well set when he was out to
Smith, but it was a day of length and spin and a bad day
for the batsman who treated those threatening portents
with less than respect. The small and jaunty figures of
Evans and Young at the wicket at the end of the day had
more of impudence than the innings had seen before. In a
day of five and a half hours a return of 264 runs indicated
either bad batting or good bowling: had it not been the
latter, the Yorkshire crowd would have been the first to

see it and would have risen from their wet places about the ground and told the players so. England's lead of 142 was more than an insurance against defeat—it seemed to promise success.

South Africa—First Innings

A. Melville, b Edrich	0
D. Dyer, c Evans b Wright . . .	9
B. Mitchell, b Butler	53
A. D. Nourse, b Butler	51
K. G. Viljoen, b Wright	5
O. C. Dawson, c Young b Butler . .	5
G. Fullerton, c Cranston b Edrich . .	13
A. Rowan, c Yardley b Edrich . .	0
N. Mann, c Edrich b Cranston . .	29
L. Tuckett, c Evans b Butler . .	3
V. I. Smith, not out	0
Extras (l-b 5, n-b 2) .	7
Total .	175

Bowling Analysis

	O	M	R	W
Butler . . .	28	15	34	4
Edrich . . .	17	4	46	3
Young . . .	17	5	31	0
Wright . . .	20	9	24	2
Cranston . .	11.1	3	24	1
Compton . .	4	0	9	0

Fall of Wickets

1	2	3	4	5	6	7	8	9	10
1	23	113	121	125	130	131	158	175	175

England—First Innings

Hutton, run out	.	.	.	.	.	100
Washbrook, b Mann	.	.	.	.	75
W. J. Edrich, c Melville b Mann	.	.	43
Compton (D.), c Mitchell b Mann	.	.	30
Barnett, c Tuckett b Rowan	.	.	.	6
N. W. D. Yardley, c Nourse b Smith	.	36
K. Cranston, c Melville b Mann	.	.	3
Evans, not out	.	.	.	.	6
Young, not out	.	.	.	.	0
Extras (b 8, l-b 8, n-b 2)	.	18

Total (for 7 wkts) . 317

Wright and Butler to bat.

Fall of Wickets

1	2	3	4	5	6	7
141	218	241	253	289	306	316

Third Day—Tuesday, July 29

Yardley declared at once on Tuesday morning, 128 runs ahead. The English tail was unlikely to be very profitable, and also the declaration gave him some psychological advantage. It would have given him less of this particular advantage in any other Test. But in this, with Melville lost so early in the first innings and England building up their lead against bowling which the South Africans knew to be the best they could produce, the South Africans were in less good heart than at any other stage of the tour.

Again Butler and Edrich opened the bowling to Melville and Dyer. The light was not bright, but better than on Monday, and the wicket was still slowish, less inclined to show the pace-signals of drying than on the day before. Again Edrich struck his blow early: in his second over Dyer mistimed him and sent a catch to Yardley. After four overs Edrich came off, and Young took his place. Mitchell had little reason to observe any change, in this match, between batting at No. 1 and at No. 3—except the absence of the loose ball often to be found in a first over, but rarely in a fifth. In each innings he was in before the end of the fourth over. Quite what happened to the ball with which Young bowled him could not be said with certainty from the pavilion, but he seemed to be both over and wide of it and South Africa had lost 2 wickets for 16 runs in half an hour—and all the rest of Tuesday and Wednesday stretched before them. It is this feeling of isolation in time that makes the four- or five-day Test such a strain even by comparison with county cricket. The time-factor in these games seems to have been conceived for giants unless the game is played on a pure batsman's wicket.

Melville was obviously anxious, but he and Nourse put on a brave front and batted resolutely. Melville, even at his most watchful, cannot conceal the grace and poise of his batting: even his slowest batting is always instinct with stroke-play. Young bowled at him gaily. Short and almost shock-headed, Young bowls as if he were eager to get at the batsman. Three or four jumpy steps and he is at the crease. His slow, left-arm, round-the-wicket deliveries are 'dug-in.' They spin wherever a ball will turn, because he *drags* the spin upon them. His length is perfect, or that fraction short of perfect which defies forcing attack. Rarely does he flight the ball or throw up the half-volley that invites the big stroke unless the pitch is much upon his side. With Mitchell's wicket already behind him, he found confidence.

Young bowled to Melville, outside the off stump. Melville moved forward and played that cover-drive which is his most characteristic stroke—bat and body were merged in the onward flow of the stroke and the ball flew away on the off side, wide of Denis Compton, stationed shortish at extra cover. Compton made a swoop at the ball and, faster than eye could tell the brain, his left hand was under the ball, and, with his fingers touching the ground, he made a catch which stunned almost every spectator. There was a pause before realization brought him a huge burst of astonished, involuntary applause. Description racked the brain for words adequate to describe the incredible speed and timing which brought hand so astoundingly to ball in that torn second of poised grace as the catch was made.

This was the most memorable moment of the game and, by dismissing Melville for the second time and when he seemed well set, Compton provided the second minor crisis of the game, after which nothing could save South Africa. Nourse shouldered his burden stolidly. He battled slowly, watching the ball with suspicion, smiting it at the last moment and cowing it before its spin could carry through. Viljoen was with him, and they laboured their way to lunch in singles or an occasional two. Target runs loomed ahead of them, towering, it must have seemed, to the sky. Viljoen was quietly thoughtful. Wright bowled four maiden overs, disturbing Viljoen. The batsman recovered from each delivery which puzzled him only for the next to come as a new problem. Butler was rarely off for long: his twelve overs before lunch cost only 13 runs; he was moving the ball through the air and off the pitch, attacking the stumps all the time and making sufficient pace off the ground to compel respect even when he was not enforcing the hasty stroke. A little before three o'clock he came on with the new ball, and in two overs he fired away the foundations of South Africa's hope of recovery. First Viljoen and then Nourse was lbw to his inswinger, which moved late and sharply and came quickly off the pitch to defeat a positive stroke played into a late line on the ball.

Dawson's innings was, from the first, one of anxiety. He was never comfortable against Butler, who by moving the ball away from him made him hesitant about the employment of his usual off-side strokes and then forbade them by use of the inswinger. He bowled Dawson with another good ball which beat a specifically defensive shot. Fullerton and Rowan stayed for forty unhappy minutes, batting with brave defensive strokes, but always giving the impression, against Butler, that they lived only from ball to ball.

Then Cranston was put on to bowl, with the best of the shine long gone from the ball. This was, one assumed, merely a rest for Butler, who would resume later and wipe out the remainder of the South African innings. Cranston was initially inspected for the duration of a maiden over, thereafter, for four overs, runs were taken off him, not heavily, but with a steadiness which had not been shown against Butler. He had had little success in his two Test Matches; indeed, little success could be expected for him in view of his lack of experience. Now, one thought, he was being given his last spell in Test cricket unless and until he justified himself afresh. His bowling was ordinary enough: taking a twelve-yard run up to the wicket from behind mid-off, he bowled high with a wristy flap which gave him some pace off the wicket. The ball bowled was little more than straight, but it was straight at the wicket, of goodish length, and occasional movement from the off prevented him from being hit freely. The ball with which he had Fullerton lbw at the beginning of his seventh over was well up to the bat and should have been driven. South Africa 184 for 7. When Cranston finished his over, South Africa were 184 all out. He had Fullerton lbw, Mann caught at the wicket by Evans, and he clean bowled Tuckett and Smith in a single over for no runs. The over read, in the score-book:

```
w   .
    .   w
w   w
```

This over saved his Test Match place for Cranston. Let us admit that it was by no means an over of outstanding deliveries. It dismissed one fair and three, by Test standards, poor batsmen. It finished off an unhappy innings played by natural, fast-wicket players on a wicket which was often drying but never dry. The South Africans had never recovered from the first-innings dismissal of Melville, and this final blow reflected more their disheartedness than superlative excellence on the part of Cranston.

England wanted only 47 runs to win, and these were scored by Hutton and Washbrook, with competence, in an hour. That hour's play, if relatively unimportant in that the win-or-lose issue was not in hazard, nevertheless contained some small gems for the connoisseur. Melville gave Tuckett, Dawson, and Mann a bowl each in case miracles were about. Off Tuckett Hutton made a few strokes, only for ones or twos, but which bore the stamp of the master-batsman. Once the ball swung into him late, and he played it away on the on side with a stroke which, it seemed, must force him to move his left leg, but the bat, like a pendulum, swung dead true and passed the barest fraction of an inch from the pad to move into the ball and persuade it away as the right leg followed into the first stride of his run. Late, very late, Mitchell was

allowed tò bowl from the grandstand end, for amusement only. He opened with a maiden of no little variety.
He would spin for you, or toy with swing, once even
with pace, and Hutton looked at him carefully, for these
matters are serious in Yorkshire. When you are equipped
with a bat and a man bowls at you, a certain dignity is
demanded. Even if you are in a net, you do not violate
the good manners of batsmanship by taking a wild swing.
Even a bad bowler may bowl the unplayable ball, and if
you treat him with contempt and are out, then you have
made a cricketing mistake. So Hutton investigated
Mitchell. Later, comfortable runs were taken from his
second and final over, but that maiden remained for him
as a source of quiet amusement. Mann fed Hutton full
tosses on the leg side to end the game, and, off one of
them, Dyer's one-handed stop on the square-leg boundary was among the finest fielding moments of the season.

England's win gave her the rubber. But most important from this game was the discovery of Butler, who,
as his figures show, bowled an honest share of the side's
overs, was always difficult to score from, and took *good*
wickets. Hutton's return to form, after the lapse which
followed his brilliant three weeks at the beginning of May,
was welcome, but it had no major effect upon selection.
Hutton, so long as he is fit and in practice, must always be
an automatic choice for England. His place is among the
great batsmen, not as the holder of the record Test score
—he made that as a restricted batsman—but as master of
every stroke and one of the most knowledgeable men
about cricket now playing the first-class game. Young
was a partial success; he bowled steadily, but, on a wicket
never unhelpful to him, he had shown no great power of
penetration. Barnett had not succeeded, but, once again,
the state of the game had demanded that he force or get

out. A forcing batsman, he had never been given real breathing space—had never gone in when the state of the game allowed him to take as long as he needed to play himself in. Cranston's one last over presumably kept him his place, although, unless they were to be too easily convinced by figures, the selectors were bound to realize that it was a statistical rather than a cricketing success.

For South Africa, they went from the fourth Test a side which had fought, but fought with less hope than so good a team should possess. Fullerton had been competent as a wicket-keeper; as a batsman he had looked better than Lindsay, but not in the class of the first five batsmen. The South African bowlers had done well. Rowan had justified himself magnificently: Mann had once again returned figures which indicated monumental steadiness in face of fatigue. Tuckett, who bowled less than in some matches, had always kept the batsmen playing. Smith had been less successful, both as run-preventer and as wicket-taker. But he was so young, and a leg-spinner was so necessary in the team, that, with the choice so narrow, his inclusion as an investment for the future was always a wise one. The major trouble for the South Africans now was loss of confidence—which had to be regained on the field of play.

South Africa

A. Melville, b Edrich	0	c Compton b Young	30
D. Dyer, c Evans b Wright	9	c Yardley b Edrich	2
B. Mitchell, b Butler	53	b Young	5
A. D. Nourse, b Butler	51	lbw b Butler	57
K. G. Viljoen, b Wright	5	lbw b Butler	29
O. C. Dawson, c Young b Butler	5	b Butler	17
G. Fullerton, c Cranston b Edrich	13	lbw b Cranston	13
A. Rowan, c Yardley b Edrich	0	not out	21
N. Mann, c Edrich b Cranston	29	c Evans b Cranston	0
L. Tuckett, c Evans b Butler	3	b Cranston	0
V. I. Smith, not out	0	b Cranston	0
Extras (l-b 5, n-b 2)	7	Extras (b 4, l-b 6)	10
Total	**175**	**Total**	**184**

Bowling Analysis

	O	M	R	W		O	M	R	W
Butler	28	15	34	4	....	24	9	32	3
Edrich	17	4	46	3	....	14	2	35	1
Young	17	3	31	0	....	19	7	54	2
Wright	20	9	24	2	....	14	7	31	0
Cranston	11.1	3	24	1	....	7	3	12	4
Compton	4	0	9	0	....	2	0	10	0

Fall of Wickets

1	2	3	4	5	6	7	8	9	10
1	23	113	121	125	130	131	158	175	175
6	16	59	130	130	156	184	184	184	184

England

Hutton, run out . . 100	not out . . . 32
Washbrook, b Mann . 75	not out . . . 15
W. J. Edrich, c Melville b	
Mann 43	
Compton (D.), c Mitchell b	
Mann 30	
Barnett, c Tuckett b Rowan 6	
N. W. D. Yardley, c Nourse	
b Smith . . . 36	
K. Cranston, c Melville b	
Mann 3	
Evans, not out . . . 6	
Young, not out . . . 0	
Extras (b 8, l-b 8, n-b 2) . 18	
Total (7 wkts dec) . 316	Total (no wkt) . 47

Wright and Butler did not bat.

Bowling Analysis

	O	M	R	W		O	M	R	W
Tuckett	18	4	48	0	....	6	1	12	0
Dawson	4	0	12	0	....	4	1	13	0
Mann	50	20	68	4	....	3.4	0	17	0
Smith	36	9	82	1	....	—	—	—	—
Rowan	46	12	89	1	....	—	—	—	—
Mitchell	—	—	—	—	....	2	1	5	0

Fall of Wickets

1	2	3	4	5	6	7	8	9	10
141	218	241	253	289	306	316	—	—	—

England won by 10 wickets.

THE FIFTH TEST MATCH

Played at the Oval on August 16th, 18th, 19th and 20th,
1947

WITH the rubber won, the selection of the English side for the fifth Test became an impossible attempt by the selectors to produce an eleven to satisfy their countless critics. To be as objective as the cricket enthusiast can be is, nevertheless, to describe the English selection as completely bankrupt. Robertson of Middlesex had made his place certain when Edrich was unable to play—the selectors indicated that Edrich was chosen, but was not fully fit (damaged shoulder muscles prevented him from bowling), and that his place would be taken by Robertson. Butler of Notts, the bowling discovery of the series, was also unfit—treatment and deferred decision made the position so far as he was concerned no better. Some thought that Alf Gover, still the fastest bowler in the country despite his age, might be given a game at the Oval for sentimental reasons: the announcement three weeks later of his retirement would have made that selection grotesque. Every enthusiast was ready to select another seam-bowler—Mallett, Trevor Bailey, young Tremlett—even Aspinall was suggested. But Bill Copson was selected as stand-by for Butler, and the strange echoes about London on that pre-Test Sunday may well have been the distant laughing-like-a-drain of Copson, holding his sides in the shadow of The Peak. The other pacer, necessary because of the absence of Edrich, was Gladwin. Already discredited by his failure at Manchester, there was no need to try Gladwin further on a wicket like the Oval, which could only force him to bowl himself

eternally out of consideration. Gladwin is a very fine
county bowler, deadly, by virtue of his length and
accuracy and inswing, to all but the twenty best batsmen
in England—a treasure to Derbyshire but a gift to
Australia—and Australia was now the problem. Barnett,
who without ever being really tested had had no great
success, was left out, and so was Jack Young. Dick
Howorth of Worcester came in to take a well-earned
place, but at the age of thirty-eight. Otherwise the combination was not disturbed. The South Africans might
well have been affronted had star English players been
rested, but, with three places to fill, had the selectors to
pick two men already discredited in Test cricket and one
other of thirty-eight? There was reason for the selection
of Howorth, and, indeed, a slow left-arm bowler, until he
is appreciably older than Howorth, can substitute experience and cunning for speed of limb so long as he can field
capably near the wicket. But how the Australians must
have rubbed their hands when they read the team.

The South Africans played the same team as at Leeds.
Both Dyer and Fullerton had justified themselves in
county games since Leeds and the combination worked
well in the field. This was Melville's best chance of gaining a prestige win.

First Day—Saturday, August 16

English cricket was still sweltering in its never-since-
1921 sunshine for the Oval Test. The grass was half-way
between jaundice and peroxide outside the diligently
greened middle, and light frocks and shirt-sleeves were in
force even within the rails of the pavilion. The Oval
pavilion watchers have a character nearer to Thread-
needle Street and its immediate neighbourhood than to

the *Debrett*-bred detachment of Lord's—and the bar is busier. With the introduction of Brian Castor to the Oval there is a new atmosphere—some of that quality which we knew among the smaller, more numerous, and more improvised Essex grounds is there now—and large, unique, and established as the Oval is, it is a happier place for the change.

At this point we shall attend to the cricket. A match between a side which has already won the rubber and one which has resigned itself to losing it has to search for its justification on the field—its justification in the balance-sheets which give first-class cricket the means of continued existence is only too plain. Take twenty-two players tired after weeks of unbroken six-day cricket, and the point of their contest needs to be strong indeed in its emphasis to urge them to the heights. It will sound strange if I attempt to plead for rain to stop play. The fact remains, however, that six-day county play, with overnight travel, sometimes over long distances and always by railways growing steadily more leisurely, is by no means a holiday. Six-day cricket is, and must remain, a purely English phenomenon, possible only in the normal English summer, which provides fortuitous rest by its rainy days. Three days of rain in the preceding four weeks would have meant rest, physical and mental. In a summer of unbroken sun, six-day cricket breeds batting records and staleness. Given an England side containing no experimental members, with the rubber won and the coming Australian visit in every English mind, and the reporter also must search for point and justification.

England won the toss and, naturally, decided to bat. The opening followed the now accustomed lines. Hutton and Washbrook, with their air of unhurrying experience and complete absence of violence, watched the shine off the ball. Once again it was obvious that they do not run together well as a pair—they seem often to lose runs which might be easily taken. On the other hand, they are capable of giving the entire innings a calm beginning, removing the shine, and imposing themselves dishearteningly upon the bowlers. Tuckett had by now had a long and arduous tour; his very virtues, steadiness and industry, had condemned him to long spells on plumb wickets. The humid atmosphere of several of the later matches had tired him: he had most obviously lost weight. Each of the opening bowlers was steady, but Hutton and Washbrook were rocklike. The entry of Mann into the strife resolved those in anxious search of relevant data to count his overs and maidens. He began to turn the ball: not much, a few inches, at even pace, but above that of Trent Bridge. Was the Oval wicket coming to life? Perhaps the sun had made it thirsty and it had grown irritable when unslaked. Eighty on the board and the two were still there and, if they seemed more like old gardeners pottering about in a long-known plot than like gallants at a tourney, gratitude for a steady start took much of the sting from demands for speed. A straightening ball from Mann found Washbrook four-square in front, his pads wide as a barn door. Neville Cardus was there to see the Lancashire tradition of lbw strong despite the passing of Frank Watson; Harry Makepeace, concentrating hard at distant Old Trafford, wagged his head and pulled at his bleached old cap.

Robertson, who looks like a gardener, sturdy and weathered for all his youth and Metropolitan setting, came in to play his first few strokes with all his usual composed dexterity. But too soon he took his eye off the ball and swung negligently, crookedly, and with head up, to send Melville, at mid-off, an easier catch than any fieldsman has a right to expect in a Test Match. Robertson walked back to the pavilion, unmoved to the eye, and allowed the entry of Compton to extract the loudest applause of the day.

Two barely possible catches flung to short leg, Hutton's confinement within the bounds of run-starved defence, and the ability of both Rowan and Mann to turn the ball, made England grateful to have lost only two wickets for her lunch-time pittance.

After lunch men sat deeper in their seats and found little to discourage slumber. A characteristic Compton stroke to the covers suggested a felicity which his total innings never achieved. Rowan and Mann spun to a length, and he could never play with the old freedom. There was promise in this innings of a Compton masterful even in cords—if not in chains—a promise not always to be detected in his more warming displays of gaiety and elegance on plumb wickets or against weaker attacks. Here was a man who could hold his ebullience subservient to watchfulness, yet hammer runs upon the slightest opportunity. It was an innings which any watching Australian spy must have observed with anxiety. But Compton was 53, and the total 178, when a ball from Rowan pitched temptingly a little wide of his off stump, and he drove it to Tuckett, who took the catch with a reassuringly lazy lurch. Then, before Compton had taken off his pads, a perfect-length ball from Mann, with a sinister puff of smoke-dust as it left the wicket, bowled the monumental Hutton for 83 runs of more labour than glory. England 178 for 4, Hutton, Washbrook, Robertson, and Compton out, and Edrich far away, battling against Goddard at Cheltenham: this was a threat of disaster. Yardley is a better junior than senior member of a partnership, and Cranston had more than his batting spurs to win in a Test

Match, being rather at the stage of struggling into his socks.

Yet these two, Yardley alternately pawky and jaunty, Cranston with a forward stroke Edwardian in manner, added 93 runs. They were slow runs, but every one of them earned, against bowlers and a field with dominance almost within their reach. Cranston is long enough in body to play forward far down the wicket, yet solid and well-balanced to do so with certainty. Batting failures, a degree of inexperience rare in a Test player, and the strained state of the game might have strangled his confidence. He was wise to play the game he knew, the old-fashioned forward stroke, executed firmly and with determination, and he succeeded. When he at length reached forward to Rowan for the spin to beat his bat and give Fullerton an eager stumping, his job, and rather more than some had expected of him, was done. Mann bowled Yardley—and then adjusted his spectacles with a prod of the index finger. Howorth and Evans saw the day down to the traditional half-past six now that D.B.S.T. was gone. In the process Evans played some strokes of mischief and Howorth, whose straight drive came like a shock to the tensely quiet game, played a single forward stroke to Mann which implied so much disaster for him that his subsequent safety and confidence came pleasantly and surprisingly to his friends. 311 for six wickets was a slow day's play. Tight bowling and fielding, and the batting side's collective and individual anxiety not to fail, restricted scoring. It was a negative success, the best thing to say about it being that it might have been worse but for the courage and industry of Hutton, Compton, Yardley, and Cranston.

England—First Innings

Hutton, b Mann	83
Washbrook, lbw b Mann . . .	32
Robertson, c Melville b Smith . .	4
Compton (D.), c Tuckett b Rowan . .	53
N. W. D. Yardley, b Mann . .	59
K. Cranston, st Fullerton b Rowan . .	45
Howorth, not out	17
Evans, not out	10
Extras (l-b 7, n-b 1) . .	8
Total (for 6 wkts) .	311

Bowling Analysis (to end of first day)

	O	M	R	W
Tuckett . . .	23	5	63	0
Dawson . . .	27	4	52	0
Mann . . .	50	21	67	3
Rowan . . .	28	7	73	2
Smith . . .	15	0	58	1

Fall of Wickets

1	2	3	4	5	6
63	80	178	178	271	290

Second Day—Monday, August 18

If Saturday's play seemed to lack urgency and grace, Monday morning threatened a tedium which the afternoon did little to relieve. Barely was the day officially begun when Howorth received a ball from Rowan which left his bat evenly, but more sharply than any Oval-burdened Surrey spin bowler of the 'twenties would have

believed. The instinctive tendency to hit a cricket ball was
superseded too late by technical knowledge that this one
should be left alone, and Fullerton sprang to his full
height, which is more than that of the stumps, to take the
catch. Evans was now partnered by Gladwin, a contrast of
styles quietly appetizing to the style-fancier. Evans's
strokes are ahead of his standing and his figures. Few
players today play the cover-drive with his complete
abandon or bat with such a combination of audacity and
handsomeness. To watch him in form is to scent an emin-
ence which is, indeed, only refuted by an inconsistency
which he may yet overcome. Gladwin watches and waits,
or else wallops. He had hardly settled in when Evans
called him for a reasonable run and he refused to step out
of his crease for the benefit of the senior partner. There
were grim and dark mutterings about Gladwin at this
run-out, which certainly seemed unpardonable. Later,
with Wright as *his* junior, Gladwin thumped at the ball in
pleasant contrast to the proceedings of Saturday. The
wicket was now playing better than on the first day, but
disconcerting clouds of dust rose from the creases at the
rare hasty movement. Wright was bowled by Mann in
attempting a stroke of great power but no synchroniza-
tion with the flight of the ball. Copson heaved his bat like
a primitive axeman and Gladwin was not out 41, partial
atonement for the destruction of Evans—atonement
grimly made. England's total of 427 was safe, and it was
due to at least eight batsmen as well as the weather and
the refusal of the Oval wicket to play tricks. The spinners
could turn, but only very slightly and at easy pace and
even height.

Mitchell and Dyer, as the first South African batsmen,
held back the threat of Melville against less fresh English
bowling, and their opening was grim indeed. If Dyer

seemed too often to be facing squarely to the bowler, this was not echoed in apparent mistiming. Neither Mitchell nor Dyer was to be hurried.

Copson bowled from the pavilion end. His feet are in-turned through a shambling run-up which threatens to throw his heavy, sandy forelock over his face, but never actually does so. He delivers the ball with a simultaneous heave of his huge shoulders and a side-to-front swing of the body. If he is less fast than of old, he is still faster than he looks and apt to have the ball upon the batsman a fraction before the stroke is ready. Pale and heavy-shouldered, he represents those colliery villages of the Notts-Derby border which have produced so many fine cricketers.

At the other end, Gladwin was a reminder of agricul-tural Derbyshire pushing its pastures into the gaps of the high hills. Tall and raw-boned, he plays silently and well within his physique. He bowled with steady length, never departing from a strictly medium pace: steadily he de-viated from straight on to the line of the middle-and-leg. If he inclined towards the off, Mitchell played him to third man where no third man was. Dyer played, with less force than he might have used, sundry strokes of polish to the covers. Each batsman was content to wait for runs to come.

The introduction of Wright was greeted with patience by batsmen who knew that their greatest hope was a drawn game and Howorth was now invited to bowl his first over in Test Match cricket. Approaching the wicket at the Vauxhall end, he measured and marked his run with an air rather of patient acceptance of his captain's whim than of enthusiasm for his task. Tilting his cap a little more towards his right ear, he approached the wicket with a slightly weary air, and launched his habitual left-hander's break-away—of flight so slow as to appear to be intended for the batsman's delectation rather than his own. Dyer, whose diet of bowling until now had been severely restricted, went hungrily for this morsel and hit it to cover, where Gladwin, nervously in manner but safely as to hands, caught it about three inches off the ground. Howorth, who, by thus taking a wicket with his first ball in Test cricket, helped to fill the reports of a somewhat dull day's play, dismissed the whole matter as no more than another eccentricity of an opening batsman. All movement at Howorth's end now virtually ceased. Viljoen treated him with deep gravity, and Mitchell met him with a batting method as grudging of unnecessary movement as Howorth's bowling action.

Viljoen's attitude towards Wright, however, was one of extreme anxiety. Wright was obviously enjoying himself as much as a man can do after sixteen months of almost unbroken cricket. He spun the ball with delight. Viljoen, once a victim of his faster ball, disliked the leg-spinner and signally failed to identify the googly. Of his courage in face of his difficulties and his resolve not to allow the bad ball to pass, there was no doubt. Then the ball played one of its rare tricks of the match by rising more steeply than the general temper of the pitch had promised, and he was caught by Evans off Wright. Mitchell had by now committed himself to a policy of defence—although he is as little predictable as George Gunn, whereby he conditions all comment upon his mood with the unspoken 'so far at least.' Nourse, as usual, came to the bowling in no spirit of kindness. He hit a four off Wright savagely, and braced himself for further hostility. Howorth delivered to him several balls which seemed to be of such delicate innocence that even Nourse could not bring himself to harm them. There was, it seemed, an air of apology about Howorth for serving such artless cannon fodder to so redoubtable a fighter. Then Nourse hit brutally at a ball which came gently to him, Yardley caught him in the covers, and Howorth's sympathy was patent.

The burden of responsibility had moved down the batting order to await Melville even at No. 5. Compton now moved into action with his newly developed 'Chinaman,' delivered, however, with less blandness than haste to be done with the over. Such haste about the rite of bowling left-arm was only to be discounted in the eyes of the languid Howorth by the fact that it was this new-fangled Fleetwood-Smith stuff that Compton was bowling. Mitchell now began to produce drives and hooks, executed with no more force than was necessary to convey them to the boundary, and to run between the wickets, when that office was required of him, with a daintiness which intended no harm to the turf and no exhaustion to himself. Melville found the necessary identification and time to check his leg-side stroke to Wright's wrong 'un with such certainty as to render the short legs no menace, little more, it seemed, than indication to the spectators of the incidence of the googly. The Wright leg-break he hit on the off side and enforced the removal thence of one of the short legs. He now batted with assurance and richness of stroke play. Howorth, who appeared a little hurt at the reluctance of the batsmen to improve their scores at his expense, was taken off. The reason for his being relieved can only have been that Yardley was tired of seeing him bowl.

Cranston, whose bowling is as straightforward as his batting, but which has length, enthusiasm, and fitness to commend it, then had Melville lbw. The event came as a surprise, shattering the assurance of the South African innings. Dawson came in to play more at his ease than in previous Tests, and he and Mitchell were not to be disturbed before play ended. Howorth, his cap twitched even farther to the right, bowled a few farewell overs of an elegant weariness, but his generosity was rejected. There was a hurt expression upon his normally kindly face as, just before half-past six, he ambled slowly in pursuit of a stroke to the third-man boundary. Mitchell, after Melville's departure a man of sweet patience, had decided, with a look at the 'set fair' sky and a jerk at his shirt, to defer his entry into three figures until the next morning. The game had developed into a tug-of-war rather than a live clash; excitement was long-term rather than open, and the English fielding was not characterized by any quality more vital than steadiness, and sometimes even that was lacking.

England—First Innings

Hutton, b Mann	83
Washbrook, lbw b Mann	32
Robertson, c Melville b Smith	4
Compton (D.), c Tuckett b Rowan	53
N. W. D. Yardley, b Mann	59
K. Cranston, st Fullerton b Rowan	45
Howorth, c Fullerton b Rowan	23
Evans, run out	45
Gladwin, not out	51
Wright, b Mann	14
Copson, b Dawson	6
Extras (b 4, l-b 7, n-b 1)	12
Total	427

Bowling Analysis

	O	M	R	W
Tuckett . . .	32	6	82	0
Dawson . . .	35	5	80	1
Mann . . .	64	28	93	4
Rowan . . .	38	9	92	3
Smith . . .	21	0	68	1

Fall of Wickets

1	2	3	4	5	6	7	8	9	10
63	80	178	178	271	290	332	358	408	427

South Africa—First Innings

B. Mitchell, not out . . .	92
D. Dyer, c Gladwin b Howorth . .	18
K. G. Viljoen, c Evans b Wright . .	10
A. D. Nourse, c Yardley b Howorth .	10
A. Melville, lbw b Cranston . . .	39
O. C. Dawson, not out . . .	28
Extras (b 3, l-b 2, n-b 2) .	7
Total (for 4 wkts) .	204

Fall of Wickets

1	2	3	4
47	62	78	164

Third Day—Tuesday, August 19

The scale was still hovering, undecided which way to tilt—whether towards an England win, or a draw—when the day began under the same sun, so same as to threaten monotony to the spectators. To the players its threat was stronger. There is no more tiring ground in England than the Oval when the weather is hot. The low walls might let in a cooling breeze but for the fact that they are backed by flats and houses and gasometers which give out steadily the heat they have absorbed. Away towards the river the chimneys fly their smoke in thick banners and the trams add noise which seems the very sound of stuffy heat. Those gusts of wind which do thread their way through the maze do little to cool—rather they whip up grit and smuts to torment the sweating cheek. The bowler's arm at the pavilion end comes out of the grey to deliver a ball which is always difficult to assess—a factor which adds to the strain on the batsmen. Above all, the earth of the Oval is hot and hard, pummelling the feet and stabbing the back. The player at the Oval must always be rising above tiredness.

From the start of the day the ball came steadily to Mitchell's bat and was as steadily pushed away. Dawson at the other end moved with a new assurance added to his customary grace. Once, however, he departed from his usual method to indulge in a swing high and wide but not particularly handsome, and which edged the ball sky-high past Evans along a course not with dignity to be marked on Ferguson's immaculate diagram of strokes.

Wright was having one of his happy mornings. Wright's happiness has no automatic connection with the taking of wickets, but this day the ball was doing as he asked. Yardley brought up three short legs for the googly and Wright swung his arm and seemed about to sing as he walked back to bowl. Nevertheless, Mitchell reached his century with the certainty of a church clock, and Dawson's fifty came, if with less solidity, with a charm for its risks. Wright suggested that he was no longer interested in the welfare of one particular googly after it had shown that it would turn on the length which makes the forward stroke uncertain and the back stroke anxious. Dawson, on the other hand, had considerable interest in its subsequent doings. He plumped for the forward stroke, no doubt because of its greater elegance, but the ball was inside the bat and the lbw decision was unanimous even from the pavilion.

With Mitchell solid at his end, there was general anticipation that Fullerton and Rowan at least of the lower-half batsmen would bat with greater confidence and effect than in those previous innings when the tail-enders alarmed one another in precarious partnership. But once again Cranston took a quick wicket—Fullerton's—Howorth in the gully making the catch off Evans's glove. Then Howorth, mildly, almost apologetically, bowled Rowan with a delivery curvingly appetizing in flight, but dropping a little shorter than the batsman expected. This completed the destruction of the late-middle batting—so often a deciding factor in the resistance of any side facing a large total.

At this juncture the advent of Norman Mann was even more spectacularly a gambler's throw than usual. He appeared to study Mitchell's methods for a brief period before deciding that they were not for any man whose patience fell below that of an average archangel. Hence a mighty blow off Howorth, some handsome drives, and other shots distinguished more by eye and the golfer's gifts than by the normal attributes of Test batsmanship. But the return of Copson finished the South African innings. Again the side crumpled in less time than it took for the spectators to complete their score-cards. Copson is now clearly less likely to fire out a great batsman by sheer speed or a ' fizzer ' than was once the case. Now, however, a considerable shrewdness and an eye for country distinguish his bowling. He uses a wicket cannily. With his county he has Pope and Gladwin to share the pace attack and, kept fresh, his powerful swing, coupled with knowledge and ability to exploit any pitch, make him still a valuable bowler. This day he persuaded Bruce Mitchell to deviate from his normal abstention and follow a rising ball outside the off stump: the resultant edged catch was simple both for Evans and the umpire. Mann thumped Copson once, but was bowled by him with a whisk of stump and bail while attempting to hit him over the pavilion. Smith contrived, by early action, to place his pads in the line of the ball to the wicket. The last three wickets had occupied Copson for just seven balls and South Africa were 125 behind on the first innings.

Hutton and Washbrook before lunch were so orthodox that one knew every move by heart—it was like a repeat performance and the 13 runs on the board were contrived out of deep knowledge—and inclination to carry on after the meal with greater time and scope. So they did. Each was the same craftsman, the touch was as certain and as long-headedly guided as ever, but they were now, obviously, on piece-work rates. Yardley's need was quick runs. This need Hutton and Washbrook realized and pushed the ball away with certainty. Twenty-eight runs in ten minutes from so normally solid a pair was still within their bounds of competence—a more assertive competence than they had shown before in the series. Thereafter there was the relative calm of Rowan and Mann wearing their patient rash upon the sun-burnt but still docile wicket. Hutton was forcing when Tuckett caught him off Mann and Washbrook was hitting Rowan hard to leg with the spin—which the wicket largely reduced to suggestion—when the ball went off the under edge of his bat on to his pad and was still a catch for Fullerton.

Thus a diligent Robertson and joyous Compton were admitted to public gaze. Robertson, no doubt chastened by his first-innings failure, seemed bent upon being anybody on earth except the self-reliant Robertson of Middlesex—but preferably some stolidly anonymous Test batsman; he laboured where he usually plays. Compton was not only the great batsman, but also the great batsman who knows luck is with him and proposes to employ but not to abuse that luck—an adjustment so rare as to be memorably rich in its dividends. His approach, justified by the state of the game, was attacking. He went down the wicket gaily; once there, he might decide not to drive, but to move bat back before ball and then to half-push-half-cut wide enough of third man to make the boundary stroke certain. Or he would hit through the covers with an ease, power, and certainty of placing which made the normal requirements for the correct playing of the cover-drive seem mere niggling pedantry. He turned the ball on his leg stump to long leg for a single with the negligence of a man who disregarded singles as he would farthings. That he made Robertson look pedestrian is no reflection upon Robertson: no batsman in the world, with the possible exception of Keith Miller, could have played anything more than a muted second-fiddle to Compton on that afternoon. If he changed his mind about a stroke, he had time to do so while lesser creatures would have been out. He hit the ball, it seemed, for fun, the impudent fun of a boy who improvises mischief upon the theme of a well-learnt lesson.

At length even the patiently industrious Tuckett could do no more. A groin at last rebelled against the strain of the body and he went off the field. With Robertson out, Yardley pressed that little too much before he had settled both feet firmly upon the game, and Cranston played for an off-break spin which Rowan, on this occasion for reasons of deceit, had failed to apply. Compton's hundred, made at more than a run a minute, gave statistical garnish to an innings whose quality was its memorable attribute. He fell to a ball from Dawson which left him, Nourse taking the ball with a catlike quickness which his immediate immobility denied.

Now there was the possibility that England's attempt to score quick runs would lead them into trouble. With their first six batsmen out, they were 380 ahead, and more than a whole day's play was guaranteed by the same unvarying sun. But Howorth, with a healthy disposition to thump, and Evans, with beauty of stroke, treated the South African bowling with swashbuckling gaiety so that Yardley could declare with them still in and England 450 ahead—a nice round figure for all concerned to memorize. Half an hour in the evening was too long for Melville to experiment with a night-watchman, but long enough for Yardley to hope for wickets against batsmen disposed to play the stroke of exaggerated caution in their anxiety to place security before runs. When Dyer touched a shortish ball from Copson to Yardley and Yardley dropped it, it seemed that England had had all the opportunity they could reasonably expect on the short innings before the night. Still the dust flew at the swish of bat or scuffle of feet inside the batting crease, but the wicket itself was peaceful. Quick changes of bowling brought Wright on while the ball still bore more shine than he is accustomed to handle, and he had Dyer lbw to end the day.

England

Hutton, b Mann	83	c Tuckett, b Mann	36
Washbrook, lbw b Mann	32	c Fullerton b Rowan	43
Robertson, c Melville b Smith	4	b Rowan	30
Compton (D.), c Tuckett b Rowan	53	c Nourse b Dawson	113
N. W. D. Yardley, b Mann	59	c sub b Mann	11
K. Cranston, st Fullerton b Rowan	45	c Mitchell b Rowan	0
Howorth, c Fullerton b Rowan	23	not out	45
Evans, run out	45	not out	39
Gladwin, not out	51		
Wright, b Mann	14		
Copson, b Dawson	6		
Extras (b 4, l-b 7, n-b 1)	12	Extras (b 6, w 2)	8
Total	427	Total (6 wkts dec)	325

Bowling Analysis

	O	M	R	W		O	M	R	W
Tuckett	32	6	82	0	....	7	0	34	0
Dawson	35	5	80	1	....	15	1	59	1
Mann	64	28	93	4	....	27	7	102	2
Rowan	38	9	92	3	....	25	1	95	3
Smith	21	0	68	1	....	3	0	27	0

Fall of Wickets

1	2	3	4	5	6	7	8	9	10
63	80	178	178	271	290	332	358	408	427
73	89	158	179	180	267	—	—	—	—

South Africa

B. Mitchell, c Evans b Copson	120	not out . . .	1
D. Dyer, c Gladwin b Howorth . . .	18	lbw b Wright. .	4
K. G. Viljoen, c Evans b Wright . . .	10		
A. D. Nourse, c Yardley b Howorth . . .	10		
A. Melville, lbw b Cranston	39		
O. C. Dawson, lbw b Wright	55		
G. M. Fullerton, c Howorth b Cranston . . .	6		
A. Rowan, b Howorth .	0		
N. Mann, b Copson . .	36		
L. Tuckett, not out . .	0		
V. I. Smith, lbw b Copson.	0		
Extras (b 3, l-b 2, w 1, n-b 2)	8	Extras (b 2, l-b 1) .	3
Total .	302	Total (for 1 wkt) .	8

Bowling Analysis

	O	M	R	W
Copson . . .	27	13	46	3
Gladwin . . .	16	2	39	0
Wright . . .	29	7	89	2
Howorth . .	39	16	64	3
Compton . .	11	4	31	0
Cranston . .	9	2	25	2

Fall of Wickets

1	2	3	4	5	6	7	8	9	10
47	62	78	164	243	253	254	293	302	302
8	—	—	—	—	—	—	—	—	—

Fourth Day—Wednesday, August 20

The last day of the last Test was magnificent.

The whole match had seemed, at its outset, to lack point. There was a complete lack of high hostility about the English cricket, and yet the South African batting had not taken advantage of it. Only Compton had saved the major English batting from looking pedestrian on a wicket which gave the bowlers occasional encouragement but no real help. But on this last day Mitchell lifted the game on to the plane of the heroic, and Nourse and Tuckett stood with him by right. Mitchell's innings was a personal triumph by virtue of the fact that it was his second century of the match and that, in it, he passed H. W. Taylor's total and became the highest scorer of runs for South Africa in Test Matches. But the greatness of his innings lay in the fact that it was not played for himself, but for his side.

I believe that the reporting of cricket is not a place for over-much personal feeling, but it is impossible for me to refrain from making personal comment at this juncture. People who followed this match by reading the complete score-sheet the next day have suggested to me that South Africa—meaning Mitchell—might have won this game, since they were only 28 runs short of winning. This statement is only possible from a person who had not seen the match, and it is one which makes my blood boil—in that it attempts to smirch great cricket played by a great cricketer. I have never known Bruce Mitchell as I have known some other cricketers—he is not an easy man to know—and I hold no personal brief for him. Only, that day at the Oval, he played an innings which was great by any standard and he deserves nothing but admiration for what he did. First, with an early wicket gone, he played himself into the day. Then, with victory a distant but not inaccessible aim, he scored much faster than his batting rate throughout the tour. With the hope of winning shot away and replaced by apparently certain defeat, he batted through exhaustion down to the end of a day which England had seemed certain to win and lost in the end only because Mitchell was invincible and his lieutenant, Tuckett, stood by him.

It was Mitchell's day. By honest valuation of the emotions of those playing and watching the match, it was, for all the brilliance of Compton's century, Mitchell's match. Compton was brilliant in his side's supremacy, Mitchell superb in attack to win a brief initiative and then epic in successful defence.

Viljoen in the morning was looking for certain runs. South Africa wanted 443 of them—at just more than seventy an hour. Anxious against Wright, he was able to fall back upon the virtues of a straight bat and his own self-reliance. It was a hard first hour. Mitchell begrudged the risk necessary to score a single. Viljoen hooked, and twice drove, with power which concealed relief. Copson and Gladwin had gone to the country. Howorth was once again humouring the batsmen from the Vauxhall end.

The slow left-hander bowling the natural spinner is not, on anything short of a sticky-dog, a penetrative bowler. The batsman must feel that, if he does not want to get out, he need not. Let him not, then, he thinks, take undue liberties and the runs will come—only headstrong play can get him out. The feeling of clash leaves him—he cannot be destroyed—can only destroy himself. So he assumes more of mastery—but the figures of the game may show that his, and his side's, position is less safe. Thus with greater assurance Viljoen played forward to Howorth. The ball from Howorth, on so tame a wicket as the Oval, makes little pace off the ground: it turns, but without hate or surprise. Always, however, his flight compels respect. The ball comes up from that lazy arm so slowly. Yet it does not pitch monotonously: sometimes what looks to be a good-length ball is up to york the batsman who tries to make it a half-volley; at other times it drops a fraction shorter than the eye had estimated. Viljoen's forward stroke groped for a ball which did not pitch as far up as he expected. Turning gently and bouncing in amiable parabola, it went through to Evans who stumped, appealed, and replaced the bail. Viljoen had scored 33 of the morning's 40 runs.

Nourse came out to join a Bruce Mitchell as solid as a rock. Melville was waiting in the pavilion. No need now for Nourse to don that mantle of care and anxiety that he had worn with such sad dignity before. This was relative security, and Nourse can fight with an easy conscience when the game runs thus. With hardly a back-lift, hardly a follow-through, he hit a ball from Copson bullet-fast for four past the bowler—and glowered after it. He spanked away a shot that was neither a hook nor a pull, but somewhere between the two, and, more relevantly, worth four runs. He cut Howorth late through slips, grimly, but with exquisite timing.

At the other end Mitchell drove on the off and hooked, but selected his ball: Nourse must be given support, and support upon which he could rely. A ball from Howorth to Nourse pitched a little outside the off stump and turned mildly away from the bat. Nourse was almost over it and went to cut again: perhaps it rose just a little, perhaps Nourse was not quite there. There is the barest knife-edge of margin for error in the late cut off the slow bowler—a stroke which must be played to *add speed* to the ball. It took the edge of his bat and went to Hutton's fast-stretch-

ing left hand at slip. Hutton dropped it: Nourse had then
30. This was the first of the crises of a day which was
usually tense and never static. Nourse did not look back
upon his escape, but rather went on with the consciousness that luck was with him. Mitchell was neat and safe—
he ventured little—but Nourse was riding the whirlwind;
to have done so at both ends would have been to take a
specifically unnecessary risk. Nourse belaboured Compton unmercifully and with relish—14 runs off his first
over, 30 from 4 overs and Compton did not bowl again
in the innings.

At lunch South Africa were 147 for 2. Nourse had
scored 63 in just under an hour and a half, Mitchell 38 in
three hours. South Africa now wanted 304 and had four
hours in which to get them—a rate of seventy-six
runs an hour, and before lunch they had been coming at
that pace. After lunch Copson and Gladwin took the new
ball and the attack should have been at its keenest. Nourse
scrutinized his first two overs and then moved back to his
earlier rate. Mitchell moved with him, rolling out strokes
which raced down on the off-side with a pace in which
timing had more share than force. Eighty runs came in
the hour. South Africa, eight wickets standing, wanted
220 runs in three hours. Since lunch Mitchell had scored
even faster than Nourse—40 runs, with six fours, to
Nourse's 34—and they were gaining on the clock.

The amiable Howorth returned once more with con-
templative air, to the Vauxhall end. Howorth is an accurate bowler: his spin is the natural and controllable spin,
and he attempts no excess of break—he does not flap the
ball out of the back of his hand. No violent variation of
pace, no experiment in swing disturbs his precision. A
ball from him, bowled at his usual pace, permits of his
'putting' the ball on a specific spot on the wicket. He

usually pitches his break-away about middle-and-off on a wicket such as that at the Oval.

Howorth now bowled to Nourse a ball which pitched on the middle stump, a little short of his usual length; it did not turn back appreciably, and Nourse, thinking it was missing the leg stump, moved across his wicket and shaped to play it to leg, but missed, and it touched the back of his leg or pad as it passed. Howorth appealed (for lbw). 'Not out,' said umpire Baldwin, adding for Howorth's benefit and possibly his own justification, 'It didn't straighten.' Evans heard a click just before he took the ball immediately behind the leg stump and he, too, appealed (for a catch at the wicket). 'Not out,' said Harry Baldwin again. 'It bowled him,' said Robertson, who was fielding on the leg side. Evans, whose eye, of course, was waiting for the ball to come into sight behind Nourse, and not watching the stumps, and Hutton (at slip) stood back from the wicket and pointed to the fallen bail. Umpire Baldwin was certain that Nourse was not lbw and that he had not played the ball to give a catch, but had been unable to see the ball as it reached the stumps for Nourse's body in the way. Since the appeal 'How's that?' covers all forms of dismissal, Baldwin may, legally speaking, have been in error, but the reasonable mind will agree that an umpire is justified in giving a man 'Not out' if he is not out *so far as that umpire can tell*; in any case, an umpire is usually correct in sensing the grounds upon which an appeal is made—and Baldwin was right in the case of Howorth's and Evans's first appeals. He looked now to umpire Smart at square leg, who unhesitatingly gave Nourse out *because he had seen the ball remove the bail*. It must be assumed that Nourse's leg or pad unusually diverted the ball on to, instead of away from, the wicket.

I have given this account of the occurrence partly because I do not think that anyone at the Oval, except those 'in the middle,' knew exactly what had happened. The scorers certainly did not know, and had to send a messenger out to the umpire to enquire before they could supply details for the score-cards with a clear conscience. I have also recorded the occurrence because I understand that there was doubt of the verdict in some quarters far from the occurrence. I have the words of Baldwin to Howorth, and of Robertson to the world in general, the report of Evans hearing a click, and the fact that umpire Smart *saw* Nourse bowled, by reliable report from the 'middle.' The remainder of the incident I saw and heard.

So Nourse was out, for 97, after an innings which had revitalized the match and placed it again in hazard. Of Nourse I say with certainty that he regretted missing his century far less than the effect of his dismissal on South African hopes of a win. Now, with South Africa, 232 for 3, wanting 219 runs in three hours, Melville came in. The English bowling was far from happy, most of the shine was off the ball, Copson and Gladwin had gone off and Cranston had gone on. Mitchell was scoring quickly; the game was in the balance, but now very slightly tilted towards a South African win.

Melville pored over the bowling. He watched ball after ball on to his bat; he pushed one or two runs, but was obviously prepared to allow the rate of scoring to fall temporarily, against his feeling full mastery. He went across, head over the ball, to play a dead-bat shot to Cranston; the ball took the inside edge of his bat and Evans made a good catch off a snick going downwards to his toes. South Africa 247 for 4. Dawson cracked a ball from Cranston hard at Howorth in the gully and Howorth caught it before anyone knew that a catch had gone up. There was a pause before the applause began. South Africa's chance of winning was gone: Cranston had done his finest piece of work and had saved England from defeat.

A quarter of an hour later Fullerton was gone too— caught by Evans off Howorth for 14. South Africa 266 for 6: two and a quarter hours to go—and the last four men of this same team had been whisked away in a single over at Leeds—three of them in seven balls in the first innings of this very Oval Test. South Africa were also, as humorists and optimists calculated, 185 runs short of winning—which they were asked to score as quickly as Nourse and Mitchell had scored with their eyes in and knowing there were good batsmen to follow them.

Mann came in at No. 8 instead of Rowan. Mann is not a cultured batsman, but he has a good eye, firm control of his nerves, and, at need, a straight bat. He watched Mitchell complete his hundred—at an average rate of twenty runs an hour—and saw him touch his cap briefly, absent-mindedly, to the applause. Mann was still with him after tea, when Yardley used Copson and Wright as his attack against the settling eye. At five o'clock Mann was caught by Hutton off Wright for 10 patient runs, made in three-quarters of an hour while Mitchell scored 38. South Africa 314 for 7: 137 runs behind, an hour and a half to go: Tuckett, Rowan, and Smith to come. It might easily be all over in five minutes, said those who had watched the team.

Tuckett came in, walking slowly, with a heavy-shouldered stoop, his face unusually solemn under his rarely worn cap, and the fieldsmen crowded round as Wright bowled to him. Tuckett was tall enough to make the bat seem small as he bent over it to watch the ball hit it and bounce away. The fieldsmen tensed and rubbed their hands. It was difficult not to admire Tuckett as he strove to stave off the inevitable. He had scored 47 runs in his eight Test innings of the series and the time to the close of play was three times as long as his longest innings in a Test. Mitchell was now responsible for the South African innings. He must stay in at all costs. If he was out the innings would collapse at once: he must shield his partner, especially from Copson and Wright, yet he must take runs whenever he could. Reserving his energy in daintily restricted movement, Mitchell stayed.

The reaction of any reasonable spectator was that South Africa's chance of winning had long disappeared and she was virtually certain to lose. At twenty-five minutes past five Mitchell was dropped by Evans. At half-past five Mitchell hit a four: as he and Lindsay Tuckett met in the middle of the pitch, easing as they recognized that the ball had gone for four, Mitchell looked at him with a puzzled expression. 'Lindsay,' he said wonderingly, 'when did Tufty get out?' There is the measure of the concentration that keeps a man at the wickets for six and a half hours on a baking day at the Oval.

Wright's short-legs and silly mid-off were staring into Tuckett's face. At twelve minutes to six Yardley took the new ball. His hope was to attack the batsmen: passive steadiness was of no service, so Gladwin was not employed, but Cranston took the new ball with Copson. Against a tight-set field Mitchell farmed the bowling as much as he could. Any five minutes of play could see the South African innings ended. Tuckett took a four off Copson. At six o'clock, with half an hour to go, South Africa, with Mitchell and Tuckett holding on grimly, needed 74 runs to win. Runs and time no longer equated even to the mathematician—they had not done so to the intelligent spectator since Melville was caught at 3.37. England needed to take three wickets to win.

Against the selected Test Match bowlers of England, a South African bowler (to be dismissed mentally but not physically as a batsman) was neither to be fired out nor tempted out. The wicket held together blandly, milder on the fourth day than on the first. At the other end stood the man who overshadowed even this heroic Tuckett. Rarely has a man so imposed himself upon a match as Mitchell upon the fifth Test of 1947. The eye sees him each time the game is mentioned, moving daintily and economically to the end, frustrating every form of attack. Copson, Wright, Cranston, Howorth had their last chances against this grim combination. Then Yardley sent away the tense and crouching close fieldsmen and Hutton attempted to lure the batsmen to suicide. Tuckett calmly added some fours to what was already his highest Test innings, and the bowling never looked likely to disturb him from good-natured steadiness. Interest endured to the last few minutes, when there was no longer time for two more batsmen to come to the wicket and be out. Fieldsmen presented Tuckett and Mitchell with bails—a rare gesture in the final scramble, for someone must go without. The final Test of 1947, revived by Mitchell from the dead to the epic, was over.

At the end of the drawn game South Africa were 27 runs behind. The margin would have been greater had runs not been tossed to them at the end of the day. South Africa had no chance to win after Nourse went: Dawson, Melville, even Fullerton, might have remade the chance, but they did not. At four o'clock the book of form said that the South Africans must lose. They were saved by Mitchell, Mann, and Tuckett—Homerically.

The English fielding had not looked of Test Match class: there was a general lack of urgency about it. The honours of the match went to South Africa because they rose above disaster and saved the game. Howorth bowled, batted, and fielded himself into further Tests; Gladwin bowled himself out; Robertson did not succeed, but must be considered again; Cranston was a very useful cricketer.

South Africa had started well at Nottingham and slumped in the next three Tests, but this was a most honourable and comforting draw.

England

Hutton, b Mann .	83	c Tuckett b Mann .	36
Washbrook, lbw b Mann .	32	c Fullerton b Rowan	43
Robertson, c Melville b Smith . . .	4	b Rowan . .	30
Compton (D.), c Tuckett b Rowan . . .	53	c Nourse b Dawson.	113
N. W. D. Yardley, b Mann	59	c sub b Mann . .	11
K. Cranston, st Fullerton b Rowan . . .	45	c Mitchell b Rowan	0
Howorth, c Fullerton b Rowan . . .	23	not out . . .	45
Evans, run out . .	45	not out . . .	39
Gladwin, not out . .	51		
Wright, b Mann . .	14		
Copson, b Dawson . .	6		
Extras (b 4, l-b 7, n-b 1) .	12	Extras (b 6, w 2) .	8
Total .	427	Total (6 wkts dec) .	325

Bowling Analysis

	O	M	R	W		O	M	R	W
Tuckett .	32	6	82	0	....	7	0	34	0
Dawson .	35	5	80	1	....	15	1	59	1
Mann . .	64	28	93	4	....	27	7	102	2
Rowan .	38	9	92	3	....	25	1	95	3
Smith .	21	0	68	1	....	3	0	27	0

Fall of Wickets

1	2	3	4	5	6	7	8	9	10
63	80	178	178	271	290	332	358	408	427
73	89	158	179	180	267	—	—	—	—

South Africa

B. Mitchell, c Evans b Copson	120	not out	189
D. Dyer, c Gladwin b Howorth	18	lbw b Wright	4
K. G. Viljoen, c Evans b Wright	10	st Evans b Howorth	33
A. D. Nourse, c Yardley b Howorth	10	b Howorth	97
A. Melville, lbw b Cranston	39	c Evans b Cranston	6
O. C. Dawson, lbw b Wright	55	c Howorth b Cranston	0
G. M. Fullerton, c Howorth b Cranston	6	c Evans b Howorth	14
A. Rowan, b Howorth	0		
N. Mann, b Copson	36	c Hutton b Wright	10
L. Tuckett, not out	0	not out	40
V. I. Smith, lbw b Copson	0		
Extras (b 3, l-b 2, w 1, n-b 2)	8	Extras (b 12, l-b 14, w 4)	30
Total	302	Total (for 7 wkts)	423

Bowling Analysis

	O	M	R	W		O	M	R	W
Copson	27	13	46	3	....	30	11	66	0
Gladwin	16	2	39	0	....	16	5	33	0
Wright	29	7	89	2	....	30	8	103	2
Howorth	39	16	64	3	....	37	8	85	3
Compton	11	4	31	0	....	4	0	30	0
Cranston	9	2	25	2	....	21	3	61	2
Hutton	—	—	—	—	....	2	0	14	0
Yardley	—	—	—	—	....	1	0	1	0

Fall of Wickets

1	2	3	4	5	6	7	8	9	10
47	62	78	164	243	253	254	293	302	302
8	48	232	247	249	266	314	—	—	—

Match drawn.

TEST MATCH AVERAGES

1947

England won three, two drawn.

ENGLAND

Batting

	Innings	Not Out	Total	Highest Score	Aver.
W. J. Edrich .	6	1	552	191	110·40
Compton (D.)	8	0	753	208	94·12
Washbrook .	10	2	396	75	49·50
Hutton .	10	2	344	100	43·00
Evans .	7	2	209	74	41·80
N. W. D. Yardley .	7	0	273	99	39·00
Barnett .	4	1	63	33	21·00
K. Cranston .	4	0	71	45	17·75

Also batted: Bedser (A. V.), 7, 2, and 0; Cook, 0 and 4; Copson, 6; Dollery, 9 and 17; Gladwin, 16 and 51* ; Hollies, 0*, 18*, and 5; Howorth, 23 and 45*; J. W. Martin, 0 and 26; Pope (G. H.), 8*; Robertson, 4 and 30; Wright, 4* and 14; Young, 0*; Butler played in one match but did not bat.

*Not out.

Bowling

	Overs	Maidens	Runs	Wickets	Aver.
Butler . . .	52	24	66	7	9·42
K. Cranston . .	82.1	23	186	11	16·90
W. J. Edrich . .	134.5	33	370	16	23·12
Howorth . .	76	24	149	6	24·83
Wright. . .	183.2	50	484	19	25·47
Hollies . . .	149.2	46	331	9	36·77
Compton (D.) .	103	29	263	5	52·60
Gladwin . .	98	37	158	3	52·66
Bedser (A. V.) .	112	24	233	4	58·25

Also bowled: Pope (G. H.), 36.2—12—85—1; Copson, 57—24—112—3; J. W. Martin, 45—6—129—1; Cook, 30—4—127—0; N. W. D. Yardley, 6—0—25—0; Hutton, 4—0—29—0; Barnett, 13—4—24—0; Young, 26—12—85—2.

SOUTH AFRICA

Batting

	Innings	Not Out	Total	Highest Score	Aver.
A. D. Nourse .	9	0	621	149	69·00
B. Mitchell . .	10	1	597	189*	66·33
A. Melville . .	10	1	569	189	63·22
T. A. Harris . .	3	0	93	60	31·00
K. G. Viljoen .	10	1	270	93	30·00
A. Rowan . .	8	3	114	38*	22·80
O. C. Dawson .	6	0	204	55	22·66
D. Dyer . .	6	0	96	62	16·00
J. Plimsoll . .	2	1	16	8*	16·00
L. Tuckett . .	9	2	87	40*	12·42
N. Mann . .	9	0	109	36	12·11
G. Fullerton . .	4	0	45	14	11·50
J. Lindsay . .	5	2	21	9*	7·00
V. I. Smith . .	6	1	12	11	2·40

Bowling

	Overs	Maidens	Runs	Wickets	Aver.
N. Mann . .	329.5	127	603	15	40·20
L. Tuckett . .	252	44	664	15	44·26
J. Plimsoll . .	39.5	9	143	3	47·66
V. I. Smith . .	155.1	35	439	9	48·77
O. C. Dawson .	158.5	33	425	8	53·12
A. Rowan . .	274.2	48	671	12	·55·91
B. Mitchell . .	2	1	5	0	—

Centuries

ENGLAND (7): Compton (D.) (4)—208 at Lord's, 163 at Nottingham, 115 at Manchester, 113 at the Oval; W. J. Edrich (2)—191 at Manchester, 189 at Lord's; Hutton—100 at Leeds.

SOUTH AFRICA (7): A. Melville (3)—189 and 104 not out at Nottingham, 117 at Lord's; B. Mitchell (2)—120 and 189 not out at the Oval; A. D. Nourse (2)—149 at Nottingham, 115 at Manchester.

SKETCHES OF THE PLAYERS

DENIS COMPTON

THE year 1947 saw Denis Compton break Hobbs's record
for the number of centuries scored in an English season
and Tom Hayward's record for a season's aggregate. Yet,
and this is the most important thing about Denis Compton,
he broke those records without ever, for a moment, adopting
the customary manner of the record-breaker. This method, as
we have seen it of recent years in almost every sport, is the
stolid, machine-like, quantitative triumph of soullessness,
attained by complete elimination of risk and beauty in execu-
tion. It is a sign of grace that Denis Compton broke two great
records without sign of such method. He went through the
warm summer of 1947 playing cricket gaily, and it happened
that in doing so he made so many runs that two records were
broken. Never, in either of his innings which finally broke the
records, was any trace to be observed of Compton doing any
other than playing just as Denis Compton always plays.

And how does Denis Compton play? He simply *plays*—
like a boy striking at a rubber ball with a paling from a fence
—for fun. He plays happily. Oh yes, many of his strokes cause
the academically minded cricket critics to turn in horror—
only to be won back at once by the air of charm which Compton lends to every game he plays. His bat may be a foot from
his left leg when he plays forward through the covers. He will
start to go down the wicket before the ball is bowled, and
then, when it cannot be driven and he is, apparently, high and
dry two yards down the pitch, he will ruefully change his shot
and, with the handle of the bat sticking into his navel, take a
casual poke at the ball to send it scuttling between cover and
third man for four runs. Rarely has a man made runs so negligently, never has a man made so many runs without seeming
to take thought for his safety or his method.

Analysis of Compton's method shows, as Alan Melville's field-placing underlined, that he plays very little between widish mid-off and widish mid-on. This gap apart, he will play the ball almost anywhere in the field with an advantage—due to an almost inhuman capacity for knowing, as he plays the ball, just where the field is. It has been observed of some great badminton players that they can take their eye off the fastest shuttle for a split second as it comes to them, or, colloquially, look out of the corner of the eye, to see, or feel, exactly where the opposition is stationed. This gift Compton possesses to an amazing degree: his strokes seem, time and again, to pass between the fielders with uncanny accuracy. He has a perfect eye and his sense of the behaviour of a ball is born in him, so that timing is to him like breathing. He must, being partly unconscious of the rarity of his own gifts, and never having known the lack of them, sometimes wonder why people make so much fuss about batting.

There is the enviable, delightful paradox, Compton obtains all the results of care and study by methods which seem negligent. He hits through the covers as hard as the greatest batsmen, yet with off-handed strokes: he shrugs the ball off his leg stump to long leg, he late cuts like a boy playing touch-last, and he seems to have more time than there is to play his hook wide of the fieldsman—yet to play that shot as a makeshift because he cannot be bothered to remember any other stroke. To watch Compton is to see the ball travelling all over the ground with bowlers and fieldsmen almost hopeless. Characteristically, he is happiest of all with the most difficult of all balls to play—the ball that leaves the bat off the pitch; Compton hits it away on the off side and will even raise a foot in a negligent kick along the line of the departed ball.

It may be that, when his magnificent eye dims a little, when his fitness diminishes with age, he will be unable to play as he does now. It may be that, when that happens, his brain will not be sufficiently utilitarian to eliminate his more risky shots. If that day comes, then we may find some of his contemporaries better batsmen in their dog-days than Compton. Then we shall know that this glorious phase of Compton was only possible in one summer, the sun's summer of a century and the summer of a man's life. And that will help to adjust perspective: then facts will confirm our impression, that we have seen, in this year of 1947, a rare fire of batsmanship that can never burn again because it was unique—the 'rose that once has blown.' It cannot go on. Never again, surely, shall we watch even Denis Compton make all the runs in the world in a few weeks, yet, so far from tiring of watching him, wish that he might go on for ever. To close the eyes is to see again that easy, happy figure at the wicket, pushing an unruly forelock out of the eyes and then, as it falls down again, playing, off the wrong foot, a stroke which passes deep point like a bullet. Never again will cold, hard figures be smashed so lightheartedly, never again will the boyish delight in hitting a ball with a piece of wood flower directly into charm and gaiety and all the wealth of achievement.

Compton is not merely a batsman, he is a cricketer, a natural cricketer who almost makes the spectator believe that there was never a genuine natural cricketer before. He fields with a dash, anticipation, and negligent assurance of hand that is the despair of all who have laboured long for less return of grace and effect.

He rarely bowls; yet he was trusted with England's slow left-arm bowling, and once he almost succeeded, once failed. Then he took bowling seriously for almost a week: as a long-scoring batsman, he did not need to bowl at all, but now batting, deep-fielding and all, he appeared bowling the 'Chinaman' and the Fleetwood-Smith googly with an accomplishment which would have been commendable after a season of practice. His bowling will obviously be better when he pauses to think and take breath between deliveries rather than trot back, turn, run up, and bowl, letting the weight of the ball swing the arm over, in a rapid, unbroken flow of action.

But are there any rules to be quoted in respect of the cricket of Denis Compton? I doubt it: if he were not so gaily, chucklingly friendly with us we might regard his batting as a kind of fairy story—and, in the end, when a younger generation, who never saw him, ridicule our stories of him behind our backs, then we shall know that it *was* all a fairy story—that it was a dream that passed across English cricket in a summer of amazing sun and lit the farthest corner of every field in the land.

D. V. P. WRIGHT

Every good cricketer who has seen, or played against, Doug. Wright knows that he is the best leg-break and googly bowler in England, and probably the best in the world.

He is certainly the fastest *true* leg-break and googly bowler cricket has ever known. He is of the type, not uncommon amongst spinners, who will bowl and spin for the sake of bowling and spinning. He seems happier at bowling a good spinner without taking a wicket than at taking a wicket with a poorer ball. His long walk back to the distant starting-mark of his run is buoyant, and there is a half-smile on his face after the ball has pitched a length and done enough to beat the bat. His run up is remarkable, and infectiously enthusiastic. Swinging into long strides almost at once, he comes up like a spring-heeled-Jack, bounding up to the crease to deliver the ball with a leap to full arm's reach above his head. The pace of his spinner is definitely medium, his faster ball is fast-medium. This latter rarely pitches straight, otherwise he would take great numbers of wickets with it, for it is not readily identifiable. Neither is his googly easily to be detected, and Viljoen at least of the 1947 South African team was never able to pick it out with certainty.

Because Wright's best ball is so good—and it is as nearly unplayable as any regularly bowled ball of any bowler now playing—he does not maintain the flat level of standard of some lesser bowlers. When he is out of form and not finding his length, the wise captain will take Wright off and send him to field, and Wright will understand and know that he is understood. In any case, he seems to enjoy fielding. But on his good days he is good on any wicket—he would be deadly on a slab of marble—and then he should be allowed to bowl to his heart's delight and he will walk back to his mark joyfully. Wright is a man of humour and considerable intelligence. He is now much more accurate than he was, and, by drawing a line a yard behind the crease, has almost eliminated his old habit of bowling no-balls, which, aside from their immediate cost in runs, unsettled him and impaired his confidence.

Watch Wright on a day when he is happy about bowling, attacking a great batsman with the support of a keen field, and you will see one of the greatest sights that modern cricket can offer, and you will see also a truly happy bowler, concerned only with bowling and not with its statistics.

A. D. NOURSE

It is deceptively easy to contrast Dudley Nourse with his captain, Alan Melville. There are the obvious points of difference—Melville tall, Nourse short, Melville slim, Nourse thick-set, Melville graceful and elegant, Nourse powerful and downright. But Melville and Nourse worked in close mutual harness to serve South African cricket, and at that point contrast must be shelved or the imagination might blind the watcher to many matters—such as Nourse's amazingly fast footwork. For, powerful as he is—and there can have been few more powerful figures in the history of Test cricket—his muscles are always in trim, never slowing him, but carrying him like a cat down the wicket after the spinning ball or across his wicket to defend. His eye enables him to play his defensive stroke very late indeed, and then he kills the ball with a stab of the bat and glowers at it as it lies dead in front of him.

Nourse was the most consistent of South Africa's Test

Match batsmen of 1947. With Melville at the other end, as at Nottingham, or Mitchell, as at the Oval, he was a great, punishing batsman. In a pinch, as at Leeds, he could be grim and determined in defence, bristling with fight and compelling confidence. As an attacking bat he was a model of the difference between the scientific hitter and the slogger. When he hit, he knew exactly what sort of delivery it was that he was hitting and exactly where he was hitting it. He drove and hooked with immense power which sprung from forearms as thick as some men's thighs, backed by mighty shoulders and the swing of a co-ordinated frame whose great strength was under minute control. He hit often with negligible backswing and no follow-through, so that the watcher was amazed at the speed of the smitten ball. Were I a cricket captain, there is no batsman in the world that I would sooner send in when things were going badly than Dudley Nourse.

In the field, his concentration and speed of foot took him quickly to the ball, whether in slips, at short leg, or in the covers. And when he threw, he did so with a lazy wave of a thick arm to send the ball, with little or no loft upon it, straight to the wicket-keeper with a smack into the gloves reminiscent of Hobbs's throw to Strudwick.

A memorable man, great son of a great cricketer, but who worked out his problems and his cricket for himself, a quiet, thoughtful captain, Nourse is a man who will be remembered by all who saw him for great Test Match batting.

Nourse is that rare type of really strong man who does not flaunt his strength, who is confident but never conceited, splendid in action but never flamboyant, grim, when necessary, but never cruel. He looks men in the eye and speaks the truth—but he never blusters. He is humorous and considerate, as good to have known as a man as to have watched playing so gallantly the game he knows so well.

(2)

GONE TO
THE TEST MATCH

Being an account of the
Test Series of 1948

To
GEORGE HAMILTON
Cordially and with
gratitude

THE DIGLIS HOTEL,
WORCESTER.

27th April, 1948.

TO-MORROW another cricket season will start, another touring team—*the* touring team—Australia, will tease the cricket prophets; another gathering of the camp-followers of cricket will wag their heads and refill their glasses.

It is ten years since an Australian side came to Worcester to start its tour of England, ten years since Bradman scored one of his recurrent Worcester centuries as the first of a series of innings planted like stepping-stones across cricketing England. To-morrow we shall see him again. What will his opening gambit be? He is old by Australian Test cricketing standards, but, surely, still a great batsman—certainly still part of the mighty legend of Australian cricket which makes our season of the Australian tour different from any other.

English cricket, since the war, has been building up to this season. The visits of the Indian and South African teams made happy summers. This one, however, will be grimmer. It is not the cricketer's fault that his occasional failure to catch a leather ball between his hands will be greeted as a national disaster. No cricketer is to blame for the fact that this year people will try to make cricket something other than a game.

Throughout the year, men who, in a normal year, do not know which team has won the County Championship, will utter such rubbish as will convince any sensible man that they have completely lost all sense of proportion. Because of this obsession, which flourishes in ignorance,

men who love the game of cricket will be unable to play
it as a game. It will be pretended that victory or defeat
in a Test Match *proves* something other than the fact
that under given circumstances eleven men of one country are a better blend of batsmen, bowlers and fieldsmen
than eleven of another. No more can be proved by a
game of cricket. But men, perhaps even countries, will
be reviled for a difference of a hundred or two runs
between two cricket teams.

Being human and an Englishman, I hope England will
win: I hope rather more—that I may see great cricket
played by great cricketers. I had sooner see England lose
with a good team than win with a bad one—and that has
occurred in past Test series.

I had sooner see England defeated than find, as I go up
and down England seeing cricket and cricketers, that the
old zest has gone. So long as cricketers talk cricket late
into Saturday night, so long as endless 'shop' analyses
Jack Walsh's 'Chinaman' to its uttermost complexity, so
long as young men are struggling with their cricket
problems, English cricket is healthy enough. Whether
or not it has yet recovered fully from the war is doubtful.
We recovered slowly after 1918, so that Australia won
overwhelmingly in 1921. But the cricketers who were
maturing in 1921 won in 1926.

The 1946 and 1947 seasons showed young cricketers
of promise all over the country: 1948, even farther from
the disorganization of war, should reveal even more. In
a year when ballyhoo will attempt to swamp cricket,
one of the rewards of watching will be the recognition
of the outstanding cricketers of the future.

Across the Severn from my window, the Worcester
ground is spickly white-painted, the wind is less sharp than
in 1946 and 1947. At this moment Reg Perks is waiting

to tell me of a winter in South Africa, and a whole season of vintage cricket is about to be decanted. My typewriter has, for the moment, no place in the scheme of things: a printed fixture-list is about to warm into the life of cricketers and cricket—and, in due time, I shall look back upon it, but for the moment I shall live it.

THE AUSTRALIAN TOURING TEAM: 1948

*D. G. Bradman, of South Australia, 39, captain.

*A. L. Hassett, of Victoria, 35, vice-captain: batsman.

*W. A. Brown, of South Australia, 35: batsman.

*S. G. Barnes, of New South Wales, 29: batsman; occasionally bowls leg-breaks.

D. Tallon, of Queensland, 32: wicket-keeper.

K. R. Miller, of New South Wales, 28: all-rounder; fast-medium bowler.

R. R. Lindwall, of New South Wales, 26: fast bowler.

I. W. Johnson, of Victoria, 28: slow off-break bowler.

W. A. Johnston, of Victoria, 26: left-arm fast-medium bowler.

C. L. McCool, of Queensland, 29· leg-break and googly bowler.

S. J. E. Loxton, of Victoria, 27: all-rounder; fast-medium bowler.

A. R. Morris, of New South Wales, 26: left-hand batsman.

E. R. H. Toshack, of New South Wales, 31: left-arm medium-pace bowler.

R. A. Hamence, of South Australia, 32: batsman.

R. N. Harvey, of Victoria, 19: left-hand batsman.

D. Ring, of Victoria, 29: leg-break bowler.

R. A. Saggers, of New South Wales, 31: wicket-keeper.

(All right-hand batsmen or right-arm bowlers unless indicated otherwise.)

Of those selected, presumably, primarily as bowlers or wicket-keepers, only Ring, W. A. Johnston and Toshack are not capable batsmen—that is, batsmen capable of scoring a century against an English county eleven. Those marked * have visited England with previous official touring teams.

CHAPTER ONE

PRELIMINARY TO THE FIRST TEST

WORCESTER opened with the invariable wind and rain. The weather stole up on the cricket overnight and chilled it. It was something warmer than for the opening of the Indian and South African tours, but not enough to make cricket watching all that it might be. The Australian team was, of course, their on-paper strongest—Barnes, Morris, Bradman, Hassett, Miller, Brown, Ian Johnson, Tallon, McCool, Lindwall and Toshack. Worcester batted first on a fairly easy wicket. It might be more accurate to say that Australia bowled first, because Lindwall had been written up to great speed and down to McCormick-like depths of no-balling. He was watched eagerly as he ran up comfortably and delivered his first ball with a low arm but uneventfully. He repaid the crowd's interest by taking a wicket with the second ball of the match and of his first over in England.

Then Eddie Cooper and C. H. Palmer scored 137 for the second wicket. Here, presumably, was the basis of the Australian team for the Tests, and two Worcester batsmen handled its bowling with relative comfort in their respective styles. Eddie Cooper, a journeyman batsman in the Lancashire manner, was safe and careful. Palmer, for his part, attacked some very ordinary-looking bowling with magnificent timing and elegant stroke-play. India and South Africa in their opening games had produced bowlers obviously of Test Match class. The Australians did not do so. Palmer appeared comfortable, even sprightly, against their spin-bowlers. He is quick on

his feet and, on a slow wicket, he went after the bowling
with little of the air of a man facing a redoubtable Test
cricket side. The Australian fielding was sound, but
Palmer and Cooper were the chief cricketers of the day
and Howorth thumped cheerfully for 37. The relatively
inexperienced batsmen in the side failed, but Worcester,
by making 233, checked many a premonition of a great
Australian attack. Lindwall did not bowl very fast, but
was obviously bent chiefly upon the avoidance of no-
balls and, in the cold, damp atmosphere, strained
muscles.

The second day was a very different story. The pace of
the wicket allowed Barnes time to play his back strokes
with careful selection of direction and he batted formid-
ably. Morris was so assured as to deny in his stroke-play
the fact that this was his first match-experience on
English wickets. Bradman was Bradman making a
century at Worcester. At the opening of his innings he
watched the slow left-arm bowling of Howorth minutely,
playing the ball fractionally short of the stumps, moving
back, making his stroke at the last second. Then, hand,
eye and wicket attuned, he proceeded, surgically, to
direct the ball through the gaps in the field, as ruthless as
ever in chastening the bad ball. There it was, happening
under our very eyes again—a Bradman century to start
the tour. To be sure there was a suggestion of stiffness
which was new, a hint of the batsman's anxiety to score
yet another hundred on this ground. But there was
no encouragement for English bowlers in this same
superb and merciless confidence. After Barnes, Morris
and Bradman had established a good credit of runs, Lindwall, McCool and Tallon, useful batsmen not selected
for their batting, were given their first taste of English
wickets, and Jackson a good meal of Australian wickets—

five of the six that fell. In the first match of his benefit
year, Jackson bowled to a length and spun neatly.
Hassett, Brown and Miller had seen English wickets
before, and winning runs were already on the board when
they went in, so that they needed merely to confirm their
memories and ours by batting characteristically until
Bradman declared on Friday morning. Miller enjoyed
himself—with barely a glance at the score-board—before
Bradman's declaration at Miller's 50 and Australia's
lead of 229. Worcester in their second innings made
good runs again. Cooper was sober, Palmer again looked
for accomplished runs and Outschoorn batted with
impressive style. Even the tail-enders, Perks and Yarnold,
were not disconcerted by the legendary Australian caps
and made almost forty between them.

In winning by an innings where India and South Africa
had lost, the Australians confirmed the impression that
their batting could be of immense weight but, on a
wicket where the ball turned only very slowly, Jackson
suggested that good-length spin bowling would have its
due and traditional reward even against such a combination of batsmen. The touring side's bowling, however,
was not impressive. Probably the bowlers were warming
up, but Lindwall showed barely the pace of Miller—
they, like Perks for Worcester, missed pace in the wicket.
McCool was extremely erratic, although he spun the
ball considerably, and Toshack and Johnson, though
accurate, were not hostile. On the scanty evidence of the
first Australian match there appeared a promise of drawn
Test Matches, with neither side able to get the other out.

Australians v. Worcestershire at Worcester, 28th, 29th and 30th April

Australians won by an innings and 17 runs.

Worcestershire 233 (Palmer 85, E. Cooper 51; Johnson 3 for 52) and 212 (Outschoorn 54, Palmer 34; McCool 4 for 29, Johnson 3 for 7).

Australians 462 for 8 wickets declared (Barnes 44, Morris 138, Bradman 107, Miller 50 not out; Jackson 6 for 135).

.   .   .   .

The second match of the tour brought in the six players who had not played at Worcester—Harvey, Hamence, Loxton, Saggers, Ring and W. A. Johnston. Again Australia won by an innings—but so would an England side against Worcestershire or Leicestershire. Again they made many runs, but through only three batsmen. Saturday threatened to be Barnes' day, promised to be Bradman's, but was eventually Miller's. Miller's first achievement was to come to the crease first wicket down when necks were being craned to see Bradman and to bow in mock appreciation of the crowd's silent surprise. When Barnes was surprisingly out, Bradman came to release the pent-up cheering and join Miller. At once he set about the warming business of making runs at one-a-minute on a cold day. The weather was arctic, but Bradman moved lightly and effectively towards another hundred and a further instalment of the crowd's readily tapped applause. He was annoyed with himself when he edged a ball from Etherington, to be caught at the wicket, and the crowd's disappointment was almost to be felt.

From that moment until the end of the Australian innings on Monday, Miller was in supreme charge of the batting: no one else made more than a dozen runs on a typically easy Leicester wicket. Neil Harvey was com-

pletely baffled by Walsh's googly, which struck back at
him while he was playing it as the ball that leaves him.
In the same over Hamence was as completely beaten by
the same bowler. It is rare to see the first-class batsman so
utterly without an idea what the ball is doing as Harvey
and Hamence facing Walsh that day. They were Walsh's
only two wickets of the innings, but Bradman himself
would not, I believe, have been unhappy to be given out
lbw to one from Walsh which he thought was a googly
only to find it a straightforward 'Chinaman'—if a 'Chinaman' can ever be straightforward. Even Miller, for several
overs, was groping, as he rarely does, for Walsh's bowling.
Five of the other eight wickets were Jackson's—the reward of an accurate length, spin and sound cricket
generalship. As Australians in England, Walsh and Jackson are unofficially disqualified from playing for either
England or Australia. Yet Jackson is certainly the best all-
rounder in English county cricket and Walsh the most
baffling spin-bowler in the world. If Walsh is sometimes
erratic, he bowls a much better length than, for instance,
Fleetwood-Smith, and he is constantly adding fresh variations and subtleties to a technique already exceedingly
complex. Jackson is an omniscient slip-fieldsman to
Walsh's bowling—constantly saving byes when even
wicket-keeper Paddy Corrall has been sent the wrong
way by one of the bowler's infinite variations on the
theme of the left-arm wrong 'un. As a bowler, Vic Jackson
is steady and tireless at medium-pace, as a batsman he has
most of the strokes built into a sound defence. These two
players play cricket the calendar round in England and
South Africa with intensity and delight. The Australian
purpose at cricket is in them, blended with the craftsman-
attitude of the English professional. They miss Test
honours because the game as they want to play it is

played only in England and they are Australians. English cricket would be the poorer without them, and Leicestershire would be struggling indeed if they left the county. Only Jackson (in each innings), Berry, Lester and Prentice, in one innings or the other, and Walsh with a flurry of swings in the first innings, showed any resistance to the Australian bowling in the shadow of a total of 448.

With the mid-order wickets falling all round him, Miller changed from the gay and experimental batsman of his partnership with Bradman to a mature and responsible general of the remainder of the innings. Then, with the tail uneasy, he farmed the bowling and took every chance of scoring. This was the innings of a man in command of every type of game and every stroke, serving his side with immense strategic sensibility and scoring almost half the team's total.

Of the bowlers, W. A. Johnston had, as yet, incomplete control of the swinging ball in the humid English atmosphere—a new and exciting medium for him. Loxton looked enthusiastic and straightforward. Ian Johnson again took wickets by virtue of a fairly good length and appreciable off-spin. Ring, the other leg-spinner of the party, replacing McCool, showed himself rather more accurate in length. His pace was near to that of O'Reilly of old, but he lacked O'Reilly's venom or McCool's extent of spin, while his flight offered no difficulties to practised batsmen.

For all the proportions of the Australians' win, the fact that batsmen short of the best in England had played the touring team's bowlers without great difficulty heartened those who hoped for England's Test chances.

Australians v. Leicestershire at Leicester, 1st, 3rd and 4th May

Australians won by an innings and 171 runs.

Australians 448 (Miller 202 not out, Bradman 81, Barnes 78; Jackson 5 for 91).

Leicestershire 130 (Walsh 33; Ring 5 for 45) and 147 (Jackson 31 not out, Lester 40; Johnson 7 for 42).

. . . .

The game against Yorkshire at Bradford, which followed, showed even the Australian batting as vulnerable. The wicket at Bradford is a very fair one. In this match it was drying, and helped the spin-bowlers, but it was still short of being 'sticky.' Miller became an off-spin bowler for the occasion, and he and W. A. Johnston twice bowled out Yorkshire. Smailes and Wardle were almost as deadly for Yorkshire, and Australia were rescued in their first innings only by Miller. Again he was the player who saved Australia when they were in trouble, this time with a hitting innings which blended eye, strength, timing and nerve to retrieve a position once as desperate as 38 for 4 wickets. In the second innings Harvey (who was missed when he had only made one) and Tallon won the game for Australia after six wickets had gone down for 31.

Australians v. Yorkshire at Bradford, 5th and 6th May

Australians won by 4 wickets.

Yorkshire 71 (W. A. Johnston 4 for 22, Miller 6 for 42) and 89 (Sellers 21; W. A. Johnston 6 for 18, Miller 3 for 49).

Australians 101 (Miller 34; Smailes 6 for 51, Wardle 2 for 28) and 63 for 6 wickets (Harvey 18 not out, Tallon 17 not out; Smailes 3 for 32, Wardle 2 for 28).

. . . .

For the match with Surrey at the Oval there was a
wicket to reassure those Australians disturbed by their
experience at Bradford. It was plumb as an Oval plumb
'un can be. Bradman made another century, Barnes and
Hassett too; while Morris and Tallon both made more
than fifty. Then, at the start of the Surrey innings, Lindwall bowled fast for a few overs. He bowled Fletcher for
one and Squires for three, and then retired into his shell.
Fishlock batted right through the Surrey first innings of
141 to make 81 not out. Once again a batsman unlikely
quite to win a place in the England side was safe and
sound against the Australian bowling. In Surrey's second
innings it was Squires who batted well, in scoring a good
50. W. A. Johnston was a vastly improved bowler by
comparison with the match at Leicester, and Bradman's
plan was now beginning to take shape. He was not
hurrying his bowlers, but allowing them runs and time
to work out their Test salvation.

The Australian batting became a nightmare to county
bowlers. After the 632 against Surrey, they made 414 for
4 wickets before declaring against Cambridge University,
but Dewes, Doggart and Bailey (66 not out) batted well
against them. Then came the incredible 721 in a day
against Essex. Runs scored day-long at a rate of 120 an
hour can become cloying: such scoring does not make
for a *match*. Barnes' opening 79 was reduced to the paltry
by Bradman's 187, Billy Brown's 153, Loxton's 120 and
Saggers' not out 104. Twice five fours were hit off an
over: in one over not a single ball was allowed to pitch
between bowler's arm and bat. Bradman scored at one
and a half runs a minute, Brown at just under a run a
minute, Loxton at one and a third to the minute and
Saggers at one a minute. Loxton and Saggers put on 166
in sixty-five minutes for the sixth wicket: four maiden

overs were bowled in the entire day. It was a mordant wit which congratulated Tom Pearce on being the first county captain to get the Australians out in a day. Loxton and Saggers showed that they could make their runs handsomely as well as a quickly, and a Bradman 100 at Southend at Whit week-end was a seaside holiday indeed. The Essex bowling was not sharp enough nor the fielding tight enough to subdue these run-hungry batsmen on a plumb wicket. Only Keith Miller took no part in the carnage. Such a situation does not attract him as a cricketer, he looks for worlds to conquer, not for the already conquered lying open for his exploitation. He removed his bat from the course of his first ball, a straight one, and returned to the pavilion—where life might produce a challenge.

On the Monday the Essex batsmen were butchered one by one to make an Australian Bank Holiday. Toshack in their first innings and Ian Johnson in the second, took wickets easily without assistance from the placid pitch until Tom Pearce and Peter Smith came together in the second innings. Now again it was the story of every match of the tour except the one at Bradford. Two batsmen of less than Test Match class made runs—fairly good runs—against the Australians by a courageous approach and the application of the basic principles of batting. Year in, year out, Tom Pearce makes bags of runs for Essex by playing forward to everything but the long-hop. If the ball turns enough to beat the bat, then it will certainly beat the wicket, for he plays solemnly 'down the track,' his right hand is sufficiently slack to prevent the edged ball carrying to slip, and he fears no bowler—now get him out! Peter Smith, with all to gain and nothing to lose, experimented with the straight bat. Those two put on 133 for the seventh wicket of the Essex second innings

—just about half of the runs scored by the county in its two innings.

The match lasted only two days, but they were days of large crowds and impressive events, if not of well-matched cricket. Despite the immensity of the Australian victory, no depression was to be observed in those salubrious cellar-haunts near Southend pier, where the attractions range from the democratic winkle to an economically priced but elegant oyster.

I append the full score of the match because it is so delightfully depressing:

Australians—First Innings

S. G. Barnes, hit wkt, b Smith (R.)	79
W. A. Brown, c Horsfall b Bailey	153
D. G. Bradman, b Smith (P.)	187
K. R. Miller, b Bailey	0
R. A. Hamence, c Smith (P.) b Smith (R.)	46
S. J. E. Loxton, c Rist b Vigar	120
R. A. Saggers, not out	104
I. W. Johnson, st Rist b Smith (P.)	9
D. Ring, c Vigar b Smith (P.)	1
W. A. Johnston, b Vigar	9
E. R. H. Toshack, c Vigar b Smith (P.)	4
Extras (b 7, n-b 2)	9
Total	721

Bowling Analysis

	O	M	R	W
Bailey	21	1	128	2
Smith (R.)	37	2	169	2
Smith (P.)	37	0	193	4
Price	20	0	156	0
Vigar	13	1	66	2

Essex

T. C. Dodds, c Ring b Miller	0	b Toshack	16
S. J. Gray, b Miller	5	b Johnson	15
A. V. Avery, b Johnston	10	c Brown b Johnson	3
F. H. Vigar, c Saggers b Miller	0	c Johnson b Toshack	0
D. J. Horsfall, b Toshack	11	b Johnson	8
T. N. Pearce, c Miller b Toshack	8	c and b Johnson	71
R. Smith, c Barnes b Toshack	25	c Ring b Johnson	0
P. Smith, b Toshack	3	lbw b Barnes	54
F. Rist, c Barnes b Toshack	8	b Johnson	1
E. Price, not out	4	not out	4
T. E. Bailey, absent hurt	0	absent hurt	0
Extras (b 2, l-b 6, n-b 1)	9	Extras (b 6, l-b 3, n-b 6)	15
Total	83	Total	187

Bowling Analysis

	O	M	R	W		O	M	R	W
Miller	8	3	14	3	....	2	1	4	0
Johnston	7	1	10	1	....	10	4	26	0
Ring	11	4	19	0	....	7	3	16	0
Toshack	10·5	0	31	5	....	17	2	50	2
Loxton	—	—	—	—	....	12	3	28	0
Johnson	—	—	—	—	....·....	21	6	37	6
Barnes	—	—	—	—	....	9·4	5	11	1

After Southend, an Australian total of 431 at Oxford was remarkable only because it included W. A. Brown's third successive hundred.

It was in the game between the Australians and the
M.C.C. at Lord's that the major paths of England and
Australian cricket first crossed. An M.C.C. team, with
four certainties for the English team and five possibles,
assisted by the best left-hander in the country (Martin
Donnelly), was expected to give the touring team its
hardest game up to then. In fact, it was another comfortable innings win for Bradman's team. Certainly Australia
had first use of a wicket which was a little more difficult
on Monday than on Saturday, but that could not have
made the difference of such a defeat. The Australian
batting was dishearteningly confident on Saturday and
gaily murderous on Monday. On that Monday morning
nine sixes were hit off Laker by the lower half of the
Australian batting. Bedser was not playing for the
M.C.C., nor his presumable Test partner as pace-
bowler; Wright was not in the side either, so there was
no great reason to be depressed by the failure of Edrich,
Cranston and Deighton to bowl out the Australians. The
batting, however, included all but Washbrook of the
main English batting strength, with a possible for No. 5
in Robertson. Edrich and Compton had run into form,
and were making many runs in county matches, and
Hutton was, on county match figures, batting outstandingly. The batting of the M.C.C. failed before fast,
medium-fast, medium and slow bowlers. Hutton's
figures were good, but he showed considerable lack of
enjoyment of the bowling of Lindwall and Miller. In the
second innings he hooked Miller badly—alarmingly
badly. Toshack's nagging accuracy in the first innings,
the spin of Johnson and McCool in the second, were, on
figures, the effective agents of the Australian bowling. In
fact, all the bowlers looked better than the batsmen, and
the poor Australian bowling form of the early matches

was becoming no more than a false impression or English wishful thinking.

In the remaining matches before the first Test, Australia did not continue unbroken the run of huge wins, but the tempering of the eleven against the Test Match became very apparent. The reserve batsmen, Harvey, Hamence and Loxton, were becoming accustomed to English cricket and wickets. W. A. Johnston was revelling in the increased assistance which English conditions afford to the medium-fast bowler, and Johnson went on steadily taking wickets. Then, at Trent Bridge against Nottingham, Lindwall cut loose with 6 wickets for 14 runs; against Sussex he took 11 wickets in the match for only 59 runs: he bowled fast.

Nevertheless, the side was by no means flawless: the spin-bowlers Hilton and Roberts of Lancashire, Knott and Bailey of Hampshire, took wickets against them on spin-responsive pitches. Hampshire, in fact, had hopes of winning until the wicket suddenly became plumb after lunch on the third day. Hardstaff (48 and 107) and R. T. Simpson (74 and 70) scored freely against them at Trent Bridge, despite Lindwall.

Australia came to the Test Match with the eleven almost selecting itself. Only one doubt may have disturbed the minds of the selectors—Bradman, Hassett and Morris —and that concerned the inclusion of a leg-break bowler. From Hordern in 1911 onwards, the Australian leg-spin bowlers—varying in method between the extremes of Mailey and Grimmett—have been an essential part of their Test sides. Neither Ring nor McCool of the 1948 side, however, had deserved a place in the Test. Ring was more impressive in his team-mates' opinion than English batsmen found him; he was accurate in length but innocuous in flight. McCool was not bowling a consistent length nor fast enough to stop batsmen going down the pitch to him on slow English wickets. The batsmen selected themselves: Morris and Barnes were an established opening pair, Bradman still a World XI No. 3, Hassett able to play either game at No. 4, Miller, potentially a great batsman, at No. 5, and Brown, an experienced Test Match opening batsman with a string of hundreds to his credit, would bat at No. 6 because the opening pair could not be disturbed. Tallon, as good as any wicket-keeper in the world, made a seventh automatic selection. Lindwall was the obvious fast bowler, and there was Miller to open with him. W. A. Johnston had been successful as a seam bowler and a medium-pace spinner, and Ian Johnson, a useful batsman and experienced slip-fieldsman, was an off-break bowler who had taken wickets regularly since the start of the tour. If the selectors decided not to break with tradition or that Toshack's batting and fielding excluded him, then Ring or McCool would play, but on bowling form Toshack had to play, and the selectors wisely accepted that position. The eleven was thus: S. G. Barnes, A. R. Morris, D. G. Bradman, A. L. Hassett, K. R. Miller, I. W. Johnson, W. A. Brown, R. R. Lindwall, D. Tallon, W. A. Johnston and E. R. H. Toshack. Neil Harvey was twelfth man.

England's side, too, almost picked itself. Washbrook, Hutton, Edrich and Compton had past and current form to establish them, and Yardley was to captain the side—there were five batsmen. Evans had settled into the side as its wicket-keeper who might at any time make brilliant runs. Bedser was back again to his power of 1946 after a winter's rest, and no one except a few county partisans doubted his right to the position of opening bowler. Thus four places remained; the problem was rather *how*

those places should be filled than who should fill them.
If it was decided that attack was the best method of
defence, then three more bowlers might be picked, with
the last place going to a batsman or even an all-rounder—
if one could be found. Again, it might be two bowlers,
one all-rounder and one batsman. If it was decided that
England would rely upon defence and the weather, then
it must be two batsmen and two bowlers. If one of the
batsmen could bowl, so much the better.

The batsmen were absolute in (county match) form.
Yardley had reported fit after an attack of lumbago.
There had been a Test Trial which had told the selectors
very little indeed, except that C. H. Palmer of Worcester
could bowl. The veteran fast bowler, Copson of Derbyshire, had been included in the Trial, doubtless to give the
English batsmen practice against fast bowling: they did
not appear to have profited from the opportunity.
Wright and Bedser confirmed the selectors' known views
of them, while Butler and Cranston, either of whom may
have been considered to support Bedser, failed to take a
wicket on the wet pitch. Howorth, who seemed to have
established himself as England's slow left-arm bowler in
the Fifth Test against South Africa was, apparently, no
longer seriously considered. He had suffered on the West
Indies tour from being fit. With many other players unfit, he had bowled too many overs in great heat, and
returned tired to the damp English spring. Fibrositis
was troubling him, and his bowling appeared deficient
in flight by comparison with his form of 1946 and
1947. Broderick of Northants, who might have taken
Howorth's place, was not impressive as a fieldsman or a
batsman in the Test Trial, although he bowled well.

Originally the selectors chose twelve players from
whom the final eleven was to be picked—plus R. T.

Simpson specifically as twelfth man; but, the day before the match, they summoned George Pope of Derby to make thirteen players for final selection. The thirteen players were:

> N. W. D. Yardley (Yorkshire),
> L. Hutton (Yorkshire),
> C. Washbrook (Lancashire),
> W. J. Edrich (Middlesex),
> D. Compton (Middlesex),
> J. Hardstaff (Notts),
> C. J. Barnett (Gloucester),
> T. G. Evans (Kent),
> J. Laker (Surrey),
> A. V. Bedser (Surrey),
> J. Young (Middlesex),

who were selected to play, and D. V. P. Wright (Kent) (lumbago) and G. Pope (Derby) who were not. In fact, the selectors had backed defence and the weather. By their final selection they admitted that England had no real chance of winning a Test against these 1948 Australians if the game was played on equal terms. Therefore they backed the batting as a defensive measure against the need to play for a draw. They included Jack Young—a safe and steady slow left-arm bowler on a plumb wicket and deadly, like all his kind, on a sticky or a fast-turning wicket—and Laker, considered the best of the young off-break bowlers. If there was rain, these two might be expected to take advantage of it. If it was fine, they and Bedser would bowl defensively, and would receive some support from Edrich, Barnett and Yardley.

I thought at the time, and think now, that the English selectors were entirely right in their approach to the first

Test Match. They realized that England's best team—and there is little doubt that it *was* the best team—must hope for the rubs of the green to win. If Yardley won the toss and the batsmen made runs—and there were enough of them for runs to be expected—and then rain came, the side had the bowling to win the match. Without rain the eleven best bowlers in England could hardly hope to bowl out the 1948 Australians twice in five days for headable totals.

CHAPTER TWO

THE FIRST TEST MATCH

Played at Trent Bridge, Nottingham, 10th, 11th, 12th, 14th and 15th June, 1948

First Day—Thursday, 10th June

IRRESPECTIVE of who should win or lose it, this Test Match, England against Australia—after ten thronged, unhappy, uncertain, dragging, war-sorry years —was a symbol. The atmosphere of a Day—more than just another opening day of another Test Match—was present at Trent Bridge, and not even the smoke-sombre cloak of the clouds nor the skirts of the rain could hide it.

It was five minutes past twelve before play could start. Then Lindwall ran, padding, accelerating smoothly and bowled the first ball easily, not yet at full pace, to Hutton. Hutton pushed it away to the region of point and scored the first run. The clouds moved in, grey and low. At a quarter-past twelve the Australian attack was driving like a gale. Hutton and Washbrook were not so certain as they would wish. Miller and Lindwall bowled. The score was 9. Miller bowled to Hutton from the pavilion end. As his arm came over high against the dark background of shadows under the pavilion balcony, the ball was hard to focus and, watched as I watched it from the level of the pavilion roof, it could be seen to move very late in its flight. It hurried, too, off the pitch, and it bowled Len Hutton, and the crowd was quiet. At 13 for 1 wicket there was rain and play stopped, there were three more minutes of play and one run just after one o'clock, and then no more until after lunch. England 13 for 1 wicket at lunch improved only Australian appetites.

Twenty minutes' play after lunch without a run led up to Ian Johnson dropping Edrich in the slips. Another maiden was bowled by Miller, and then Edrich took a single off Lindwall. Two balls later Lindwall bowled a ball slightly short of a length along the line of Washbrook's leg-stump. Washbrook hooked hard and high— the first sign of a fighting stroke since lunch. The ball passed in a swinging arc towards the long-leg boundary, and there Billy Brown judged it, ran smoothly into its path and caught it: 15–2–6.

With Compton and Edrich together there were memories of great partnerships against South Africa. Now, although there was none of the dominance of those days, they bore straight bats and struggled with hope towards command and ease. Compton hit Miller through the covers for four and the weather seemed finer; Compton smiled at Edrich, and a man near me spoke, uninvited, to a stranger. Compton suppressed much of the Compton in him, eschewing even his favourite sweep of the ball outside the leg-stump. Edrich was a struggling fury under the weight of Miller and Lindwall. Johnston came on for Lindwall and bowled a maiden over. Soon Toshack bowled for Miller. There was a perceptible lessening of tension—the sort of easing which can be fatal if accompanied by careful bowling. A four off each bowler and England were fighting; the stranger spoke back to the man near me. Then Bill Johnston bowled Edrich for the 18 runs of a grim hour and a quarter. About now the light became poorer, poor enough for Hardstaff to hang out a bat more of enquiry than of hope to Johnston, whence Miller caught him with superb agility at slip: 46–4–0. Miller came back and bowled Compton: 48–5–19. It was all very sad for those who had hoped, and one always hopes for one's friends.

Barnett, threatening to stand no nonsense, hit a four off
Toshack: Bradman looked surprised, and moved a fieldsman eighteen inches and Johnston bowled Barnett:
60–6–8. Yardley, who had gathered two singles in a
quarter of an hour, watched Evans make strokes while he
himself played to prevent the ball from hitting his wicket.
Evans hit a catch to Bradman at cover and Bradman
dropped it. We remembered Evans' Trent Bridge
innings of 1947 and hope stirred faintly again. But Morris
caught Evans off the tireless, enthusiastic and accurate
Johnston, and Yardley was lbw to a ball from Toshack
which straightened. England at tea: 75–8–3: Laker not
out 1, Bedser not out 0. Bill Johnston had taken 4 wickets
for 20, Miller 2 for 15. Englishmen were downcast
indeed; there was no hope left: this was not only defeat,
but defeat without a shred of credit. Only Edrich had
shown the will, the heart and the ability to defend against
these bowlers: 75 for 8 indeed!

Between a quarter to five and five minutes to six Jim
Laker and Bedser doubled the English score. It did not
need excessive sensitivity to feel the gratitude of the
crowd going out to the two batsmen. When Laker
pushed the ball for a firm single, every Englishman on the
ground was proud of him and relished the fact that Laker
played for England. Laker made strokes. He made the
strokes of a practised batsman, the strokes the men before
him should have made. Lindwall (strained groin) did not
bowl after tea, but Miller, Johnston, Johnson and Toshack did. Bedser stood defensive beside Laker, while the
pair put on 89 runs for the ninth wicket. The wicket was
a little easier than in the morning, when an occasional ball
had lifted or skidded—but the difference was not such as
to cause hesitation in the best batsmen in England at one
moment, confidence in tail-enders at the next. The light,

too, improved, but nothing can detract from the courage of Laker and Bedser nor from Laker's stroke-play—particularly in the off-drive. With Young, last man in, Laker was caught by Tallon standing back to Miller. The English total of 165 was poor, but a relief after the *mauvais quart d'heure* of tea-time. The bowling of Johnston and Miller had been fine almost beyond praise: they lacked nothing of the art of the pace-bowler.

Barnes and Morris had twelve minutes of the evening in which to treat the bowling of Edrich with disrespect and that of Bedser with calm certainty while promising to prove 165 a hopelessly inadequate total.

England—First Innings

L. Hutton, b Miller	3
C. Washbrook, c Brown b Lindwall . .	6
W. J. Edrich, b Johnston	18
D. Compton, b Miller	19
J. Hardstaff, c Miller b Johnston . .	0
C. J. Barnett, b Johnston . . .	8
N. W. D. Yardley, lbw b Toshack . .	3
T. G. Evans, c Morris b Johnston . .	12
J. Laker, c Tallon b Miller . . .	63
A. V. Bedser, c Brown b Johnston . .	22
J. Young, not out	1
Extras (b 5, l-b 5)	10
Total . . .	165

Bowling Analysis

	O	M	R	W
Lindwall . .	13	5	30	1
Miller . .	19	8	38	3
Johnston . .	25	11	36	5
Toshack . .	14	8	28	1
Johnson . .	5	1	19	0
Morris . .	3	1	4	0

Fall of Wickets

1	2	3	4	5	6	7	8	9	10
9	15	46	46	48	60	74	74	163	165

Australia—First Innings

S. G. Barnes, not out	6
A. R. Morris, not out	10
Extras	1

Total (for no wkt)   .   .   .   17

Bowling Analysis

	O	M	R	W
W. J. Edrich	2	0	11	0
A. V. Bedser	2	0	5	0

Second Day—Friday, 11th June

The second day was a little finer and a little clearer than the first had been. It was also Australia's day and a day of characteristic five-day Test cricket. Here were all the merits and demerits of the five-day match plainly laid out as if for exhibition and judgment. Australia built themselves an embattled position, and had time to build it without risk or hurry on a gentle and accommodating Trent Bridge wicket. Given a winning opportunity, it is characteristic of the Australians that they will never dissipate it by over-anxiety or by carelessness.

Morris and Barnes wore the mantle of ease from the start of the day. Bedser made the ball move into Barnes and away from Morris quite late in its flight, but neither showed undue concern. Barnett, opening with Bedser after the unceremonious treatment of Edrich on the previous evening, bowled the inswing. Barnett, while the ball retains some of its shine, is a very useful run-checker against Australian batsmen because he keeps the ball well up to the bat. In fact, on this morning he wisely concentrated, at little more than medium pace, on bowling only fractionally short of half-volley length. Barnes in particular was reluctant to drive the swinging ball, and Barnett was allowed to bowl most economically for some time. It may be argued that Barnett to some degree bowled the batsmen in—if so, it was for lack of any other member of the side likely to bowl them out. For half an hour Morris and Barnes walked about their creases with the air of men pottering comfortably at home in their own back-gardens. Then, the left-handed Morris; going across his wicket to play Bedser as he so regularly did, played at a ball which he might safely have left unplayed and edged it to Evans—who dropped it. Morris middled the next few balls punctiliously, and the fifty was up after the innings was an hour old. Young bowled a full-toss to Morris as his first ball, but immediately his mechanical arm slipped into gear and its customary grooved accuracy. Laker, bowling in his first Test against Australia or before an English crowd, bore himself with the self-possession of the Yorkshire league cricketer he was before he joined Surrey. He sauntered up to the wicket and bowled. He was pushed away firmly for a single in his first over. In his next he achieved a maiden with a casual air. In his third over he stunned the crowd by bowling to Morris a ball which the batsman pulled on to his wicket while ostensibly playing it to leg. Regaining consciousness, the watchers cheered, and Australia were 73 for 1 wicket.

Bradman came in under a hail of cheering, such as would have disturbed most men. At once he put everything aside but the problem of Laker, whom he inspected almost fastidiously. A stabbed stroke brought him three

runs, but not yet comfort. Bedser then bowled to him a ball
which came quickly in off the pitch, and Bradman's stroke
to it was so late as to verge on the posthumous. Then
Laker pitched a ball outside the great man's off stump,
and Bradman played to cut, only to find the ball running
fast away from him. With the reflex of a born batsman,
he went on with the stroke and edged it hard, and there
was not quite a catch—had he half-checked his stroke he
must have put the ball up to slip. Perhaps Bradman of
1948 takes longer to consolidate than he did in his prodigy
days: the entry of the full artillery is delayed if he is judged
by his old standard. There is that spell when Bradman is
frankly, humanly and unashamedly, scratching himself
an emplacement. Catch him then and he will go uncom-
plaining. Fail and you have the Bradman of old to deal
with.

Bradman's playing-in notwithstanding, the hundred
came just before lunch, after 125 minutes' batting, and
Australia were 104 for 1 wicket at lunch. Lunch at
Trent Bridge is a well-ordered meal, but was accepted on
this day with apathy fitting a game whose issue was
virtually settled after it had run only a quarter of its way.

At 2.15 Laker and Young bowled, and Barnes seemed
to be achieving comfort after his meal when he played
late to a ball from Laker which went with the bowler's
arm. It took the edge of Barnes' bat low down—the type
of low-edged stroke which, as a rule, scuttles away to fall
short of slips. This ball went on to Evans' instep and flew
into the air—Evans turned as it flew up over his head and
took the catch gratefully. Miller did not score off the
remaining four balls of the over. Bradman played a
precise maiden over from Young. Then Miller played a
ball from Laker which was going away from him all the
time, to give Edrich a catch at slip, and Australia were,

most unexpectedly, 121 for 3 wickets. Laker had taken 3 for 22—two wickets in two overs for no runs.

The new ball was now available. Whether Yardley should have persevered with Laker—whose tail was up—and Jack Young—who was dropping on a spot—is questionable. By taking the new ball he could turn Bedser, fresh and armed with the full shine of the ball, at Brown—who was newly at the crease—and Bradman, whose respect for Bedser is considerable. Laker, on the other hand, had already risen to the occasion twice in the match, and Bradman had had half an hour since lunch to get his eye in again. Forty minutes passed, 43 runs on the board, and Edrich and Bedser had employed the shine of the new ball without taking a wicket—and Laker and Young were on again.

Then, almost as an afterthought it seemed, Yardley himself bowled—and Brown was lbw to him for 17— Australia 185 for 4 wickets. Here was England's first opportunity to recover some degree of the initiative she had gained when Yardley won the toss—and which had been lost from the moment of Hutton's dismissal.

It was a situation much to the taste of Bradman and Lindsay Hassett, who now came out to bat with him. Hassett batted cold-bloodedly, in the knowledge that the wicket was innocuous, that no English bowler was likely to come dangerously off it by virtue of any extra gift of pace or spin, and that, above all, there was no need whatever to hurry—not only was the morrow also a day, but Monday and Tuesday as well were within the limits of the match. So tantalizingly, humorously—but with a wry humour—he delighted in having his bat waiting, already in position, for the bowled ball to hit it.

Bradman, from time to time, hit past mid-off or mid-on with immense force: he forced the ball away off his

back foot and straightforwardly made a hundred. Once
he had played himself in, there was never any real doubt
that Bradman would make a century and, once the inevitable had occurred, more than one spectator considered honour satisfied and the price of his seat money
well spent. Hence a steady trickle of homegoers inter-
rupted the view of the faithful during the last half-hour
of the day. England bowled well. Young in particular
compelled quietness from the batsmen. A slow left-arm
bowler, bowling against batsmen well set, on a wicket
which gives him so little assistance that he is bowling
with six fieldsmen on the leg side and no slip, does well
to bowl thirty-two overs at less than two runs an over.
Laker, slightly more expensive in terms of runs per over,
had taken 3 good Australian wickets for 77 runs.

The control of the game had passed completely back
into Australia's hands with Bradman and Hassett putting
on 108 in their unfinished fifth-wicket stand, and denying
England a wicket between twenty minutes to four and
the close of play—when the score was:

England—First Innings—165 (Laker 63; Johnston 5 for 36,
   Miller 3 for 38)

Australia—First Innings

A. R. Morris, b Laker	31
S. G. Barnes, c Evans b Laker . .	62
D. G. Bradman, not out . .	130
K. R. Miller, c Edrich b Laker . .	0
W. A. Brown, lbw b Yardley . .	17
A. L. Hassett, not out . . .	41
Extras	12
Total (for 4 wkts) . .	293

Bowling Analysis

	O	M	R	W
Edrich	11	1	42	0
Bedser	31	9	66	0
Barnett	12	5	17	0
Young	32	12	53	0
Laker	33	9	77	3
Compton	2	0	9	0
Yardley	15	3	17	1

Fall of Wickets

1	2	3	4
73	121	121	185

Third Day—Saturday, 12th June

Edrich, in a rare fury, and Bedser addressed their bowling selves to Hassett, Bradman and the morning prompt at 11.30 in the novelty of sunlight. Almost at once those who had come prepared with statistics startled the less well-informed by applauding Bradman's thousandth run of the season. Barely had the enquirers been satisfied as to the reason for the outburst when they themselves burst out cheering as Bradman took a hasty flick at a ball from Bedser which came in upon him and sent it to Hutton at short fine leg, who caught it.

Half the play until half-past three is accounted for by Lindsay Hassett. In the main he was light-footedly passive, pushing the ball away or deflecting it neatly. On the other hand, when Yardley called for the new ball, Hassett was violent with it to the disturbance of the shine and any offensive plan which England's captain may have entertained.

Hassett made his runs so slowly that only his grace and concealed humour made his innings tolerable. If a Test

were allocated only five hours, then Hassett would be the
rapid-scoring stroke-maker we know he can be. Given
five days in which to win a Test, Hassett knows his team
would place runs before fireworks, so he sets out to make
as many runs as are consistent with perfect safety at a
five-day scoring rate. Blame the authority which arranges
the five-day match if you will, but not Hassett, who carefully weighs the conditions of a game and then plays it
as effectively as possible within those conditions. Hassett
made 137 in almost six hours, and he hit twenty fours and
one six. He commanded one end while Johnson, Tallon
and Lindwall made their runs with fair certainty and built
a lead which saw their side safe beyond the normal
requirements of safety.

Hassett timed his exit to a nicety: he was bowled by
Bedser, and retired at once, with a smile, to allow that
earnest batsman Ernie Toshack to join his colleague Bill
Johnston. Johnston makes a number of powerful strokes,
some of which call for last-minute adjustments of several
limbs if the bat is to continue upon the course Johnston
has chosen for it. Hence he may suddenly remove his legs
from the line of a stroke which he has already half-
completed—with amazing consequences. Alternatively,
he will change the direction of the half-played stroke in
such a manner as to convince a fieldsman that intelligent
anticipation is of no value in fielding. Toshack, one feels,
bats because he will not otherwise be allowed to bowl.
He has an earnest, almost helpful air as of one not un-
willing to co-operate with the bowler. His strokes are
executed with less than the maximum co-ordination of
limbs. But both Toshack and Johnston scored more runs
than several recognized batsmen on the England side—
and they made them in a manner calculated to interest
and amuse. At once spontaneously and inimitably they

added 33 runs for the last wicket, to increase Australia's
first innings lead to 344 which, although history has seen
it exceeded, was calculated to give satisfaction to those
concerned on the credit side.

England had just over two and a half hours to bat
when Washbrook and Hutton went out to open the
second innings. Lindwall, although he had been able to
run well enough between the wickets when batting, did
not bowl. Moreover, he did not field, his place being
taken by Neil Harvey, who is probably the best outfield
in the world—which was at least part-compensation to
Bradman for the loss of a fast bowler.

Four of the five runs on the board were leg-byes when
Washbrook glanced Miller to leg and Tallon caught him
for the one run scored from the bat. Then Hutton hit a
four off Johnston and Edrich one off Miller, and everyone
felt that this was better than the first innings. Then Bradman brought on Johnson instead of Miller. There was a
degree of steady certainty about the batting to hearten
Englishmen until Edrich groped for a ball from Ian
Johnson and again Tallon caught and howled successfully. The price of reserved tickets for the fifth day's play
at once dropped several more points.

Hutton and Compton, the two finest batsmen in
English cricket to-day, came together and rose to their
greatest heights. Depression lifted from the crowd like
mist before the sun. Miller bowled round the wicket to
Hutton and Hutton hit him through extra-cover as hard,
surely, as cricket ball could be hit. Denis Compton was,
perhaps, not that Compton of gaiety who laughs his way
to mastery of bowling short of the greatest. He curbed
his natural ease just so much as would guarantee that
it contained no hint of carelessness. Once he threw his
bat at a ball from Johnston which was floating away

from him and the stroke flew past cover-point for four.

Test teams have been grateful to be saved before now by batting which was grim and determined, graceless and slow. But Hutton and Compton played strokes of power and delight on the offside, and their partnership was already worth 82, made at more than a run a minute, when play ended until Monday. At the end of the day Keith Miller went on to bowl at his fastest. So high is his action, so perfect his body-swing and follow-through, that a ball from him need be only slightly short of a length to rear high even on so placid a turf as that of Trent Bridge.

Now, with the game apparently within their grasp, Australia were threatened by two great batsmen batting at their greatest. Hutton had often been uncomfortable against the short rising ball on the leg-stump—so Miller bowled him a bouncer. Trent Bridge is the last pitch in the world on which an Australian should bowl a bouncer if he wishes to retain the affection of the crowd. Trent Bridge remembers Larwood and, bitterly, remembers that it lost Larwood and, roughly speaking, why it lost him. Nottingham, moreover, is not far from Yorkshire, and Yorkshiremen would certainly have travelled to Trent Bridge, if only to see Len Hutton bat. So, when Miller bowled a bouncer to Hutton, there was an angry surge of voices round the ground. Miller tossed back his hair, grinned and bowled another short riser to Hutton: Hutton ducked. The crowd began to boo Miller angrily. Miller grinned again and threw back his hair twice and bowled again to Hutton—a ball which struck Hutton on the shoulder. The boos increased and, through savage muttering, the day's play ended with the end of Miller's over, and the spectators, still fulminating against Miller, pressed forward angrily to the pavilion, forming a crowd through which the players must pass on their way in. No one, not even the crowd itself, I fancy, was sure what would happen. This was a deeply angry and bitter crowd. Last of the Australian players to enter the gaunt-let, his sweater on his arm, smiling and throwing back his head, came Keith Miller—to saunter easily and un-molested up the pavilion steps. The air cleared again, the poisonous atmosphere of mob-anger was gone. If in-dignation remained, it was honest indignation which may, on any subject, be right or wrong. Trent Bridge was only a big cricket ground after a day's play—propor-tion was restored—but a sickness remained with me.

England—First Innings—165 (Laker 63; Johnston 5 for 36, Miller 3 for 38)

Australia—First Innings

A. R. Morris, b Laker	31
S. G. Barnes, c Evans, b Laker . . .	62
D. G. Bradman, c Hutton b Bedser . .	138
K. R. Miller, c Edrich b Laker . . .	0
W. A. Brown, lbw b Yardley . . .	17
A. L. Hassett, b Bedser	137
I. W. Johnson, b Laker	21
D. Tallon, c and b Young	10
R. R. Lindwall, c Evans b Yardley . .	42
W. A. Johnston, not out	17
E. R. H. Toshack, lbw b Bedser . . .	19
Extras (b 9, l-b 4, w 1, n-b 1) . . .	15
Total . . .	509

Bowling Analysis

	O	M	R	W
Edrich .	18	1	72	0
Bedser .	44·2	12	113	3
Barnett	17	5	36	0
Young .	60	28	79	1
Laker .	55	14	138	4
Compton	5	0	24	0
Yardley	17	6	32	2

Fall of Wickets

1	2	3	4	5	6	7	8	9	10
73	121	121	185	305	338	365	472	476	509

England—Second Innings

L. Hutton, not out	63
C. Washbrook, c Tallon b Miller .	1
W. J. Edrich, c Tallon b Johnson .	13
D. Compton, not out	36
Extras (b 1, l-b 6, n-b 1) .	8
Total (for 2 wkts)	**121**

Bowling Analysis

	O	M	R	W
Miller .	12	5	34	1
Johnston .	13	5	31	0
Toshack .	8	3	22	0
Barnes .	4	1	11	0
Johnson .	14	5	15	1

Fall of Wickets

1	2
5	39

Fourth Day—Monday, 14th June

After Saturday's sun, the blanket of cloud descended on the cricket on Monday. With a new ball imminent, Ian Johnson and Toshack bowled tidily but mildly at Hutton and Compton for the first ten minutes, which the batsmen gratefully used to settle in. Then came Miller and Johnston, both moving the new ball sharply in a poor light and humid atmosphere. The batsmen made their one permitted appeal against the light—Umpires Chester and Cooke discussed the matter and decided that play should go on. Within ten minutes rain and thunder stopped play for a quarter of an hour.

Then Miller, as in the first innings, produced a superb ball out of the dark pavilion behind him, to bowl Hutton for 74 runs, which were handsome, memorable and worth their number in dollars to England. Again Hardstaff came in to face fast bowling in the gloom. Again he flicked at a rising ball to send a catch which was dropped at slip. He was agonizingly uncertain until the umpires stopped play for bad light in an eerie yellow gloom which bathed the ground in half-light.

After half an hour, with the light barely more than a half candle-power better, Compton and Hardstaff came out to bat until lunch-time. Again, despite circumstances of sight and score which weighed upon the batsmen, they scored at a run a minute and, for an hour after lunch, charmed and conquered their difficulties. It seems that Hardstaff now grips his bat lower on the handle than he used. Certainly in this game, after a dangerous early existence, he seemed to play the late defensive stroke better than formerly, without losing the majesty of his offside play. Compton was content often to score singles where he might in county games have risked a harder hit, but his batting was beyond detailed praise. In its manner, its style and its context it must rank with any innings he has ever played. To every man who watched Compton on that dull June day his innings will remain a Test classic.

Hardstaff and Barnett both lost their wickets in the gloom; there was another stoppage for bad light, just before Compton reached his century. Yardley was dogged for over an hour beside Compton—an innings which gave a solid core to the support of Compton. Johnston again bowled with heart and stamina, and stamped himself as the most resourceful of left-arm fast-medium bowlers—without reckoning his considerable capabilities as a medium-pacer or as a pure spin-bowler.

Miller with the new ball had Compton dropped at slip and almost caused him to play on. Johnson, Johnston, Miller and Toshack bowled well all day: the wicket allowed a little more spin, but was never truly difficult; the light, on the other hand, was never good and occasionally atrocious. Runs had to be earned, and they were earned gallantly. Harvey's fielding and looks came in for considerable admiration: Tallon was sound.

But it was Compton's day—even when, as most of the crowd sought untrammelled exits, Sid Barnes was allowed to experiment with his feints to turn from leg—without effect upon the score-card which showed England, surprisingly if not impressively, just one run on with four wickets standing.

England—First Innings—165 (Laker 63; Johnston 5 for 36, Miller 3 for 38)

Australia—First Innings—509 (Bradman 138, Hassett 137; Laker 4 for 138)

England—Second Innings

L. Hutton, b Miller	. . . . .	74
C. Washbrook, c Tallon b Miller	. . .	1
W. J. Edrich, c Tallon b Johnson	. . .	13
D. Compton, not out	. . . .	154
J. Hardstaff, c Hassett b Toshack	. .	43
C. J. Barnett, c Miller b Johnson	. .	6
N. W. D. Yardley, c and b Johnson	. .	22
T. G. Evans, not out	. . . .	10
Extras	. . . .	22
Total (for 6 wkts)	. . .	345

Bowling Analysis

	O	M	R	W
Miller . .	33	9	91	2
Johnston . .	43	12	99	2
Johnson . .	38	15	62	1
Toshack . .	33	14	60	1
Barnes . .	5	2	11	0

Fall of Wickets

1	2	3	4	5	6
5	39	150	243	264	321

Fifth Day—Tuesday, 15th June

The astutest detective might have been baffled to deduce the position of the batting side and their respective scores from the look of the two batsmen, Compton (154 not out) and Evans (10 not out) as they walked to the middle to start the day's play in an attempt to increase England's lead of 1 run. Evans was obviously eager to get at this Australian bowling. He walked with a taut, balanced, impatient, flickering half-trot, and held himself with a brisk uprightness. Beside him Denis Compton was apparently thinking of other but pleasant things; trailing his bat behind him as if his possession of it were an afterthought of which he was not yet fully convinced.

The two Australian bowlers presented something of a similar contrast. Big Bill Johnston was exuberant as ever, plonking down his feet, bucking and heaving with delight, as he chased up to bowl. Joyously he tried cut, swing and spin, yet watchful of length: his pace from the wicket seemed to match, as well as to spring from, his enthusiasm. At the other end Ian Johnson rolled good-naturedly up to the crease from only a yard or so behind it, and bowled with the laziest of arms.

Evans played his own confident game. He had scored thirteen of the morning's runs to Compton's nine before, at ten minutes to twelve, rain stopped play for forty minutes. Play started again in a deep gloom. The crowd was quiet, sensing the final dominant of the game; matches flared like tiny beacons as men lit their pipes in the backs of the stands. With the approach of untimely darkness Miller again went on to bowl at the pavilion end, and the batsmen appealed against the light—unsuccessfully.

Compton had just overtaken Evans on the morning's batting when Miller took the new ball in a steady drizzle. The rain meant that the shine would remain on the ball for, at most, a couple of overs from each end. It may be that Bradman hoped, by a combination of the new ball and poor light, to take a quick wicket which would wreck this last appreciable barricade of the English batting. But the rain could not damp Evans nor the new ball cause him to swerve from his purpose. He hit Johnston impudently through the covers, and scored ten

while Compton made five before rain stopped play
again.

Ten minutes later, and still in doubtful light, the batsmen had to play themselves in afresh. Miller, from the
pavilion end, was as hostile as ever, but Compton was
184, and he had apparently settled in again, batting with
a quiet certainty. It seemed possible that he might baulk
Australia. At such a time Miller is Australia's man. He
bowled Compton a short ball which rose sharply along
the line of the leg-stump. Compton shaped to hook it—
actually started to hook. Part-way through the stroke he
decided not to hook—presumably having misjudged the
speed of the ball. He simultaneously ducked, pulled back
his bat, and moved across the wicket. This triple opera-
tion was too much for him on the slippery turf, and he
fell, delightfully comically, on to his wicket. Compton—
hit wicket, bowled Miller, 184. It was, in some ways, an
unsatisfactory end to so great an innings. Yet Compton
was trapped into an error of judgment as to the pace of
the ball.

The Miller-Compton duel was always most absorbing.
They are probably the two closest friends from the opposing sides in these matches, being much together after play
has ended. Each obviously respects the other's cricketing
ability. In this match the injury to Lindwall increased the
importance of Miller's bowling, while the first innings
failure of the England batting made Compton's wicket
a vital objective for Australia. The poor light and the
stoppages which forced Compton constantly to play
himself in afresh were advantages to Miller. The easy
pace of the Trent Bridge wicket favoured Compton.
The honours went to Compton, yet Miller did in the end
beat him—and who knows but that Compton and Evans
might have played on into the afternoon and changed the

shape of the game but for that one ball from Miller.

Laker was subdued until lunch and out immediately after. That he did not repeat his great success of the first innings merely emphasized the exceptional quality of his earlier 63. Evans followed him for 50 self-confident runs from good strokes varied by occasional 'ifs.' England, all out just after half-past two, left Australia 98 to make to win in so much time that they might well have made them with the proverbial bus-ticket.

Barnes took three fours off Bedser's opening over— two of them from no-balls. He took a four off Edrich also, and Australia were 24 for no wicket after the first four overs with the new ball. Yardley at once put on Young in place of Edrich, and Morris hit Young for four. Then Bedser steadied and bowled two intent and intense overs to Morris before clean bowling him with a ball which moved the other way—an inswinger to left-handed Morris. Bradman came in, and at once Yardley brought Edrich on again in place of Young. But Edrich never bowled a ball to the new batsman. As in the first innings, Bedser bowled Bradman a ball which swung in late to him, again Bradman flicked it in a rather untidy leg-glance—and again Hutton was waiting at backward short-leg to catch it. This was Bradman's first duck in a Test in England, and when the spectators recovered their breath, several of them said, 'Well, I never.' Australia 48 for 2—and, as if stage-managed, a large and very black cloud—very black even for this match—began to roll up the line of the Trent towards the ground, casting its cold shadow before it. It looked to hold half a summer's rain —and if rain came now. . . . Hassett hit Bedser hard and high to long-on. Young came back for Edrich. Hassett hit Bedser hard and high to long-on again. The cloud was now blotting out half the sky to the south.

At this point England appeared to have a chance of saving the match—if Barnes should forget himself and, from sheer force of habit, appeal against the light. Barnes, however, unusually for him, tried to drive Young straight—the bowler saw it coming, moved to the catch —and dropped it. Hassett pulled Bedser just as hard but not so high to long-on. The score stood at 93, and the cloud was almost straight overhead when Barnes hit Young for four and, almost before the ball reached the boundary, grabbed a stump and raced to the pavilion and up the pavilion steps and into the pavilion. Several people performed counting operations on their fingers, Denis Compton smiled at the world in general, and the other players remained on the field. At 97 the scores were equal. Only Barnes could have laughed that off. He jog-trotted back, replaced the stump, watched Hassett hit the winning single, and refrained from taking a souvenir stump. The cloud blew away: Australia had won the first Test by 8 wickets. They had been winning ever since the first day, and are not of the temper to allow even the gentlest of miracles to wrest won games from them. England had saved honour, if not the game, by her second innings. Compton and Hutton as batsmen, Bedser as a bowler had held their own, but the English fielding was somewhat stiff-limbed for an international side, even in a wet summer.

England

L. Hutton, b Miller . .		3	b Miller . .	74
C. Washbrook, c Brown b Lindwall . . .		6	c Tallon b Miller .	1
W. J. Edrich, b Johnston .		18	c Tallon b Johnson	13
D. Compton, b Miller .		19	hit wkt b Miller .	184
J. Hardstaff, c Miller b Johnston . . .		0	c Hassett b Toshack	43
C. J. Barnett, b Johnston .		8	c Miller b Johnston	6
N. W. D. Yardley, lbw b Toshack . . .		3	c and b Johnston .	22
T. G. Evans, c Morris b Johnston . . .		12	c Tallon b Johnston	50
J. Laker, c Tallon b Miller . . .		63	b Miller . .	4
A. V. Bedser, c Brown b Johnston . . .		22	not out . . .	3
J. Young, not out . .		1	b Johnston . .	9
Extras (b 5, l-b 5) . .		10	Extras (b 12, l-b 17, n-b 3)	32
Total . . 165			**Total . 441**	

Bowling Analysis

	O	M	R	W		O	M	R	W
Lindwall .	13	5	30	1	....	—	—	—	—
Miller .	19	8	38	3	....	44	10	125	4
Johnston .	25	11	36	5	....	59	12	147	4
Toshack .	14	8	28	1	....	33	14	60	1
Johnson .	5	1	19	0	....	42	15	66	1
Morris .	3	1	4	0	....	—	—	—	—
Barnes .	—	—	—	—	....	5	2	11	0

Fall of Wickets

1	2	3	4	5	6	7	8	9	10
9	15	46	46	48	60	74	74	163	165
5	39	150	243	264	321	405	413	423	441

Australia

A. R. Morris, b Laker	. 31	b Bedser . .	9
S. G. Barnes, c Evans b Laker	62	not out . .	64
D. G. Bradman, c Hutton b Bedser	138	c Hutton b Bedser	0
K. R. Miller, c Edrich b Laker	0		
W. A. Brown, lbw b Yardley	17		
A. L. Hassett, b Bedser .	137	not out . . .	21
I. W. Johnson, b Laker .	21		
D. Tallon, c and b Young .	10		
R. R. Lindwall, c Evans b Yardley	42		
W. A. Johnston, not out .	17		
E. R. H. Toshack, lbw b Bedser	19		
Extras (b 9, l-b 4, w 1, n-b 1) . . .	15	Extras (l-b 2, w 1, n-b 1) .	4
Total. . .	509	Total (for 2 wkts)	98

Bowling Analysis

	O	M	R	W		O	M	R	W
Edrich .	18	1	72	0	....	4	0	20	0
Bedser .	44·2	12	113	3	....	14·3	4	46	2
Barnett .	17	5	36	0	....	—	—	—	—
Young .	60	28	79	1	....	10	3	28	0
Laker .	55	14	138	4	....	—	—	—	—
Compton	5	0	24	0	....	—	—	—	—
Yardley .	17	6	32	2	....	—	—	—	—

Fall of Wickets

1	2	3	4	5	6	7	8	9	10
73	121	121	185	305	338	365	472	476	509
38	48	—	—	—	—	—	—	—	—

Australia won by 8 wickets.

CHAPTER THREE

THE SECOND TEST MATCH

Played at Lord's, 24th, 25th, 26th, 28th and 29th June, 1948

THE Australian selectors had no need to puzzle about selection once it was established that treatment, wise resting and careful but increasingly searching use had rendered Miller and Lindwall fit after injuries. No member of the Trent Bridge side had had time to lose form in the nine days between the two matches. Neither, fortunately, had any other member of the party shown such outstanding form as to embarrass the selectors in leaving him out.

The English selectors were anxious to make good the ground lost at Trent Bridge. The second innings of that Test, however, had been good enough to earn most of that team another chance. And, that performance apart, the selectors, all mature cricketers, knew that at least eight members of the English eleven at Trent Bridge were so clearly the best men in England at their particular cricketing jobs that if we could not beat Australia with them, we should certainly not do so with any of the available alternative choices. The country in general appeared to be less well equipped with cricket sense. A tired bowler had only to return good analyses on two or three bowlers' wickets, or a batsman need but score three centuries against weak bowling on plumb wickets and everyone even remotely connected with first-class cricket was swamped with letters demanding those players' inclusion in the Test side.

Barnett had been unlucky in having to bat twice at Nottingham in doubtful light, but his county form did not argue his retention and Hardstaff was not fit to play. In place of these two, George Emmett and 'Tom' Dollery, both of whom, Dollery in particular, were in outstanding county form, were picked to attend at Lord's.

Pope, who had been among the thirteen for final selection at Trent Bridge, was not again asked—his place went to Coxon of Yorkshire. The selection of Coxon was undoubtedly a further attempt to find a Test-class all-rounder. He had for some years held the reputation of a game and hard-working bowler, a plucky and dour batsman and a keen field anywhere. He had had a sound bowling spell for his county against Australia at Sheffield, and this, coupled with the need of a seam bowler better than Edrich, must have clinched his selection. It might be argued that Coxon was not of Test standard in any department of the game, but he was a man of good heart and experience—and what other all-rounder in the country (if Pope was not to be picked) had better claims to inclusion? Several batsmen-bowlers, certainly, were in good county form, but, without exception, they were men likely to give away in the field more runs and wickets than they were themselves worth.

Wright was fit again, and, of course, became one of the basic thirteen players for the match. N. W. D. Yardley, L. Hutton, C. Washbrook, W. J. Edrich, D. Compton, H. E. Dollery (Warwickshire), A. Coxon (Yorkshire), T. G. Evans, J. Laker, A. V. Bedser and D. V. P. Wright made up the finally selected eleven. G. Emmett of Gloucester became twelfth man, and J. Young was omitted. Comparison of team-balance with the eleven for the first test, shows an all-rounder (Coxon) coming in for a batsman (Barnett or Hardstaff) and a leg-spin bowler (Wright) for a slow left-arm bowler (Young).

Thus the emphasis had been slightly shifted from the defensive in the leaving out of one batsman and one of the two wet-wicket bowlers.

First Day—Thursday, 24th June

The captains thumbed the wicket portentously before they tossed, but Bradman did not hesitate to bat when he won. Bedser ambled up from the Nursery end to bowl the first ball, and Barnes played the over decorously and ritualistically as a maiden. Then Coxon bowled from the pavilion end. Coxon takes a long, winding run-up to the wicket, planting his feet down very hard and looking very fierce, but his actual delivery, possibly because his body is rather squared up, is not so fast as the preliminaries promise. He bowls the currently popular inswing, and it was off an inswinging ball that he had Barnes caught at backward short-leg by Hutton when Australia had made only 3.

Bradman made so stammering a start, even for him, that many spectators had to take a second look to be sure that it was indeed *le maître*. He almost played his first ball into his wicket, and immediately afterwards he was thumped upon the pad, and at the instant-roared appeal for lbw he looked up with the air of one who has enough troubles already without outsiders presuming to add to them. Then Yardley barely failed to make enough ground to catch a ball that Bradman popped up gently towards short-leg.

Coxon was bowling a good length, moving the ball in to the bat and getting all the pace to be hoped for from so friendly a wicket. One ball from him did not follow the course of his customary swing, and Morris played it hastily, defensively and with an aggrieved air. Thirty-two in the first hour was not the best Australian rate, but

First Test Match:
Hutton and Washbrook go out
to open the England innings

First Test Match:
...er bowling to Hutton
(arrow indicates
ball)

First Test Match: Washbrook, caught Tallon, bowled Miller: 1
First Test Match: Hardstaff plays Miller through the slips

Bradman in play during his century in the First Test

th Test Match—the end. The players are, left to right, Cranston, Harvey, Evans,
Bradman, with Pollard in the background

Top: *First Test Match: Yardley caught and bowled Johnston: 22. Miller is at slip,*
Tallon the wicket-keeper

Bottom: *Second Test Match: Miller catches Compton off W. A. Johnston. Ian Jo*
is at slip, Tallon wicket-keeper and Hasset mid-on

Top: *The England team receives Bradman with cheers for his last Test innings at the Oval,*
Fifth Test Match

Bottom: *Third Test Match: Hutton plays Miller. Fieldsmen, left to right, W. A. Johnston,*
Sidney Barnes (back to camera), Ian Johnson, Tallon

Top: *Third Test Match: Barnes catches Emmett at forward short leg off Lindwall*

Bottom: *Lindwall bowling in the touring side's first match—Australia v. Worces.*
The batsman is C. H. Palmer; the umpire, Fred Root

Top: *Fourth Test Match: Crapp about to catch Hassett*

om: *Third Test Match: Bedser bowling to Morris. Fieldsmen, left to right, Dollery,*
Pollard (back to camera), Edrich, Evans, Crapp, Young, Yardley

Top: *Tallon's great one-handed catch off Lindwall to dismiss Hutton in the first in* *of the Fifth Test. The other fieldsmen, left to right, are W. A. Johnston, Barnes and N* Bottom: *Second Test Match: Miller has driven Bedser straight to the Pavilion for*

it reflected the respect with which Bradman and Morris were treating the English bowling. Then Bradman edged Bedser near to Hutton at backward short-leg, but the ball was not quite within reach. Edrich disturbed neither batsman, but Wright bowled well enough to deny the batsmen full confidence, and Laker's few overs were neat indeed. Through their difficulties Bradman and Morris were unhurriedly prepared to wait for the bad ball and, since the bad ball rarely came, they were only 82 for 1 at lunch—but Bradman and Morris were still not out.

Immediately after lunch Bradman *did it again*. Bedser bowled him a ball which came in to him, and he—Bradman—flicked *another* catch to Hutton at backward short-leg and again Hutton caught it: Bradman, *c Hutton b Bedser*, 38. Again, just as at Nottingham, men shook their heads in wonder. Two wickets down for 87.

Hassett, looking smaller and slighter than ever, walked out with his dryly comical toddle, and Bedser bowled well to him. Morris, too, was busy to defend against Bedser, who was now bowling in such a manner that no one watching could doubt the fact that he is England's best fast-medium bowler. He is so very powerful that he can bowl easily at a pace likely to compel a grunt from most bowlers. He is always bowling so completely within himself that close control comes relatively easily to him. Hassett played him so gently that the watcher felt power thwarted by delicacy. Wright, however, made Hassett hurry into a stroke of no dignity with a leg-break that bit and turned.

Laker derived no life from the pitch, and Coxon was little more than industrious at mid-afternoon, but Bedser and Wright bowled well enough to keep the spectators from appreciating their seat-backs. Morris's bat seemed all middle, but largely defensive middle, though he twice beat cover-point with drives of exquisite timing. Bedser laboured to make him edge the ball that left him—the ball Bedser bowls so well to the left-hander. Again and again Morris moved across his wicket to Bedser, sometimes so far that all three stumps showed clear behind him. Bedser and Coxon took the new ball, but Morris firmly hit it for two fours to make his first Test century in England. It was a hundred of resource, precision and immense maturity of judgment, confirming, if confirmation were needed, that Arthur Morris at twenty-six was established among the classic batsmen.

When the right-hander was batting, Hutton was fielding in the position where he had three times caught Bradman, backward short-leg, and then, moving a few yards to his left, he became gully to the left-handed Morris. And now Morris cut a ball from Coxon to him and Hutton again held the catch. Bedser immediately afterwards missed Hassett. To have caught him would have been a great moral advantage to the English bowlers, because his attitude of toying with the bowling takes some of the fire from a bowler.

Bedser put himself right with himself immediately afterwards by getting Miller lbw before he had settled in, and Australia were 173 for 4 wickets. And then Billy Brown was the next batsman—an experienced opener in Test Matches against England and another discouraging batsman to bowl at. To have got out Barnes, Morris, Bradman and Miller, and then to find yourself bowling at Hassett and Brown was to realize, depressingly, what it meant to bowl against Bradman's 1948 Australians. Brown and Hassett were patiently careful and assured about the business of batting until tea, which they achieved.

Yardley is not a particularly good bowler, not good

enough, at all events, to bowl much more than once a month for Yorkshire. He swerves the ball a little, bowls an occasional cutter, and in general swings his arm more from a sense of duty than pride in his own powers. He put himself on to bowl as the day moved into its last phase, largely to take a fair share of the late labour, and began with two maidens, but he was probably contemplating taking himself off when he suddenly clean bowled Hassett to general surprise and delight. In his next over Brown picked two over-pitched balls off his toes and hit them hard to midwicket for four apiece, went to hit the next ball, which came through a fraction quicker, and was lbw. Yardley's figures for the spell were 2 for 14, and Australia's 225 for 6 was due cause for English cheering. Ian Johnson pored over the bowling of Yardley, Wright and Coxon, and scored a run every ten minutes. Edrich presents no problem to the Australian batsman on a straightforward wicket such as is prepared for a Lord's Test. So, against Edrich, after three-quarters of a patient hour's defence, Johnson took a slash outside the off-stump and was caught by Evans standing back. Australia 246 for 7. Tallon's batting was as hard-bitten as the man himself, and Lindwall, at No. 9, was as assured as only an Australian tail-ender can be when his side is in trouble. They could prevent any more catastrophes, but they could not, even by batting to the end of the day, dispel England's belief that her bowlers had done nobly. With first innings on a relatively easy Lord's wicket, Australia had been pegged down to forty-three runs an hour, and her seven best batsmen were out with the three hundred still an hour's steady batting away.

Australia—First Innings

S. G. Barnes, c Hutton b Coxon 0
A. R. Morris, c Hutton b Coxon . . . 105
D. G. Bradman, c Hutton b Bedser . . 38
A. L. Hassett, b Yardley 47
K. R. Miller, lbw b Bedser 4
W. A. Brown, lbw b Yardley . . . 24
I. W. Johnson, c Evans b Edrich . . . 4
D. Tallon, not out 25
R. R. Lindwall, not out 3
    Extras (b 1, l-b 6, n-b 1) 8
                                  ─────
        Total (for 7 wkts) . . . 258

Bowling Analysis

	O	M	R	W
Bedser	34	12	67	2
Coxon	29	9	62	2
Edrich	5	0	15	1
Wright	21	8	54	0
Laker	7	3	17	0
Yardley	15	4	35	2

Fall of Wickets

1	2	3	4	5	6	7
3	87	166	173	216	225	246

Second Day—Friday, 25th June

Friday's spectators took their seats early and eagerly, with the expressions of theatre-goers, well-dined, who settle down to watch a play which they know in advance will end happily. Coxon and Bedser with the new ball were expected to exploit the wicket's morning freshness. Lindwall and Tallon placed the meat of the bat firmly against the ball like good, but not great, batsmen. They added another seventeen runs before Bedser bowled Lindwall at 275. The additional runs were annoying from an England point of view, but the happy ending was now, surely, at hand.

The remaining batsmen were the wicket-keeper and that now celebrated comedy duo, Johnston and Toshack. Between them they added another seventy-five runs while the spectators, formerly gaily anticipatory, passed from annoyance to alarm and from alarm to an admiring despair. Tallon was straightforwardly practical, but Johnston and Toshack were gaily incorrect: but their strokes figure in the score-book if not the book of style. The eye saw the ball and the arms guided the bat to it in violent collision. There were fifty laughs and thirty runs to the last wicket partnership. The morning's play gave Australia ninety-two runs in seventy minutes—and seized dominance from England. Two hundred and seventy-five would have been a good score to have settled for the Australian innings: 350 was a different matter—and an invitation to recall the excellence of Bradman's bowling. There was rueful reflection on the three dropped catches of Thursday and on Yardley's morning reluctance to use Wright—who took a wicket as soon as he was put on.

The wicket was still good—not perhaps so easy as that at Nottingham, but to be relied upon as playing truly and uniformly. And the Australian resistance of the morning had changed the balance of the game—indeed, it had changed the entire feeling of every watcher. There was a feeling of anti-climax after the fighting attack of the first day. Australia went into the field with a moral advantage freshly won from her opponents.

Lindwall began to bowl from the pavilion end. He was

careful of the newly-mended groin, running up, at first
easily, to bowl below his fastest. Then he began to
accelerate. Between balls he walked lazily back to his
starting-point, revolving, one could suspect, the formula
for his next ball. His first over was a maiden. Miller, with
haunch-bone trouble, did not bowl, and Johnston began
from the Nursery end. Hutton took a three and Washbrook a four off his first over. The opening partnership
began to move into gear: so did Lindwall. The second
ball of his fourth over was at full Lindwall pace, a little
short of a length, and it rose quickly—it was too fast for
Washbrook's thought to tell his reflexes not to touch it
before he had edged a catch to Tallon.

Edrich stayed with Hutton until lunch and for a quarter
of an hour after lunch. Then Hutton, away from the
storm of Lindwall, played forward to a slow, well-
pitched-up ball from Ian Johnson, which turned inside
his bat and he was bowled—bowled by so peaceful-
looking a bowler as Johnson after weathering Lindwall!
When Lindwall bowled Edrich—and Dollery—England
were 46 for 4—and the batting was dangerously spilt.

Solemnly Compton and Yardley shouldered their now
accustomed task of digging England out of trouble.
Compton was characteristically Compton—even that
gaily absent-minded leg-sweep was brought into action—
to startle Hassett's contemplation of the horizon from
long-leg. Yardley was grim and watchful, a game he
seems temperamentally fitted to play. He gathered his
runs thriftily from the on side, content to wait long for
the hittable ball and then to handle it in utilitarian fashion.
His batting was memorable, not for its quality, but for its
value to England at that moment.

Yardley and Compton batted faithfully for eighty-five
runs, and in just under two hours they were out within

five minutes and one run of each other—to Lindwall and
Johnston and the new ball. Laker and Coxon contributed
their worthy mites and applause which echoed bitterness
and relief greeted Wright's stroke, just before the end of
play, which saved England from the danger of following-
on.

It was Lindwall's day. He bowled at great but well-
varied speed and at several lengths. He knew where he
was putting the ball, but he never allowed the batsman
the comfort of automatic bowling: he was working out
variations, not only of length and pace, but also on the
themes of the outswing and a sharply cut ball which came
back off the pitch, in every over. Bradman handled him
carefully, never allowing him to bowl otherwise than
fresh, and the fieldsmen served him eagerly and well.

Johnston was enthusiastic and varied in technique, Ian
Johnson patiently and steadily spinning and Toshack
always there or thereabouts. At the end of the day
England were 143 behind with only one wicket to fall.

Australia—First Innings

S. G. Barnes, c Hutton b Coxon	.	.	.	0
A. R. Morris, c Hutton b Coxon	.	.	.	105
D. G. Bradman, c Hutton b Bedser		.	.	38
A. L. Hassett, b Yardley	.	.	.	47
K. R. Miller, lbw b Bedser	.	.	.	4
W. A. Brown, lbw b Yardley		.	.	24
I. W. Johnson, c Evans b Edrich	.		.	4
D. Tallon, c Yardley b Bedser		.	.	53
R. R. Lindwall, b Bedser	.	.	.	15
W. A. Johnston, st Evans b Wright		.	.	29
E. R. H. Toshack, not out	.	.	.	20
Extras (b 3, l-b 7, n-b 1)	.	.	.	11
Total	.	.	.	**350**

Bowling Analysis

	O	M	R	W
Bedser .	. 43	14	100	4
Coxon .	. 35	10	90	2
Edrich .	. 8	0	43	1
Wright .	21·3	8	54	1
Laker .	. 7	3	17	0
Yardley	. 15	4	35	2

Fall of Wickets

1	2	3	4	5	6	7	8	9	10
3	87	166	173	216	225	246	275	320	350

England—First Innings

L. Hutton, b Johnson	20
C. Washbrook, c Tallon b Lindwall . .	8
W. J. Edrich, b Lindwall	5
D. Compton, c Miller b Johnston . .	53
H. E. Dollery, b Lindwall	0
N. W. D. Yardley, b Lindwall . .	44
A. Coxon, c and b Johnson . . .	19
T. G. Evans, c Miller b Johnston . .	9
J. Laker, c Tallon b Johnson. . . .	28
A. V. Bedser, not out	6
D. V. P. Wright, not out	8
Extras (l-b 3, n-b 4)	7
Total (for 9 wkts) . . .	207

Bowling Analysis

	O	M	R	W
Lindwall .	. 23	6	66	4
Johnston .	. 22	4	43	2
Johnson .	. 31	10	68	3
Toshack .	. 18	11	23	0

Fall of Wickets

1	2	3	4	5	6	7	8	9
17	32	46	46	133	134	145	186	197

Third Day—Saturday, 26th June

As an apéritif to the Australian orgy of triumphs to come, Lindwall took Bedser's wicket—played-on—before midday. Then, on a perfect wicket, Australia, taking advantage of the generosity of the English fieldsmen, proceeded to increase her lead to 478 with six second innings wickets in hand.

Barnes wanted a big score. He played himself in carefully, he examined each new bowler with almost superstitious care and, when he was seeing the ball really big, he hit it very hard indeed. He was fortunate not to be stumped when he was at least two yards down the wicket to Laker and missing—the ball passed close to the leg-stump and went for byes. In the same over Barnes might have been caught. In the next Morris gave a difficult chance. Australian batsmen cannot be let off on so comfortable a wicket. Relief came with Morris playing Wright to leg when a leg-break *did*: Morris had only sixty-two—almost a minor victory for the bowling side in a Test Match.

For the first few overs of his innings Bradman was a very unhappy man. His methods in the treatment of the elementary off-break as bowled by Laker inspired no confidence and achieved only occasional contact. He settled slowly and uncomfortably into the day's batting, but, once settled, went firmly along, it seemed, to his accustomed century.

Barnes, meanwhile, positively achieved a century, and began to force the pace. He went down the wicket to Laker again, missed again and *was* missed again—Evans

failed to stump him. Bradman was receiving frequently
from Bedser the ball which swings into or outside the leg-
stump. Again and again he shaped to turn it down the
leg side—and *remembered*—and stopped it coldly—or
allowed it to swing safely away to Evans. He did not
propose to give Hutton another catch at backward short-
leg. The first Australian wicket, Morris's, had fallen at
122, just before three o'clock; five chances had been
missed, and Bradman and Barnes were still together, for
the second wicket, at 296 and a quarter to six. Three
chances had been missed off Laker, and now he was being
hit for sixes. Yardley, with his uncanny sense, apparently,
of knowing when a wicket is about to fall, was taking one
of his bowling spells, for friendship's sake, when Barnes,
anxious to show his appreciation, hit him hard and high
to long-leg for Washbrook to make a catch which both
dismissed Barnes and saved another six.

Hassett, who had been wearing his pads for almost four
hours, came out to bat in the knowledge that it did not
matter particularly whether he batted or not. Yardley
swung his arm and bowled Hassett first ball. Australia
were 296 for 3 wickets—but even 296 for 9 wickets would
barely have given an England reason for cheerfulness. At
329 Bradman edged a ball from Bedser to Edrich at slip.
Slip catches after six o'clock to a man who has been in the
field all day may pardonably be dropped, for the hair-
trigger concentration of the slip-field may well have relaxed by the last half-hour. Edrich, however, never nods,
he caught the ball as he fell, and Bradman had *not* made a
century—329–4–89.

Miller and Brown whiled away the rest of the day,
Miller, in fact, enlivened it by offering a couple of
chances which a kindly field forbore to hold. A lead of
478—more than the record England-Australia fourth

innings—was a pleasant thought for Australia. The game now retained no more than an academic interest. For England the main consolation was that no side in the world could drop Miller, Barnes and Morris, in all, seven times on a plumb wicket and come well out of the innings. Bedser had bowled well—and so had the unfortunate Laker: Wright had taken a good wicket and also had at least two catches dropped. Coxon had laboured up his furious track and bowled hard, but more than heart and enthusiasm are demanded of the man who is to bowl to such a batting side on such a wicket.

Australia

S. G. Barnes, c Hutton b Coxon	.	.	0	c Washbrook b Yardley 141
A. R. Morris, c Hutton b Coxon	.	.	105	b Wright . . . 62
D. G. Bradman, c Hutton b Bedser	.	.	38	c Edrich b Bedser . 89
A. L. Hassett, b Yardley			47	b Yardley . . 0
K. R. Miller, lbw b Bedser	.	.	4	not out . . . 22
W. A. Brown, lbw b Yardley	.	.	24	not out . . . 7
I. W. Johnson, c Evans b Edrich	·	.	4	
D. Tallon, c Yardley b Bedser	.	.	53	
R. R. Lindwall, b Bedser			15	
W. A. Johnston, st Evans b Wright	.		29	
E. R. H. Toshack, not out	.	.	20	
Extras (b 3, l-b 7, n-b 1)	.	.	11	Extras (b 17, l-b 4, n-b 1) . . . 22
Total			350	Total (for 4 wkts) . 343

Bowling Analysis

	O	M	R	W		O	M	R	W
Bedser	. 43	14	100	4	....	21	5	51	1
Coxon	. 35	10	90	2	....	19	3	47	0
Edrich	. 8	0	43	1	....	2	0	11	0
Wright	. 21·3	8	54	1	....	19	4	69	1
Laker	. 7	3	17	0	....	28	6	96	0
Yardley	. 15	4	35	2	....	13	4	36	2
Compton	. —	—	—	—	....	3	0	11	0

Fall of Wickets

1	2	3	4	5	6	7	8	9	10
3	87	166	173	216	225	246	275	320	350
122	296	296	329	—	—	—	—	—	—

England—First Innings

L. Hutton, b Johnston	20
C. Washbrook, c Tallon b Lindwall	8
W. J. Edrich, b Lindwall	5
D. Compton, c Miller b Johnston	53
H. E. Dollery, b Lindwall	0
N. W. D. Yardley, b Lindwall	44
A. Coxon, c and b Johnson	19
T. G. Evans, c Miller b Johnston	9
J. Laker, c Tallon b Johnson	28
A. V. Bedser, b Lindwall	9
D. V. P. Wright, not out	13
Extras (l-b 3, n-b 4)	7
Total	215

Bowling Analysis

	O	M	R	W
Lindwall	. 27·4	7	70	5
Johnston	. 22	4	43	2
Johnson	. 35	13	72	3
Toshack	18	11	23	0

Fall of Wickets

1	2	3	4	5	6	7	8	9	10
17	32	46	46	133	134	145	186	197	215

Fourth Day—Monday, 28th June

Did Bradman remember the fifth Test of 1938? Even in face of possible shortening of the match by rain he continued to batter England from a position of defeat to one tragi-comical. His side was 478 on at the start of play. Notwithstanding interruptions by rain, their lead was 544 at lunch. And still Australia batted into the afternoon to set England 596 to win. Bradman was merciful, in that he did not expose England to the possibility of more runs by Johnston and Toshack. Perhaps those worthies themselves protested against such sadistic employment of their specifically light-hearted batting.

Miller spent a gay morning, batting happily between the showers. He refused to be checked by the new ball; indeed, he cut it with a stroke which would have been memorable in any cricketing company of any period. He drove Bedser with magnificence and gaiety, and he hooked Coxon with strokes which were fours before the field could move.

Billy Brown, Miller's early-morning partner, was spruce, neat and unhurried as ever. He batted like a demonstrator, polished, almost detached, as he picked the overpitched ball off his toes and sent it precisely away on the on side. Lindwall hit firmly and with a disheartening certainty against bowlers who, with every reason to despair, did not slacken. Two more chances were missed, but it barely mattered to notice them. Bradman's declaration, on the stumping of Lindwall, at a non-round figure in the lead was presumably made on the grounds that since Tallon had his pads on he might as well keep wicket in them.

The ground before the pavilion was a surprising scene of comings and goings at the beginning of the English innings at twenty past three. Bradman brought his fieldsmen out, rain started and they turned back into the pavilion. Before they were all in the rain stopped and they came back on to the field and joined the umpires just as rain began to fall again and they all came back to the pavilion—all this before a ball had been bowled in England's second innings.

The rain was sufficient to liven the wicket to the desire of Lindwall and Johnston. Hutton was obviously ill at ease, and at once edged a leaping ball from Johnston into slips where it was not caught. Washbrook was struggling with inclination, refraining from touching the ball rising over or outside his off-stump, partly by self-denial, partly by playing too late. Lindwall bowled magnificently to Hutton, who had little relish for the rising ball along the line of the stumps. He received the first ball of the innings but, including a forty-minute stoppage for rain, did not 'get off the mark' until an hour and twelve minutes later. Several times he fenced with it as he would certainly not have done with a similar ball bowled by one of the less fast county bowlers of his daily experience. Washbrook was struggling, but seemed to enjoy a grim pleasure in his mountainous task.

Hutton, at length, timed a lifting ball from Lindwall sufficiently well to send a catch to Ian Johnson at slip, and he was out for thirteen of the first wicket's forty-two. Edrich crouched low over the bowling or, alternatively, crouched *under* several deliveries from Lindwall which were dropped short. On several occasions his crouch was so low that the bails were to be seen above his head. But, whether he crouched or played, he never moved back from the line of the ball.

Lindwall came off for Toshack, and there was an English sigh of relief as the fast bowler struggled into both sweaters and walked to point. Toshack appeared an extremely amiable antagonist, nay, almost a collaborator, after the hostility of Lindwall. Such a reaction may well have been in Bradman's mind—many wickets were obtained by other bowlers in this series who exploited the relief of the English batsmen at the resting of Lindwall. Washbrook hit Toshack's first ball for four—and Toshack mentally rubbed his hands, for his success depends upon batsmen trying to hit him rather than resting patiently upon defence before his accuracy. Next, Washbrook took a single and gave the bowling to Edrich, who had made one scoring stroke in twenty minutes. At once Edrich went out to drive Toshack, was not quite to the pitch of the ball, and edged another catch to Ian Johnson at slip: England 52-2-2.

Denis Compton came out with that engaging air of eagerness which he brings to the heaviest of undertakings. He joined Washbrook in a short partnership of watchfulness and steady middling of the ball. Washbrook was beginning to find his feet and was willing to hit the bad ball hard, or to push anything a little less than good for a workmanlike single. Then with England 65 for 2, Toshack bowled Washbrook, most unusually, a fulltoss. Washbrook played to drive it and remarkably misjudging its swing, he edged it, and Tallon took another brilliant catch: 65-3-37.

In the first innings Dollery's first ball from Lindwall had beaten him for speed, he was relatively inexperienced in Test cricket, and there was a certain amount of doubt as to his achieving much more in this innings. Bradman

brought Lindwall on for Toshack as soon as possible, but
not until Dollery had enjoyed the feel of the ball in the
middle of the bat with a single off Toshack and a two
and a one off Johnston. Now, in the dull grey of late
afternoon, Dollery and Compton seemed like giants to
those who clung to hope for England. Here at last men
were putting bat to Lindwall as if he were an ordinary
bowler. To be sure, Dollery was uncertain with one ball
which leapt, but otherwise, stepping boldly into the line
of the ball, he played it firmly. Dollery is burly of build,
to make the bat in his hands seem a slight weapon; he
has, too, a walking-stick manner with the bat, which
adds to the impression of confidence in his play. He and
Compton played the Australians with steady certainty,
and a warmth went out to them from the intent watchers.

They stayed for half an hour, the most heartening
half-hour of English batting in the series so far. In that
half-hour the major bowling danger at Bradman's command looked no more than a straightforward problem,
difficult but not impossible for honest batsmen. England
were still, with 106 for 3 wickets, 489 runs behind: there
was no hope of victory, but it was possible that rain and/
or Compton might save England from defeat.

Australia—First Innings—350 (Morris 105, Tallon 53; Bedser 4 for 100)

Australia—Second Innings

S. G. Barnes, c Washbrook b Yardley	141
A. R. Morris, b Wright	62
D. G. Bradman, c Edrich b Bedser	89
A. L. Hassett, b Yardley	0
K. R. Miller, c Bedser b Laker	74
W. A. Brown, c Evans b Coxon	32
R. R. Lindwall, st Evans b Laker	25
I. W. Johnson, not out	9
Extras (b 22, l-b 5, n-b 1)	28
Total (7 wkts dec.)	460

Bowling Analysis

	O	M	R	W
Bedser	34	6	112	1
Coxon	28	3	82	1
Edrich	2	0	11	0
Wright	19	4	69	1
Laker	31·2	6	111	2
Yardley	13	4	36	2
Compton	3	0	11	0

Fall of Wickets

1	2	3	4	5	6	7
122	296	296	329	416	445	460

England—First Innings—215 (Compton 53; Lindwall 5 for 70)

England—Second Innings

L. Hutton, c Johnson b Lindwall . . . 13
C. Washbrook, c Tallon b Toshack . . 37
W. J. Edrich, c Johnson b Toshack . . 2
D. Compton, not out 29
Dollery, not out 21
Extras (b 4) 4
                                                 ——
Total (3 wkts) 106

Bowling Analysis

	O	M	R	W
Lindwall . .	13	3	47	1
Johnston . .	18	10	27	0
Toshack . .	11	1	28	2

Fall of Wickets

1	2	3
42	52	65

Fifth Day—Tuesday, 29th June

The second ball of the day was bowled by Bill Johnston to Compton, and it virtually ended the match. Compton went forward to it, and it was the left-arm bowler's break-away, it pitched a good length, found the edge of the bat and flew into slips. There Keith Miller, who was so frequently the instrument of the tragedies of English Test cricket in 1948, made a brilliant catch at the second attempt. Yardley, faced with an impossible task, made the invariable honest, hard-working Yardley response and put his head down and played. He was bowled by Toshack.

Coxon took the next ball, walked into it, and there was an appeal for lbw—'Not Out'—he promptly walked into the next ball also and this time *was* lbw. Dollery's manly innings ended next—joint top-scorer with Wash-brook with 37.

Laker, Bedser and Wright were fully conscious of their own inadequacy in face of a deficit still greater than 400. Evans, however, was there again to bat gaily and well and to make every man turn to his neighbour and say, 'If Evans can do it, why can't the others?' If the neighbour did not know, he at least put up some pet theory and found conversational consolation even in adversity.

Australia won by 409 runs, which was, presumably, big enough even for Bradman. This time Toshack had the most impressive figures, but the chief agent of destruc-tion was again Lindwall. When he so patently disturbed Hutton he struck a blow at the morale of the England batting which was never overcome. Again, all the Aus-tralian bowlers were supported by magnificent fielding and wicket-keeping.

Australia

S. G. Barnes, c Hutton b Coxon 0	c Washbrook b Yardley . . 141
A. R. Morris, c Hutton b Coxon 105	b Wright . . 62
D. G. Bradman, c Hutton b Bedser 38	c Edrich b Bedser 89
A. L. Hassett, b Yardley . 47	b Yardley . . 0
K. R. Miller, lbw b Bedser . 4	c Bedser b Laker 74
W. A. Brown, lbw b Yardley 24	c Evans b Coxon 32
I. W. Johnson, c Evans b Edrich 4	not out . . 9
D. Tallon, c Yardley b Bedser 53	
R. R. Lindwall, b Bedser . 15	st Evans b Laker 25
W. A. Johnston, st Evans b Wright 29	
E. R. H. Toshack, not out . 20	
Extras (b 3, l-b 7, n-b 1) . 11	Extras (b 22, l-b 5, n-b 1). 28
Total . . 350	Total (7 wkts dec.) . . 460

Bowling Analysis

	O	M	R	W		O	M	R	W
Bedser .	43	14	100	4	....	34	6	112	1
Coxon .	35	10	90	2	....	28	3	82	1
Edrich .	8	0	43	1	....	2	0	11	0
Wright .	21·3	8	54	1	....	19	4	69	1
Laker .	7	3	17	0	....	31·2	6	111	2
Yardley .	15	4	35	2	....	13	4	36	2
Compton	—	—	—	—	....	3	0	11	0

Fall of Wickets

1	2	3	4	5	6	7	8	9	10
3	87	166	173	216	225	246	275	320	350
122	296	296	329	416	445	460	—	—	—

England

L. Hutton, b Johnson	.	20	c Johnson b Lindwall	13
C. Washbrook, c Tallon b Lindwall	. . .	8	c Tallon b Toshack	37
W. J. Edrich, b Lindwall	.	5	c Johnson b Toshack	2
D. Compton, c Miller b Johnston	. . .	53	c Miller b Johnston	29
H. E. Dollery, b Lindwall		0	b Lindwall	. .	37
N. W. D. Yardley, b Lindwall	. . . .	44	b Toshack	. .	11
A. Coxon, c and b Johnson		19	lbw b Toshack	.	0
T. G. Evans, c Miller b Johnston	. . .	9	not out	. . .	24
J. Laker, c Tallon b Johnson		28	b Lindwall	. .	0
A. V. Bedser, b Lindwall		9	c Hassett b Johnston	9
D. V. P. Wright not out	.	13	c Lindwall b Toshack	4
Extras (l-b 3, n-b 4)	.	7	Extras (b 16, l-b 4)	20
	Total .	215	Total .	186

Bowling Analysis

	O	M	R	W		O	M	R	W
Lindwall .	27·4	7	70	5	....	23	9	61	3
Johnston .	22	4	43	2	....	33	15	62	2
Johnson .	35	13	72	3	....	2	1	3	0
Toshack .	18	11	23	0	....	20·1	6	40	5

Fall of Wickets

1	2	3	4	5	6	7	8	9	10
17	32	46	46	133	134	145	186	197	215
42	52	65	106	133	133	141	141	158	186

Australia won by 409 runs.

CHAPTER FOUR

THE THIRD TEST MATCH

Played at Manchester, 8th, 9th, 10th, 12th and 13th July,
1948

CRICKETING England and, more especially, non-cricketing England, which had heard or overheard the news, were full of woe and anger. Old men wagged their heads sadly, and uttered, as original, a statement to the effect that men (in this case cricketers) were not what they were. Others proposed various remedies, outstandingly, 'Sack the lot.' The selectors were not to be stampeded. It would be remarkable if they did not contemplate the series of 1921, when Armstrong's team was almost as successful as Bradman's. In that season the selectors semi-panicked to include in the England team a number of charming men and good county cricketers who should never have been asked to play in a Test Match.

The selectors did, however, take one drastic step: they omitted one of the two best batsmen in England—Len Hutton. Hutton, at Lord's, in the M.C.C. *v.* Australia match and the Yorkshire–Australia match at Sheffield, had been much below his true stature in playing the pace bowling of Miller and Lindwall. Hutton is so good a batsman and so thoughtful, knowledgeable and conscientious a cricketer that the situation inevitably caused him considerable mental anxiety which was reflected in his play, and which must certainly have affected to some degree the confidence of his team-mates, all of whom hold him in considerable respect. This was certainly the result that the Australians, who are realists in their cricket strategy, must have

desired. It was well known that the English batsman they
most feared was Hutton. Their fast bowlers had worked,
on every conceivable occasion, to shatter Hutton's confidence, and they had succeeded. Wright was also dropped.
His lack of results at last overcame the recognition of his
real greatness as a bowler—which is still a cricket fact
whatever statistics say. The experiment with Coxon at
Lord's had failed and, temporarily at least, it seemed
to have convinced the selectors that to include an all-
rounder who was not good enough was less wise than to
admit the fact that none of the available all-rounders was
good enough. Emmett and the left-hander Crapp, of
Gloucester, both batsmen with good reputations as
players of fast bowling, were brought in for the first
time in a Test Match. Pollard, experienced on the Old
Trafford wicket, successful there against the Indians in
1946 and in good current form, was wisely chosen to open
the bowling with Bedser. The twelve were:

> N. W. D. Yardley (Yorkshire)
> C. Washbrook (Lancashire)
> G. Emmett (Gloucestershire)
> W. J. Edrich (Middlesex)
> D. Compton (Middlesex)
> J. F. Crapp (Gloucestershire)
> H. E. Dollery (Warwickshire)
> T. G. Evans (Kent)
> A. V. Bedser (Surrey)
> R. Pollard (Lancashire)
> J. Young (Middlesex)—

all of whom played in the match—and J. Laker (Surrey)
who did not—although his poor figures at Lord's might
be laid to the account of his fieldsmen rather than to
Laker. John Wardle, the Yorkshire slow left-arm bowler,

who had bowled well against the Australians for his county at Sheffield, was nominated as twelfth man.

In this selection England once again played only one bowler—Young—as a winning agent in the event of bad weather. The side included only three bowlers—Bedser, Pollard and Young—and, in the absence of a good all-rounder, the change-bowling of Yardley, Edrich and Compton would barely have satisfied a good county captain.

The Australians brought in Loxton in place of W. A. Brown. Loxton was in good form as a forcing batsman, his fielding had been consistently superb, and he was a fast-medium bowler of enthusiasm and probably of pace as great as that of any English bowler. He thus gave Bradman another pace-bowler against the continued inability of Miller to bowl, for Old Trafford is a wicket usually sympathetic to pace bowling.

First Day—Thursday, 8th July

The Old Trafford wicket of recent years had developed a reputation for being occasionally 'green.' So, when Yardley won the toss and batted, more than one spectator envisaged Messrs. Lindwall and Johnston receiving from the pitch assistance which previous evidence suggested they did not need.

Washbrook was moved, minutely, but significantly, from No. 2 to No. 1, and opened the innings with Emmett. Lindwall bowled the first over comfortably, and Washbrook and Emmett got, slightly less comfortably, off the mark. Johnston was the other opening bowler, and, although he bowled a maiden, Emmett and Washbrook started confidently. Emmett batted neatly, and, if he is not tall, he was well over the ball in playing his strokes and looked to be perfectly self-possessed in his first Test innings. The wicket, even as Lindwall worked up to pace, remained as amiable as Denis Compton.

Emmett and Washbrook were unhurried, almost composed, for the first half-hour, during which they scored twenty-two runs, and no ball behaved other than with strict decorum. Then Johnston began an over by bowling to Washbrook a ball which started on, or slightly outside, the leg-stump: it 'floated' a little and was farther up to the batsman than it first promised to be. This was a ball that Johnston bowled from time to time during the tour and which batsmen constantly misjudged—even when it went away wide of the off-stump. Washbrook was playing to push this particular ball to mid-on when it yorked him, off-stump, and the first wicket had counted only twenty-two.

Edrich played out the remainder of the over most decorously. Emmett then played a maiden from Lindwall. In Johnston's next over Edrich hit a four, but Emmett was content to defend, playing well within himself. Then, as the first ball of an over, Lindwall bowled one of his fastest to Emmett, just short of a length on the leg-stump. Emmett was back in line with the ball, when it jumped—and so did Emmett, lifting his bat quickly to push the most simple catch to Barnes fielding on the bat at forward short-leg. England 28 for 2: men sighed and cursed their optimism and resigned themselves to things being as bad as ever.

Compton came in to Edrich, who was making heavy weather of the bowling, and who was rendered no more comfortable by a ball which came sharply back to hit him on the pad while he was playing to mid-off. Compton at once took a two off Lindwall and then a single. When he had made five, he went to hook a short ball from Lindwall which rose comparatively sluggishly (by Lindwall's standards). Compton hooked a trifle early and the ball flew off the upper edge of his bat on to his forehead. The Australians were sympathetic, but disaster was upon England once again. Compton was helped off the field with blood coming from a cut above the eye.

In his place, placidly as a man starting a day's work in the fields, came Jack Crapp. Twenty-eight for two, plus England's best batsman retired hurt, and Lindwall bowling, is not the position at which most men would chose to begin their Test career. Crapp took guard, adjusted himself comfortably into his stoop and contemplated the approaching Lindwall with an air as of one with a straw in his mouth. He played his first ball square towards third man for a single, lest getting off the mark should disturb his well-wishers.

Lindwall, Johnston, Toshack, Johnson and again Lindwall bowled in the hour remaining to lunch, but no further wicket fell. Crapp with a calm watchfulness, Edrich with a bristling defensive care, scored twenty-four grim runs in that time. Toshack began his spell with five consecutive maiden overs. But the rate of run-scoring was of little importance to the spectators by comparison with the spirit of this defence. Here, at last, was a fighting quality akin to that of the Australians. I believe that the Australians must have sensed the antagonism of the batting and that they reacted in taut sympathy—there was less than the usual amount of banter, neither Edrich nor Crapp was inclined to conversation or any distraction from their concentrated resistance. The bowling and fielding was tight as a vice. England were 57 for 2 at lunch—with news that Compton would probably bat after all.

Before lunch Ian Johnson had bowled ten overs to Edrich and Crapp for seven runs. The same number of

runs came off his first over after lunch. First Edrich
pushed him away for a single, and then Crapp, effort-
lessly, hit him straight over the sight-screen at the Manchester end. A man dallying on his way back from lunch
dropped his glass at the sight: Crapp, for his part, stood
motionless with the air of a boy pretending he *hadn't*
broken a window. Edrich was bent upon giving nothing
away: he knew, I am sure, that he was not in conquering
form, but will-power, care and a keen eye kept him at the
crease. Crapp played a ball from Toshack into the hands
of Barnes fielding at short-leg disturbingly close to both
bat and line of wicket-to-wicket. Barnes dropped the
catch and Toshack looked the other way. Now Toshack
settled into his steady routine of bowling the unhittable—
fourteen overs for eight runs.

Just before three o'clock Lindwall was to be seen cart-
wheeling both arms and doing a knees-bend at gully,
and Umpire Davies fingered the new ball in his coat
pocket. Lindwall limbered up with a maiden over and
then took the new ball. The crowd became quiet. Crapp,
calm as ever and playing the ball very late indeed, hit
him for two cracking fours, one square on the offside,
the other past mid-off. He was seeing Lindwall clearly
and playing him with confidence and the middle of the
bat.

Lindwall began his third over with a delivery which
started outside the line of Crapp's off-stump. (Crapp, of
course, is a left-hander.) Early in the ball's flight Crapp
threw his bat over his shoulder and his pad outside the
line of the off-stump. It was Lindwall's swinger; in the
last yard before pitching it curved in like a boomerang—
more sharply than I have ever seen a ball swing before
from a bowler of such pace. Crapp had apparently
judged that it could, at most, swing to his pad, *outside* the

off-stump. In fact, it hit him on the heel and he was patently lbw. He slouched out, quietly disappointed in himself, and, indeed, he had given the impression of knowing precisely what to do with every ball he received up to Lindwall's masterpiece—a superb ball of pace, length and swing.

Dollery came next, and was at once bowled by a well-pitched-up inswinger from Bill Johnston—and England were 97 for 4, which almost cancelled out the Edrich-Crapp stand. Yardley at once began to score more quickly than Edrich, yet without exceeding his own normal rate; meanwhile Edrich, on his solemn and valuable way, remained unshaken by a ball from Lindwall which took his bat's edge and flew away through slips. He had scored thirty-two in just over three hours when he went too far across to a ball which Lindwall pitched on the off-stump and swung away: too late Edrich tried to pull his bat away, and he gave Tallon a catch behind the wicket. Edrich and Crapp had scored only sixty-nine between them, but they had given the English innings a core of hard fight and English spectators a grim pride.

And now Compton, with a plaster across his forehead, came out again—applauded all the way to the wicket. Compton and Yardley put on twenty-two together before, with Yardley out to Toshack, England were 141 for 6 wickets, and only Compton of the recognized batsmen was left. Evans walked jauntily to the crease, took a single off his first ball, and then proceeded to score almost run for run with Compton. Even the return of Lindwall could not stop them, although, off him, Compton gave a low and difficult chance to Tallon—it was not held. Seventy-five runs in seventy-five minutes was the gayest resistance of the day, and England were 216 for 7 when Evans went—fittingly—caught cracking at Lindwall.

For the last twenty minutes Bedser, as Compton's sleeping partner, was content with four runs, made from one stroke. England's 231 for 7 wickets was not too good, but it was much better than it might have been—and Compton was there against the morrow.

England—First Innings

C. Washbrook, b Johnston . . .	11
G. Emmett, c Barnes b Lindwall . . .	10
W. J. Edrich, c Tallon b Lindwall .	32
D. Compton, not out	64
J. Crapp, lbw b Lindwall . . .	37
H. E. Dollery, b Johnston	1
N. W. D. Yardley, c Johnson b Toshack .	22
T. G. Evans, c Johnston b Lindwall .	34
A. V. Bedser, not out	4
Extras (b 2, l-b 13, n-b 1). . . .	16
Total (for 7 wkts) . . .	231

Bowling Analysis

	O	M	R	W
Lindwall . .	26	6	64	4
Johnston . .	30	7	46	2
Loxton . .	7	0	18	0
Toshack .	28	17	36	1
Johnson .	27	14	51	0

Fall of Wickets

1	2	3	4	5	6	7
22	28	96	97	119	141	216

Second Day—Friday, 9th July

The period between the start of play and lunch-time on the second day at Old Trafford was epic cricket for

England. Even Lindwall and Johnston with the new ball did not move Compton and Bedser while, in two stirring hours, they scored ninety-two runs. Compton's nearest approach to error was when he glanced a ball from Lindwall to fine leg and Tallon, covering much ground, almost turned a legitimate stroke into a dismissal. Bedser, for his part, defended impassively, except during one over from Toshack, when at least five of the six balls completely beat him. Toshack gave him a sad wag of the head. Altogether Compton and Bedser scored 119 for the eighth wicket in two and a half hours—only five short of the English test record against Australia held by Hendren and Larwood.

Compton's innings was again one in which he curbed his natural exuberance and batted with care—but even care could not conceal the natural and graceful ease with which Denis employs bat against ball. This was his eighth century in ten Tests against Australia—a magnificent record and a fair index of his standing among Test batsmen. Bedser included six fours in his thirty-seven, a leg-glance off Lindwall, and an off-drive from an overpitched ball by Johnston were strokes to satisfy any batsman.

The failing of the pair as a pair was in their running between wickets. The partnership ended when Compton played a ball towards Bradman at extra-cover, Bradman misfielded, and Compton called Bedser for a run. Bedser started slowly, but it is doubtful if the promptest run would have defeated Loxton's rapid pick-up and throw-in as he dashed in behind Bradman.

With Pollard as his partner Compton attempted to keep the bowling. Bradman set out to counter the plan. For the first four balls of the over when Compton had the strike, the fieldsmen were deep about the boundary to prevent the four: for the last two balls of the over they closed in to stifle the short single which would give Compton the bowling for the next over. On several occasions this stratagem succeeded. On one occasion it pinned down Pollard to face the bowling of Ian Johnson. Johnson bowled a ball a fraction over-pitched, which stopped on middle-and-off and turned in to the leg-stump. Pollard swung a not-quite-straight bat at full arm's length into the turn of the ball and brought the full meat of the blade to bear. Barnes was at forward short-leg, not so close to the bat as he had been, but very close indeed by normal standards. He turned away from the line of Pollard's stroke, but the ball struck him under the ribs and felled him. The stroke was of such power as to have carried the long-on boundary. Barnes was carried to the pavilion in a state of collapse. Even those who, from the start of the tour, had expressed the hope that some strong batsman would 'shift' Barnes, shared the general depression at the occurrence, and Pollard himself was considerably distressed. Twenty-six runs came for the last two wickets, and Compton was not out at the end of England's most encouraging innings of the series.

The Australian innings lacked Barnes as an opening batsman, and the ready-made substitute, Brown, had been omitted, so Ian Johnson opened with Morris. Almost at once Bedser made a ball hurry off the pitch, Johnson played hastily back, 'got a touch,' and Evans, standing up to the stumps, caught him head high—3–1–1. Bradman started more certainly than at any other time in the series, playing every ball, from the first, in the middle of the bat. England's attack, however, was a sharper opening combination than at Trent Bridge or Lord's. Pollard is a man of strong and gay resolve, always particularly dangerous at Old Trafford. The first ball of his third over was of fiery pace and Bradman was plumb lbw—13-2-7—and England were in their best position of the series.

Hassett, delightfully elegant in difficult circumstances, played Bedser to long-leg for four almost with negligence. The pace-bowlers, Bedser, relieved for two overs by Edrich, and Pollard who was not rested, bowled from half-past three until half-past five with only the tea interval as relief. Pollard, with his long, padding, flat-foot run, seemed to bowl steadily faster and faster. His stamina is immense: apart from growing even redder in the face, he shows little sign of the long bowling spell. He, to a greater extent than Bedser, could compel the hasty stroke even from Hassett, that master of timing in defence. He might well have taken—and deserved—three wickets from his seventeen overs, off which only twenty-five runs were scored.

Morris played several balls unpremeditatedly with his pads, but in the main he was a sheet-anchor of power and reliability, taking runs where they were to be had, never pressing when the bowling was 'tight.' When Young was brought on for Pollard, Hassett at once hit him against the spin for four to long-on: in trying to repeat the stroke to a ball which turned sharply, he gave Washbrook a catch at cover, and Australia were 82 for 3 wickets with fifty minutes to watch away to the end of the day.

Miller and Morris together were an interesting contrast. Miller was looking for runs, even his defensive back strokes hit the ball crisply, and he hooked a short ball from Pollard to the square-leg boundary with crushing force. Morris was the height of steadfast circumspection. At the end of the day Australia were 237 behind and three of their wickets were gone.

England—First Innings

C. Washbrook, b Johnston	11
G. Emmett, c Barnes b Lindwall . . .	10
W. J. Edrich, c Tallon b Lindwall . .	32
D. Compton, not out	145
J. Crapp, lbw by Lindwall	37
H. E. Dollery, b Johnston	1
N. W. D. Yardley, c Johnson b Toshack .	22
T. G. Evans, c Johnston b Lindwall .	34
A. V. Bedser, run out	37
R. Pollard, b Toshack	3
J. Young, c Bradman b Johnston . . .	4
Extras (b 7, l-b 17, n-b 3) . . .	27
Total	363

Bowling Analysis

	O	M	R	W
Lindwall .	40	8	99	4
Johnston .	45·5	13	67	3
Loxton .	7	0	18	0
Toshack .	41	20	75	2
Johnson .	38	16	77	0

Fall of Wickets

1	2	3	4	5	6	7	8	9	10
22	28	96	97	119	141	216	337	352	363

Australia—First Innings

A. R. Morris, not out	48
I. W. Johnson, c Evans b Bedser . . .	1
D. G. Bradman, lbw b Pollard . . .	7
A. L. Hassett, c Washbrook b Young .	38
K. R. Miller, not out	23
Extras	9
Total (3 wkts)	126

Bowling Analysis

			O	M	R	W
Bedser	.	.	21	6	51	1
Pollard	.	.	20	5	34	1
Edrich	.	.	2	1	5	0
Yardley	.	.	4	0	12	0
Young	.	.	6	2	15	1

Fall of Wickets

1	2	3
3	13	82

Third Day—Saturday, 10th July

The English team shamed the pessimism of Englishmen on this grey Manchester Saturday—by bowling and batting which were more than a match for Bradman's Australians. They finished the day in at least an impregnable position, probably a winning one. Moreover, four of the English batsmen fully established themselves as capable batsmen against the full Australian bowling combination of Miller, Lindwall and Johnston, in action together for the first time since the first day at Trent Bridge.

Bedser and Pollard loosened their arms with the old ball for the first ten minutes of the morning before they attacked Miller and Morris with the new ball. In a new-ball spell of an hour and a quarter they took the wickets of Morris (51) and Miller (31). After Miller was out, Barnes very bravely tried to bat. He struggled, in obvious pain, for half an hour to score one run, and then collapsed and was carried off again. Lacking Morris to block up one end, Loxton, Tallon and Lindwall wisely played strongly for quick runs, but Bedser and Pollard bowled steadily, and never lacked life from a wicket dulled by early-morning rain. The partnership of Johnston and Toshack

was so short as only to hint, this time, at its comic potentialities before Pollard made Johnston play an edged
stroke towards first slip (Edrich). Evans ran across and
tried to catch it, but only deflected it off his gloves;
Edrich, already moving one way, turned and grabbed at
it on its new course and missed. Evans and Edrich looked
at one another in dismay, the crowd groaned, when suddenly, with a left-arm movement of amazing speed,
Crapp made a prestidigitatorial attempt to catch the ball
from behind Edrich's right ankle and only failed by half
a finger-tip to catch the uncatchable. In the next over
Johnson played the same stroke off Bedser, the ball going
away from Crapp's right hand at slip. Crapp took two
walking strides to his right, caught the ball, and without
breaking stride, continued into the pavilion, and the
Australian innings was over for 221, with Toshack once
more proudly not out.

So England began their second innings in good heart
and a lead of 142. Washbrook took the first ball solemnly,
played the second firmly for one, and to the third ball
Emmett hung his bat to dry to earn the now familiar
epitaph 'c Tallon b Lindwall.' England 1-1-0.

Miller bowled the second over. Was it again to be a
story of the Australian fast bowling hurling out the
English batting? The crowd shared the pent-up anxiety
of Edrich, bowed in his customary intense care over his
first few balls. Washbrook then recalled that this was Old
Trafford and that he was Washbrook. He hit three fours
off Lindwall and one off Miller in the space of four overs,
and assumed his county-match stature. Once or twice his
bat was attracted to the rising ball outside the off-stump
as by a magnet. Each time, however, he pulled it away or
was providentially late with his stroke.

Under this influence Edrich found his feet and moved

with his own assurance, and the hour and a half to tea passed with Washbrook scoring fifty in seventy minutes and Edrich steadfast at the other end. Once Washbrook swung Lindwall hard and high to Hassett at long-leg, and as that safe fieldsman moved under the ball we reached with a sigh for our score-cards; but Hassett missed it, and his gestures of self-reproach were not entirely humorous in conception.

After tea Edrich began to hit hard indeed, and sacrilegiously smote Toshack for four and a six, whereupon Toshack's private and left-handed gods decreed that he should be run out. England were now 125 for 2 wickets, and Edrich and Washbrook had put on 124 in slightly over two hours.

Compton was again cheered in, but at once Miller caught him at slip off the righteously indignant Toshack. Thus Crapp came out for his second Test innings after 2 wickets had fallen for 4 runs. At once Washbrook hit another catch to Hassett at long-leg and again Hassett dropped it. Once more Crapp was the man for the occasion. He played with Washbrook to the end of the day, when England were 316 runs on with 7 wickets to fall.

England—First Innings—363 (Compton 145 not out; Lindwall 4 for 99, Johnston 3 for 67)

England—Second Innings

C. Washbrook, not out	85
G. Emmett, c Tallon b Lindwall	0
W. J. Edrich, run out	53
D. Compton, c Miller b Toshack	0
J. Crapp, not out	19
Extras (b 9, l-b 7, w 1)	17
Total (for 3 wkts)	174

Bowling Analysis

	O	M	R	W
Lindwall	14	4	37	1
Miller	14	7	15	0
Johnston	14	3	34	0
Loxton	8	1	29	0
Toshack	12	5	26	1
Johnson	7	3	16	0

Fall of Wickets

1	2	3
1	125	129

Australia—First Innings

A. R. Morris, c Compton b Bedser	51
I. W. Johnson, c Evans b Bedser	1
D. G. Bradman, lbw b Pollard	7
A. L. Hassett, c Washbrook b Young	38
K. R. Miller, lbw b Pollard	31
S. G. Barnes, retired hurt	1
S. J. E. Loxton, b Pollard	36
D. Tallon, c Evans b Edrich	18
R. R. Lindwall, c Washbrook b Bedser	23
W. A. Johnston, c Crapp b Bedser	3
E. R. H. Toshack, not out	0
Extras (b 5, l-b 4, n-b 3)	12
Total	221

Bowling Analysis

	O	M	R	W
Bedser	36	12	81	4
Pollard	32	9	53	3
Edrich	7	3	27	1
Yardley	4	0	12	0
Young	14	5	36	1

Fall of Wickets

1	2	3	4	5	6	7	8	9
3	13	82	135	139	172	208	219	221

Fourth Day—Monday, 12th July

On Monday it rained: it rained: it rained. England had fought to a winning position, and now we stood by and watched it all washed away.

Fifth Day—Tuesday, 13th July

On Tuesday it rained. But it did not rain enough. It stopped to allow a mockery of a match to take place. Yardley declared and, after Johnson had been early caught by Crapp at slip off Young, Bradman and Morris batted, and five English bowlers, including Compton, bowled to finish the day even to the end of the ordained hours of play. There was never a real prospect of a finish after the loss of Monday. Australia retained the Ashes which no one begrudged them, but a win, her first post-war win, would have done England and English cricket much moral good—and England had fairly earned a win.

England

C. Washbrook, b Johnston	11	not out . .	85
G. Emmett, c Barnes b Lindwall	10	c Tallon b Lindwall	0
W. J. Edrich, c Tallon b Lindwall . . .	32	run out . .	53
D. Compton, not out .	145	c Miller b Toshack	0
J. Crapp, lbw b Lindwall .	37	not out . .	19
H. E. Dollery, b Johnston .	1		
N. W. D. Yardley, c Johnson b Toshack . .	22		
T. G. Evans, c Johnston b Lindwall . . .	34		
A. V. Bedser, run out .	37		
R. Pollard, b Toshack .	3		
J. Young, c Bradman b Johnston . . .	4		
Extras (b 7, l-b 17, n-b 3)	27	Extras (b 9, l-b 7, w 1) . .	17
Total . .	363	Total (3 wkts dec)	174

Bowling Analysis

	O	M	R	W		O	M	R	W
Lindwall .	40	8	99	4	....	14	4	37	1
Johnston .	45·5	13	67	3	....	14	3	34	0
Loxton .	7	0	18	0	....	8	1	29	0
Toshack .	41	20	75	2	....	12	5	26	1
Johnson .	38	16	77	0	....	7	3	16	0
Miller .	—	—	—	—	....	14	7	15	0

Fall of Wickets

1	2	3	4	5	6	7	8	9	10
22	28	96	97	119	141	216	337	352	363
1	125	129	—	—	—	—	—	—	—

Australia

A. R. Morris, c Compton b Bedser	51	not out . .	54
I. W. Johnson, c Evans b Bedser	1	c Crapp b Young	6
D. G. Bradman, lbw b Pollard	7	not out . .	30
A. L. Hassett, c Washbrook b Young . . .	38		
K. R. Miller, lbw b Pollard .	31		
S. G. Barnes, retired hurt .	1		
S. J. E. Loxton, b Pollard .	36		
D. Tallon, c Evans b Edrich	18		
R. R. Lindwall, c Washbrook b Bedser . . .	23		
W. A. Johnston, c Crapp b Bedser	3		
E. R. H. Toshack, not out .	0		
Extras (b 5, l-b 4, n-b 3)	12	Extras (n-b 2)	2
Total . . .	221	Total (for 1 wkt)	92

Bowling Analysis

	O	M	R	W		O	M	R	W
Bedser	36	12	81	4	....	19	12	27	0
Pollard	32	9	53	3	....	10	8	6	0
Edrich	7	3	27	1	....	2	0	8	0
Yardley	4	0	12	0	....	—	—	—	—
Young	14	5	36	1	....	21	12	31	1
Compton	—	—	—	—	....	9	3	18	0

Fall of Wickets

1	2	3	4	5	6	7	8	9
3	13	82	135	139	172	208	219	221
10	—	—	—	—	—	—	—	—

Match drawn.

CHAPTER FIVE

THE FOURTH TEST MATCH

Played at Leeds, 22nd, 23rd, 24th, 26th and 27th July, 1948

ENGLAND'S good showing at Manchester did not
blind the selectors to possible improvements. Their
primary task was the selection of batting which could
assume mastery over the Australian pace bowlers. But
there was no bowler of comparable pace to Lindwall and
Miller in English county cricket. So the only trial for a
batsman was to play him in a Test Match unless his county
had an immediate match against the Australians. Meanwhile, the selectors could but pick men adequate to deal
with the fastest bowling momently available in county
cricket.

In a winning side it is possible to carry a player of
whose quality the selectors are convinced even if he
makes some poor scores. But in a losing series it is not
good cricket politics to do so unless the player is of
unquestionably outstanding quality, like the pre-war
Edrich. So Dollery and Emmett were dropped—although
Emmett was recalled from the West Country the day
before the match to become one of the thirteen players
for final match-selection.

Hutton, who had made some good scores in county
matches, was recalled—but any reasonable judge must be
satisfied that county form would not very strongly have
influenced the selectors. Hutton, I am convinced, was recalled because the selectors believed that his temporary
omission would have sharpened him to key pitch.
Cranston, the Lancashire captain, was also picked—an

indication that the selectors were again hankering after the non-existent Test all-rounder. He had not taken large numbers of wickets nor scored many runs, but he had achieved runs and wickets when they were most needed in county games. The thirteen players were:

> N. W. D. Yardley (Yorkshire)
> L. Hutton (Yorkshire)
> C. Washbrook (Lancashire)
> W. J. Edrich (Middlesex)
> D. Compton (Middlesex)
> J. C. Crapp (Gloucestershire)
> K. Cranston (Lancashire)
> T. G. Evans (Kent)
> A. V. Bedser (Surrey)
> J. Laker (Surrey)
> R. Pollard (Lancashire),

who became the eleven for the match—G. Emmett (Gloucestershire), who was, after all, twelfth man, and J. Young (Middlesex), who was left out. Thus, in their final selection the selectors included only one bad-weather bowler, and flirted once more with the idea of an all rounder.

Australia, too, made changes. Barnes had not recovered from the blow he had received at Old Trafford and Tallon was also injured. Instead of including the obvious choice —Brown—as replacing an opening batsman in Barnes, the Australian selectors chose Harvey. With the Ashes retained, it was good policy to 'blood' this promising young player in a winning eleven—particularly since he had fielded superbly as twelfth man in preceding Tests. Saggers, only less good than Tallon, was chosen to keep wicket—without the least anxiety to the Australian party. Their side was otherwise the same as at Old Trafford.

First Day—Thursday, 22nd July

Yardley won the toss again, and again, of course, batted—on a wicket which promised to be peaceful. Optimism from Manchester conflicted with memories of Trent Bridge and Lord's in the minds of the spectators, and few were inclined to do more than wait and see: the threat of Lindwall still hung over the English batting.

Back in the English team *at Leeds* was a challenge to Hutton, and the cheers of the crowd as he walked out with Washbrook were both a spur and a reminder of a faith and an affection that had never faded. Lindwall and Miller bowled: the crowd was quiet and watchful, hardly daring but to fear disaster, for never in the series had England's first wicket outlasted the spell of the opening bowlers. In Miller's second over Hutton drove him for four and the batsman and the crowd looked happier. Johnston came on for Miller, then Miller for Lindwall, Toshack for Johnston, Johnston for Miller—all in fifty minutes—fifty minutes of Washbrook and Hutton, their batting growing, like the work of experienced gardeners, from the nursed seedlings of defence towards the full growth of stroke-play.

Washbrook led Hutton—25 to 24—at the fifty after seventy-five minutes. Then, in Loxton's second over, Hutton gave an untaken chance to Hassett, who was fielding in a retreat version of Barnes's position at short-leg.

Lindwall came back before lunch, and suffered the indignity of being struck for five fours in six overs—one cover-drive from Hutton was a stroke to stir the romantic cricketer to extravagance. As Hutton overtook Washbrook, he was himself again—a great batsman. England were eighty-eight for no wicket at half-past one, and gratitude and relief as well as congratulation were in the applause which ushered the batsmen to their lunch.

Before half-past two—after 131 minutes to give the event its statistical setting—Hutton and Washbrook had seen the hundred up for the first wicket. They were, perhaps, behind the clock, but they were ahead of expectation—even abreast of hope. Three times rain stopped play before Lindwall came again. He swung his arms, bent his knees, handed his sweater to the umpire, walked slowly to his mark, touched his toes, swung his arms again, first both at once and then separately. Then he swept into his run, and Hutton hit him past cover for two. The next two balls were to a length, and Hutton played them steadily back to the bowler.

Lindwall turned to the umpire and asked for the new ball. He bowled again, in a close-watching silence. Hutton hit him for four with the glory of batsmanship, the drive past extra-cover. Lindwall almost rocked in his swinging run-up for the next ball; Hutton moved across too late and was bowled off-stump. The first wicket fell at 168: the partnership was more than the vindication of Washbrook and Hutton, it was the symbol of an English professional cricketer holding his place as the practitioner of an enduring and still vital craft.

Edrich stayed grimly with Washbrook, for Edrich, like the Australians, can be grim in refusing to relax a fraction of an advantage. These two stayed through Lindwall, Johnston, Miller, Johnston, Johnson, tea and Toshack. The score grew, only slowly but very surely, and the crowd enjoyed it. This was five-day cricket: there was an echo of the Oval in 1938 as the batsmen set their eyes on a huge total. This time the advantage was not allowed to slip.

Washbrook came with the certainty and smoothness

of an express train to his hundred, and then laid out the
delights of stroke play. He hit a four past mid-on with
the walking-stick ease and the perfect timing of a Frank
Woolley. Edrich hit the loose ball as if he hated it. But
loose balls were few. There was not the relaxation of
Australian out-cricket there had been at Old Trafford:
Johnson and Johnston were both steady, and Loxton and
Harvey fielded eagerly and cleanly among uniformly
good fielding. Saggers kept wicket with quiet ease, and
was as quick as a Tallon to move over to the leg-side
ball.

Edrich followed behind, a hundred behind, Washbrook to the last over of the day. Then, as the crowd
waited to bestow its gratitude once more on him, Washbrook made the stroke of a tired man and was caught at
slip by Lindwall off Johnston. Bedser came massively and
amiably to the wicket as the most solid of night-watch-
men, and the day's score went out to bring a minor but
definite warmth to the stomachs of men who, day by day,
found little of cheer in their newspapers.

England—First Innings

L. Hutton, b Lindwall	81
C. Washbrook, c Lindwall b Johnston . .	143
W. J. Edrich, not out	41
A. V. Bedser, not out	0
Extras (b 1, l-b 2)	3
Total (for 2 wkts) . . .	268

Bowling Analysis

			O	M	R	W
Lindwall	.	.	19	5	46	1
Miller	.	.	12	2	33	0
Johnston	.	.	21	6	48	1
Toshack	.	.	22	5	58	0
Loxton	.	.	15	1	39	0
Johnson	.	.	17	6	41	0

Fall of Wickets

1	2
168	268

Second Day—Friday, 23rd July

The sky was dull and the clouds low over Headingley as the crowd settled into seats or footholds and waited to see whether Alec Bedser would swindle a few runs out of Lindwall and Johnston before he was out. Certainly for half a dozen overs he was not a comfortable man. Several of his strokes were uncertain, but he gives the impression of being unhurried in playing fast bowling, towering massively over the line of the ball and watching it right on to the bat.

Lindwall did not look a dangerous bowler, but on such a wicket as Headingley on the 23rd July, 1948, no pace bowler in the history of cricket would have worried the good batsman when well set. Lindwall tried furiously hard with arm and cricketing brain to take a wicket, but he had no weapon to overcome the pacifism of the wicket.

The first hour brought twenty-two runs, and Edrich's fifty—at four minutes a run. Hereabout Toshack roused himself from his contemplation of eternity at points distant as the spirit moved him from the position of mid-off. He hoisted up the sleeves which he keeps down for fielding and all non-bowling activities, and prepared to put a firm stop to any scoring at all. He wheeled his arm and dropped a pin-pricking length on the leg-stump, swinging in a little, sometimes tending to straighten off the pitch, sometimes not. He called a tune in very slow time, and Edrich and Bedser, harmonizing with his accuracy and his meticulously placed field, played that tune.

Bedser attacked Toshack in a manner which might well have destroyed the faith in human nature of any man less amiable than Toshack. Bedser actually struck him for fourteen runs in one over. Toshack, a forgiving man, no doubt made allowance for the fact that Bedser was not really a batsman, but only a promoted fast-bowler. Nevertheless, he stopped bowling and went back to mid-off, and thereafter utterly ignored Bedser. Johnson replaced him, and Bedser at once treated him in the same fashion—fourteen runs from an over, including a mighty six over long-on. Bedser, now at his ease, played firm and steady strokes, hitting the ball hard in attack, playing coolly in defence.

Edrich still refused to give the Australians the slightest breath of encouragement. As soon as Johnston came off Lindwall went on, Loxton relieved Lindwall and Miller relieved Loxton, so that there was constantly one of the fast bowlers bowling tight at one end. While the slower bowlers operated, Bradman cushioned the blows of Bedser with a deep-set field. Again two English batsmen batted from the start of the day to lunch without the loss of a wicket. Edrich's innings had denied hope to the Australian bowlers, and every run scored by Bedser could be regarded as sheer profit. The score was 360 for 2 wickets at lunch, Edrich and Bedser still in and Compton, Crapp, Yardley, Cranston and Evans were still to come.

In face of Lindwall and Johnston, Edrich and Bedser dug themselves in after lunch.

Morris came on to bowl the 'Chinaman': Bedser, after preliminary puzzlement, pigeon-holed the phenomenon, and hit one specimen of it off the full-toss for a furious four. Runs were coming at almost two a minute. Edrich reached his century with Bedser not far behind him, and looking likely to make his hundred also when the partnership was broken. Bedser hit Ian Johnson with the spin towards mid-on, and Johnson dived across to make a catch as he fell sideways. Edrich and Bedser had put on 155 for the third wicket. His seventy-nine was Bedser's highest score in a Test. On a wicket perfect for batting, Bedser, with a straight bat in defence and a heavy one in the drive, had made his hay with relish.

Almost immediately Edrich played only half an Edrich-pulled drive and was caught by Morris. Four hundred and twenty-three for three wickets was a setting in which Compton could hardly have hoped to find himself in this series, but it was one which he proceeded to exploit. Despite the loss of Edrich, he showed Crapp how pleasant it all was. He played a late cut off Toshack—which is impossible—and it went perfectly for four. He experimented with Ian Johnson's spin, playing it through an array of angles about short-leg.

Perhaps Crapp was bemused by this virtuosity, at all events he most uncharacteristically played over a ball from Toshack and was bowled. Yardley, received by Lindwall with the new ball, hit him and it for four. Then Compton glanced Lindwall to leg, and Saggers, in the manner of Tallon, caught him. Loxton, with a little aid from Miller, then rolled up the remainder of the English innings like a shutter. On a plumb wicket the third England wicket fell at 423, a hundred minutes later the entire side had been put out, on the same plumb wicket, for only seventy-three more runs. Yardley's stroke-play was the only redeeming feature of the collapse.

The crowd was silenced by the landslide, but moved to mirth when, on Pollard coming to the crease, Hassett, fielding in the position Barnes had been when Pollard hit him at Old Trafford, skipped fearfully out of the way in a perfectly timed piece of clowning. The final score emphasized the worth of Edrich's fierce resistance in face of out-cricket so unrelenting that it swept away the entire innings through the first chink of relaxation.

Like Lindwall and Miller before them, Bedser and Pollard laboured to extort life from the lethargic wicket: like the Australians, they found the task beyond human endeavour. Neither Morris nor his new partner Hassett hurried his stroke, and there was surprise in the applause which hailed Morris having holed out at midwicket off Bedser. One ball from Pollard had Bradman groping slightly, but, with the history of his great scores at Headingley echoing about him, Bradman settled commandingly into the game, and had more than twice as many runs as Hassett by the end of the day, when Australia were 433 runs behind. Englishmen, with two of his hook-strokes still pictured in the mind, went home for the night convinced that 433 was not a very large number.

England—First Innings

L. Hutton, b Lindwall	81
C. Washbrook, c Lindwall b Johnston . .	143
W. J. Edrich, c Morris b Johnson . . .	111
A. V. Bedser, c and b Johnson . . .	79
D. Compton, c Saggers b Lindwall . .	23
J. C. Crapp, b Toshack	5
N. W. D. Yardley, b Miller . . .	25
K. Cranston, b Loxton	10
T. G. Evans, c Hassett b Loxton . .	3
J. Laker, c Saggers b Loxton . . .	4
R. Pollard, not out	0
Extras (b 2, l-b 8, w 1, n-b 1) . .	12
Total . . .	496

Bowling Analysis

	O	M	R	W
Lindwall .	38	10	79	2
Miller .	17·1	2	43	1
Johnston .	38	13	86	1
Toshack .	35	6	112	1
Loxton .	26	4	55	3
Johnson .	33	9	89	2
Morris .	5	0	20	0

Fall of Wickets

1	2	3	4	5	6	7	8	9	10
168	268	423	426	447	473	486	490	496	496

Australia—First Innings

A. R. Morris, c Cranston b Bedser . .	6
A. L. Hassett, not out	13
D. G. Bradman, not out . . .	31
Extras (b 4, l-b 9)	13
Total (for 1 wkt) . . .	63

Bowling Analysis

	O	M	R	W
Bedser	8	1	18	1
Pollard	9	2	13	0
Cranston	3	0	3	0
Edrich	2	0	16	0

Fall of Wickets

1

13

Third Day—Saturday, 24th July

Bedser and Pollard ruefully surveyed the harmless wicket and a ball whose early shine had departed the previous evening as Bradman, alertly, and Hassett, at a toddle, came out to bat before a Saturday crowd at Headingley—the concentration of Yorkshire cricket-samplers. Throwing all his energy into an attempt to take advantage of the unsettled eye of morning, Bedser brought a ball back fiercely to hit Bradman a thunderous blow on the hip which, even after rubbing, was reflected in the batsman's thoughtful frown.

At the other end Pollard turned from the pink of healthy effort to the scarlet of joy when he made a ball lift and leave Hassett's bat by way of the outside edge and fly to Crapp at slip. Crapp caught it with the air of one to whom it was all in the day's work: 65-2-13.

Miller hit his first ball for three to give Bradman the benefit of Pollard. Pollard bowled to Bradman with his always-generous enthusiasm: Bradman's stroke was half-decided and half-cock and he was bowled. The cheering rolled like thunder, and Pollard's face was the roundest, happiest, rosiest sight seen in Yorkshire since the previous evening's sunset: 68-3-33: Morris, Hassett and Bradman out, and Australia 428 behind. Neil Harvey now faced his first Test innings. He played the remaining two balls of the over calmly—calmly, at least, to distant view. Australia were in trouble and here again was Miller. He hit his first ball from Bedser for four and the next for one. Eight runs off his first three balls. Pollard found yet another scrap of life in the wicket to bring the ball on to Harvey's bat before Harvey planned, and the stroke scuttled unpremeditatedly to third man. Now for an hour and a half Miller played like an emperor. He hit Pollard majestically through the covers, straight-drove Bedser like a gale and hit Laker's first ball for six.

Miller looked greater than the ordinary common sense of batting in an innings of which every stroke would have been memorable but that each ousted its predecessor from the appreciation. Miller's was not merely a great innings, but I cannot believe it possible for a cricket brain to conceive of any innings which could be greater.

Harvey settled in the warmth of Miller's innings and, once satisfied that the ball would find neither life nor turn in the wicket, he too played magnificently. Had Miller not batted, Harvey's innings would take all the superlatives. Miller was there and his innings stands alone. Yet Harvey's must, surely, have been the best innings ever played by a batsman in his first Test.

There was little time for more than an occasional rueful recollection that the English bowling was being punished. Here, before our very eyes, two of the greatest innings of all Test cricket were being played. He would have been a poor cricketer who could allow partisan feeling to mar his delight in such greatness.

In face of this thunder and lightning, Yardley himself amiably came on to bowl. Miller, to compensate for playing the first ball of his over defensively, hit the next two for four apiece. The last ball of the over lifted and touched Miller's glove, hit Evans on the head and went to slip, where Edrich dived and caught it. Miller's fifty-eight at Headingley will remain in mind if every other innings I have ever seen is forgotten. He came to a precariously balanced innings, raised cricket to a point of æsthetic beauty, and then went, leaving the innings firm-set.

Loxton began with a few gangling strokes not good enough to obtain fatal contact outside the off-stump. He soon discovered, however, that the honest Loxton manner would pay its dividends, and then he was happy. Miller and Harvey hit 121 in 95 minutes, Loxton and Harvey 105 in 96 minutes.

Harvey, with the self-possession of a mature cricketer and the characteristic off-side power of the left-hander, hit fours through every angle between point and mid-off —yet to bowl on his legs was merely a cue for his typically Australian hook. If he appeared to have a weakness on this wicket, it was in playing square on the off-side, yet he gave no chance in that direction, but merely scored handsome runs.

The swinging ball did not disturb these batsmen and the pitch suppressed all pace and spin. The only conceivable weapon against these batsmen was flight, and no England bowler possessed the degree of flight that Wilfred Rhodes would have put into throwing his hat across a table—if indeed Wilfred Rhodes would perform so careless an act with his well-brushed trilby.

Harvey hit seventeen fours in his 112, Loxton five sixes and nine fours in 93—and was bowled trying to hit Yardley out of sight. Loxton's innings, like Loxton himself, was rugged, strong, straightforward and enthusiastic. Lindwall was equally rumbustious, slightly more rugged and almost as prolific. Johnson and Saggers were mercifully brief, and Bill Johnston his usual acrobatic and astounding batting self. The normal partnership of Toshack and Johnston did not take place owing to Lindwall's insistence on staying in longer than Johnston.

Toshack appeared with a hobble and a knee injury, calling for a runner. This was not a method of obtaining the sympathetic company of Bill Johnston at the batting crease, but sheer necessity. Johnston's simplest duty was that normally required of a runner for an injured batsman, which is the running between wickets and making good his ground. His real difficulty lay in deciding for Toshack whether that injured worthy should stand at square leg or at the crease—at which end he ought to be—and advising him loudly that he, Bill Johnston, was there to do the running and would he, Toshack, please withdraw from the fairway after playing the ball.

Johnston interspersed these well-thought-out duties with an amazing turn at the crease, in which his length of limb and the sabre-like curve of his bat recalled the famous Pyramid advertisement of the handkerchief spinning on end.

The act continued to the end of the day to bolster the sinking spirits of those Englishmen who had counted themselves happy about the game only twenty-four hours before and whose hopes were being shattered. Even Pollard, the hero of the morning, was submerged beneath the flood of strokes, though he and Bedser bowled gamely all day. Neither Cranston nor Laker, however, posed any problem sufficiently grave to give the batsmen pause. From the disasters of the morning, the Australian innings had developed power, grace and many runs, and Lindwall and Toshack (his Test batting average precariously intact) awaited the morning only thirty-nine runs behind England.

England—First Innings—496 (Washbrook 143, Edrich 111, Hutton 81, Bedser 79; Loxton 3 for 55)

Australia—First Innings

A. R. Morris, c Cranston b Bedser	. .	6·
A. L. Hassett, c Crapp b Pollard .	. .	13
D. G. Bradman, b Pollard	. .	33
K. R. Miller, c Edrich b Yardley .	. .	58
R. N. Harvey, b Laker	. .	112
S. J. E. Loxton, b Yardley .	. .	93
I. W. Johnson, c Cranston b Laker	. .	10
R. A. Saggers, st Evans b Laker .	.	5
R. R. Lindwall, not out	. .	76
W. A. Johnston, c Edrich b Bedser	.	13
E. R. Toshack, not out .	. .	12
Extras (b 9, l-b 14, n-b 3) .	. .	26
Total (for 9 wkts) .	.	457

Bowling Analysis

	O	M	R	W
Bedser . .	31	4	92	2
Pollard . .	37	6	103	2
Cranston . .	14	1	51	0
Edrich . .	3	0	19	0
Laker . .	30	8	113	3
Yardley . .	17	6	38	2
Compton. .	3	0	15	0

Fall of Wickets

1	2	3	4	5	6	7	8	9
13	65	68	189	294	329	344	355	403

Fourth Day—Monday, 26th July

Australia's one remaining wicket scored only one run in seven minutes, and then Lindwall edged a ball from Bedser to second slip, where Crapp nonchalantly caught it instep-high. Lindwall's seventy-seven had had a considerable effect on the feeling of the game as well as helping to reduce England's lead as low as thirty-eight. Toshack, not out, hobbled back to the pavilion beside Lindwall, bowed a little under the weight of his Test batting average of fifty-one.

Lindwall and Miller again bowled to Hutton and Washbrook. The wicket was still as peaceable a wicket as ever was seen on a fourth day, and the batsmen went steadily about their business. Although Lindwall occasionally brought the ball back off the pitch to strike him about the thigh or hip, Washbrook went undisturbedly on with his batting. Lindwall began with two maidens, but the next five overs of his opening spell cost him twenty-one runs: Miller's opening six overs cost five runs. Then Miller and Lindwall were off for Bill Johnston and Loxton; and then they were on again, and off again, and Hutton and Washbrook were still together: they had put on seventy-two at lunch, and Headingley ate its lunch happily.

After lunch Hutton and Washbrook put up the hundred, and thus made an opening partnership of a hundred in each innings of a Test match, as they did at Adelaide in 1946–7. It is a record for the same pair *twice* to put on an opening hundred in each innings of a Test Match. Now each in his own way began to move faster. At 129, Hutton hit Johnson for a long six to square leg and played his own handsome cover drive off Miller; Washbrook used his feet to get down the pitch to Ian Johnson and drive him straight for four. Washbrook pull-drove

Johnston to long-leg for what appeared to be a one-bounce four. But Harvey raced across, at toppling speed, and made the catch with his hands almost touching the ground, never checking in his full-stretch run. It was a catch which took the breath, and the applause for it and Washbrook were for some time indistinguishable. Then, to the first ball of Ian Johnson's next over, Hutton went down the wicket to drive, found the ball, dropping shorter than he had judged, was still not up to him, and hit it uncertainly up to mid-off, for Bradman to make an easy catch.

With the wickets of Hutton and Washbrook falling at the same total, several responsibilities devolved upon Edrich and Compton. Primarily England's task of the day was to score runs quickly so as to give Australia a fairly high total to go for on the fifth day of the match. Hutton and Washbrook had legitimately and wisely concentrated first on playing themselves into a sound start before attempting to force the game. Now they were out, and the new ball and Lindwall were only six overs away. Edrich and Compton needed quick runs against a sharp attack. They could go for the runs, but they knew that their dismissal might mean another England collapse and, if that happened, Australia, barring weather, would win easily.

Edrich, with an assurance born of his first-innings century, was the more certain of the two. Compton was obviously and consciously taking risks when he cut Ian Johnson and again when he had to move very quickly indeed to complete his intention of making another ball from the same bowler into a full-toss. The two Middlesex batsmen recalled their partnerships against South Africa when Lindwall and Miller took the new ball.

There was no spectator on the ground who did not

appreciate the immensity of the danger of these two bowlers when employing the new ball or recall the damage they had already done to English batting in the series. Yet Compton and Edrich, against this background of anxiety, treated the pace attack with, by Test standards, something approaching hilarity. Compton played a square cut off Lindwall so late that his stroke was within a sparrow's blink of being posthumous. Edrich made a ball from Miller into a half-volley, and hit it to the long-off boundary with a valedictory wave of the bat.

At the 200 England were appreciably behind a rate of a run a minute, but Compton was batting with assurance and had overtaken Edrich. Together they saw away the new ball and tea and the immediate post-tea fast spell. As the crowd breathed more freely, Bradman brought on Ian Johnson with a deep-set off-side field—which reflected the paucity of hope of either bowler or captain that the ball would turn appreciably.

Edrich overtook Compton with a savage burst of hitting against Ian Johnson—4, 4, 4, 6 off four consecutive balls. On the kill, Edrich is almost frightening, his feet take him on savage tip-toe to the ball, and his whole body is contorted with the violence of the blow he strikes. The innings was on the heels of the run-a-minute mental pace-maker when Edrich played forward confidently to Lindwall and was lbw. Crapp's orders were obvious. Taking barely half a dozen balls to play himself in, and playing his stroke characteristically late, he began to force the ball away powerfully and with good placing.

At this time it seemed possible that England would make good a threat which had been constant throughout the afternoon except for a few minutes after the Hutton-Washbrook dismissals—the threat to collar this hitherto swordlike Australian attack. It is certain that the absence of Toshack, nursing a troublesome knee and his batting average in the pavilion, had something to do with the situation. Toshack is incomparably good in shutting up one end: he cannot be hit safely away from his fieldsmen. But now Bill Johnston came on to bowl the cut leg-break from over the wicket. His long arms made the ball move off even the recalcitrant Headingley wicket, and he compelled respect even from the impassive but belligerent Crapp and a Compton who was promising every moment to become his most incalculable self.

Then Crapp, in attempting to force Lindwall off his back foot, played the ball on to his stumps—Johnston, in two overs, dismissed Yardley, Cranston (first ball) and Compton—and England were 278 for 6 wickets—316 runs ahead, with seven and a quarter hours' play left in the match.

Evans and Bedser (four fours in a score of seventeen) set confidently about reviving the innings; they went racing away and, after Bedser was out, Laker stayed with Evans to put on another thirty-two runs before the close of play, when England were exactly 400 runs on with 2 wickets to fall. The tail end had justified the efforts of the first four batsmen after the middle batting had sagged—as indeed it did regularly throughout the series. It had been a good day's cricket, not, perhaps, achieving the heights of Australia's innings of Saturday, but adding up, with the three preceding days, to a magnificent Test match—an even matching with brilliance from players on both sides, constant fluctuations and steadily good cricket.

England—First Innings—496 (Washbrook 143, Edrich 111, Hutton 81, Bedser 79; Loxton 3 for 55)

England—Second Innings

L. Hutton, c Bradman b Johnson . . .	57
C. Washbrook, c Harvey b Johnston . .	65
W. J. Edrich, lbw b Lindwall . . .	54
D. Compton, c Miller b Johnston . .	66
J. C. Crapp, b Lindwall	18
N. W. D. Yardley, c Harvey b Johnston .	7
K. Cranston, c Saggers b Johnston . .	0
T. G. Evans, not out	47
A. V. Bedser, c Hassett b Miller . .	17
J. Laker, not out	14
Extras (b 4, l-b 10, n-b 3). . . .	17
Total (for 8 wkts). . . .	362

Bowling Analysis

	O	M	R	W
Lindwall . .	25	5	84	2
Miller . .	20	5	52	1
Johnston . .	29	5	95	4
Loxton . .	10	2	29	0
Johnson . .	21	2	85	1

Fall of Wickets

1	2	3	4	5	6	7	8
129	129	232	260	277	278	293	330

Australia—First Innings—458 (Harvey 112, Loxton 93, Lindwall 77, Miller 58; Bedser 3 for 92, Laker 3 for 113)

Fifth Day—Tuesday, 27th July

Yardley batted again on the fifth morning, only to be entitled to use the roller. In the now-established tactic, he called for the heavy roller in the hope of breaking up the very dry wicket, thus making it reactive to spin. Evans and Laker made three runs off the two overs bowled before Yardley declared (345). Australia needed to make 404 runs in five and three-quarter hours to win. Thus the match resolved itself into a three-sided question of the state of the wicket, the fall of wickets and the relation of runs to clock.

Not for seventy years had a side won a Test match against a declaration, and England had not in the match reached the rate of scoring Yardley now challenged Australia to achieve—in the fourth innings and on the fifth day. On the other hand, the declaration was not the usual deadeningly safe declaration of the Test captain in fear of the pillory. Again, a draw was of no use to England and, if Yardley was to win, he had to offer Bradman an objective within possibility or the Australians would put up the shutters. The outfield was fast, as it had been throughout the match; the state of the wicket after Yardley's use of the heavy roller was not certainly predictable, but it would definitely be a little dusty.

Morris and Hassett opened again and scored six sober runs off the first six overs, bowled by Bedser and Pollard. Then Bedser was taken off after only three overs and Laker was called up. This was the first major climax of the day. If the ball turned appreciably, Laker might well bowl England to a win. He set two slips and a gully close to Morris's bat. Morris and Hassett took thirteen runs off the over: one ball of the over pitched to a length. Pollard bowled a maiden from the other end. In Laker's next over one or two balls turned, but not quickly. Bedser took over from Pollard, who had bowled six overs, four of them maidens, on a wicket patently useless to a bowler of his type. At one Hassett should have been stumped off Bedser. Laker's third, fourth, fifth and sixth overs were maidens, only a single was scored from his seventh—two runs off six overs since his disastrous start.

Forty-four runs had come in the first hour: Australia were behind the clock. Bedser and Pollard could, for the moment, keep the batsmen quiet, but there seemed no possibility that they could do anything to beat a good batsman on this wicket or through this dry air. So now Yardley put Denis Compton on to bowl the 'Chinaman.' There was no slow left-arm bowler in the side and no established leg-breaker; thus Compton was England's best chance, if possibly an expensive one, of turning the ball on the Headingley wicket. His first over cost ten runs, his second was a maiden, during which Morris went down the wicket to him and missed—and was not stumped—Evans did not gather the ball. Laker at the other end bowled two maidens. Then Compton caught and bowled Hassett with a fierce effort. Australia, 57 for 1 wicket in 73 minutes, were still behind the clock.

Bradman came in, and Laker posted three short legs close to his bat. Bradman at once hit him for four to long-off, against the spin. In his next over Laker bowled a ball to Morris which turned and lifted. Every pair of field-glasses on the ground was trained upon the wicket, but Laker did not repeat the feat.

Australia, 74 for 1 wicket in 83 minutes, were still behind the clock. Now England wanted a win, not a draw, and defensive bowling could at best only draw the match. The wicket was, if anybody's—and, for most of the England bowlers, anybody might have it as a gift—if anybody's, it was a leg-spinner's. There was no member of the England side who bowled the leg-break at all except Hutton. In his ten previous Test Matches against Australia, Hutton had bowled three overs and taken no wicket. In 1947, for Yorkshire, he took 4 wickets at 44 runs each. But he was the only leg-spinner in Yardley's eleven at Leeds, and Yardley used him—at a time when England had a runs-time advantage to gamble against wickets. Hutton might be punished—but a similar risk had just been taken with Compton and had succeeded. Hutton was Yardley's gamble for a win—he *had* to gamble.

Five fours were hit off five full-tosses in Hutton's first two overs. The Yorkshire crowd's cold unhappiness could be felt. His third over was a maiden; his fourth cost another ten runs. Yardley took Hutton off and put Compton on. Bradman edged Compton's googly to Crapp at slip, and Crapp, one of the two best slip fieldsmen in England, dropped it. At lunch Australia, with ninety-five runs in ninety minutes, were pressing hard on the clock.

After lunch Bradman gave an early chance, but then settled in with Morris, and together they marched down the afternoon. They were 288 at tea, and Bradman had been missed twice in consecutive overs. All afternoon England lacked a bowler who could flight the ball and spin. Compton looked the best of them, and he was at one stage hit for six fours in eight balls.

Bradman and Morris made their runs steadily, running like well-planned trains to their time-runs schedule, despite all Yardley could do to check them. Had the English fielding been as good as the Australian, the story might have been different. Eight chances were missed, and a batsman of the class of Bradman or Morris cannot be let off three times without the fielding side suffering.

None of the chances was absolutely easy, but none of them would have been called remarkable if taken. They should have been accepted by Test cricketers; since they were not, the side which missed them deserved to lose. Yardley took his regular wicket—that of Morris—and Miller was playing carelessly when Cranston had him lbw. Bradman was in with Harvey when Harvey made the winning hit at a quarter-past six. The great match of the first four days had spluttered out—on a day when the Australian batting outclassed an England side woefully short of a spin-bowler of flight and whose out-cricket was not good enough for a Test Match. Laker had not the flight to beat great batsmen on a quasi-perfect wicket.

It is almost impossible to leave the Fourth Test without saying that Wright or Hollies, even Jenkins of Worcester, would probably have won the match for England had they been in the team. Even among the natural spinners, Jack Young, or, better still, those bowlers of subtler flight, Roberts of Lancashire, Wardle of Yorkshire or John Clay, might have bowled out Australia.

For Australia it was a triumph of skill, stamina, strategy, good heart and great cricket. Morris, Bradman, Miller, Harvey, Loxton, Johnston, Lindwall had personal triumphs, but it was a great eleven that won.

England

L. Hutton, b Lindwall	81	c Bradman b Johnson	57
C. Washbrook, c Lindwall b Johnston	143	c Harvey b Johnston	65
W. J. Edrich, c Morris b Johnson	111	lbw b Lindwall	54
A. V. Bedser, c and b Johnson	79	c Hassett b Miller	17
D. Compton, c Saggers b Lindwall	23	c Miller b Johnston	66
J. C. Crapp, b Toshack	5	b Lindwall	18
N. W. D. Yardley, b Miller	25	c Harvey b Johnston	7
K. Cranston, b Loxton	10	c Saggers b Johnston	0
T. G. Evans, c Hassett b Loxton	3	not out	47
J. Laker, c Saggers b Loxton	4	not out	15
R. Pollard, not out	0		
Extras (b 2, l-b 8, w 1, n-b 1)	12	Extras (b 4, l-b 12, n-b 3)	19
Total	496	Total (8 wkts dec)	365

Bowling Analysis

	O	M	R	W		O	M	R	W
Lindwall	38	10	79	2	....	26	6	84	2
Miller	17·1	2	43	1	....	21	5	53	1
Johnston	38	13	86	1	....	29	5	95	4
Toshack	35	6	112	1	....	—	—	—	—
Loxton	26	4	55	3	....	10	2	29	0
Johnson	33	9	89	2	....	21	2	85	1
Morris	5	0	20	0	....	—	—	—	—

Fall of Wickets

1	2	3	4	5	6	7	8	9	10
168	268	423	426	447	473	486	490	496	496
129	129	232	260	277	278	293	330	—	—

Australia

A. R. Morris, c Cranston b
Bedser . . . . 6　c Pollard b Yardley 182
A. L. Hassett, c Crapp b
Pollard . . . . 13　c and b Compton . 17
D. G. Bradman, b Pollard . 33　not out . . 173
K. R. Miller, c Edrich b
Yardley . . . 58　lbw b Cranston . 12
R. N. Harvey, b Laker . 112　not out . . 4
S. J. E. Loxton, b Yardley . 93
I. W. Johnson, c Cranston b
Laker 10
R. A. Saggers, st Evans b Laker 5
R. R. Lindwall, c Crapp b
Bedser 77
W. A. Johnston, c Edrich b
Bedser 13
E. R. H. Toshack, not out . 12
　Extras (b 9, l-b 14, n-b 3) 26　Extras (b 6, l-b 9,
　　　　　　　　　　　　　　　　n-b 1) . . 16

　　　　Total . . 458　Total (for 3 wkts) 404

Bowling Analysis

	O	M	R	W		O	M	R	W
Bedser	31·2	4	92	3	....	21	2	56	0
Pollard	38	6	104	2	....	22	6	55	0
Cranston	14	1	51	0	....	7·1	0	28	1
Edrich	3	0	19	0	....	—	—	—	—
Laker	30	8	113	3	....	32	11	93	0
Yardley	17	6	38	2	....	13	1	44	1
Compton	3	0	15	0	....	15	3	82	1
Hutton	—	—	—	—	....	4	1	30	0

Fall of Wickets

1	2	3	4	5	6	7	8	9	10
13	65	68	189	294	329	344	355	403	458
57	358	396	—	—	—	—	—	—	—

Australia won by 7 wickets.

CHAPTER SIX

THE FIFTH TEST MATCH

Played at the Oval, 14th, 16th, 17th and 18th August, 1948

WITH Australia 3–0 up at the last Test, the English selectors wisely looked to the future and, where changes were to be made, they introduced young men of promise to blood them early against Australia. Of the players at Leeds, Cranston was omitted because he had been a gamble and had not come off. Pollard and Crapp were left out, presumably on grounds of age. Laker's form at Leeds precluded him from selection even on his own county ground. Three of the four fresh players had already done well against the Australians—J. G. Dewes of Cambridge University and R. T. Simpson of Notts as batsmen, and Eric Hollies as a bowler. The fourth fresh player, Allan Watkins of Glamorgan, had shown promise as a left-handed bat, was useful as a medium-pace bowler in county cricket, and he was the best short-leg fieldsman in England. Jack Young, left out of the thirteen at Leeds, was included in the twelve players for final selection. Before the match Washbrook was declared unfit, and Crapp was summoned to take his place. The eleven was finally:

N. W. D. Yardley (Yorkshire)
L. Hutton (Yorkshire)
J. G. Dewes (Cambridge University and Middlesex)
W. J. Edrich (Middlesex)
D. Compton (Middlesex)
J. C. Crapp (Gloucestershire)
A. Watkins (Glamorgan)

T. G. Evans (Kent)
A. V. Bedser (Surrey)
J. Young (Middlesex)
E. Hollies (Warwickshire)

and Reggie Simpson was twelfth man, as he had been for the Trent Bridge match.

Toshack was still suffering from knee trouble, but Barnes was once more able to play. Ian Johnson was left out, and Ring, a leg-break bowler, came in in his place.

First Day—Saturday, 14th August

Alarming rumours of flooding of the Oval ground brought early comers to inspect the wicket—if they could. They could not. They had to be satisfied with the firm state of the outfield and the lightish colour of the distant middle as seen through field-glasses for their advance information. Yardley won the toss and chose to bat.

When play started, half an hour late at midday because of earlier rain, Hutton went in first with John Dewes, a thickly built and cheerfully boyish-looking left-hander. Each batsman was off the mark with a single in the first over—which was bowled by Lindwall with no indication of any liveliness in the wicket. The second over was from Miller, whose first ball had Dewes groping for a late in-swing—a most unusual ball for the left-hander to receive in England to-day—and it bowled him. Miller had bowled three overs and taken one wicket for 2 runs—a stroke by Edrich—when he came off for Johnston. Edrich, after going decorously for twenty minutes, hooked hard at Johnston, and was well caught by Hassett just behind the square-leg umpire.

Denis Compton received some short balls from Lindwall which rose because they *had* to, not from any evil in the wicket. One of these knocked his bat out of his hand and flew along the ground to Hassett at long-leg. Compton was a little flustered: he thought he would take a run, started to run, decided to go back for his bat—and yet run—and was so stranded that Hassett might easily have run him out. Hassett, with a smile completely friendly, refused even to try to run him out and allowed him to regain his crease. The gesture made little difference: Compton hooked a short ball from Lindwall very hard and downwards, only for Morris to make a brilliant catch in the position where Hassett had caught Edrich.

Miller now came back for Lindwall, and Crapp, who had done nothing at all for twenty minutes at the crease, was caught at the wicket off a motionless bat. Miller had now taken two wickets for 3 runs.

All this time Hutton, at the opposite end from these disasters, was playing calmly and safely. He made few run-scoring strokes, certainly took no risks, but, on the other hand, he never looked like being out. There still, and men were thankful, was an unruffled Hutton, who had not played a single hurried shot in the ninety minutes to lunch—and England were 29 for 4 wickets.

Immediately after lunch Yardley was bowled by a very fast ball from Lindwall which kept a little low—35 for 5. Watkins followed him, to be struck a crushing blow straight on the point of his left shoulder by another short-pitched ball from Lindwall. He was lbw to Johnston just afterwards for 0, and returned to the pavilion in much pain —42 for 6. Then Lindwall took the remaining four wickets, three of them clean bowled. Hutton batted calmly and extremely well through a disastrous innings. Near the end he hit Lindwall hard and high to the Vauxhall end boundary for the only four of the innings. Next he played a sound leg-glance, also off Lindwall, and Tallon made about three yards to catch it one-handed— *left*-handed—a bare two inches off the ground. It would have been a brilliant catch made by a bare-handed fieldsman unhampered by pads—for a man padded and gloved it was memorable—and no other wicket-keeper in the world, I fancy, could have made it a chance.

England were out for 52—their lowest total against Australia in England—Lindwall 6 for 20—Miller 2 for 5 —and Ring, included as a leg-spinner, did not bowl! Although sawdust was necessary for the bowlers' run-ups, the wicket had been covered, and there was Hutton's play to prove that there was nothing wrong with the wicket—only one ball at which Hutton played passed his bat.

The triumph was Lindwall's, a reward for the peak performance of a thoughtful and enthusiastic season's bowling and an historic feat by a man with a firm place in cricket history.

If anyone retained any suspicion that there was life in the wicket, Barnes and Morris at once removed it when they began the Australian innings. Watkins, still in considerable pain from his heavily bruised shoulder, made no mention of his injury, but bowled, and, of course, could not bowl well. A number of critics who had, presumably, seen him struck by Lindwall did not enquire whether Watkins was suffering from the blow, but hurried into bitter criticism of him. Meanwhile Barnes and Morris batted like a civic procession, each in character, and, in just over two hours, they scored 117 for the first wicket.

Then Hollies—who had bowled his leg-break patiently, accurately and with well-controlled flight—persuaded Barnes to play at a leg-break pitched well outside his off-stump. Having once played out at it, away from his body,

Barnes was bound to snick it, and Evans made a very good catch.

The huge crowd had waited long for Bradman to make his last Test appearance—and now they cheered him all the way to the wicket. Yardley went to meet him and shook hands with him, and the English team gave him three cheers. Bradman played his first ball from Hollies firmly in the middle of the bat. The second was a googly: Bradman played outside it and was bowled—was his eye a little misted at his reception I wonder? A lesser man's might well have been. After such a reception a man could hardly do other than score a duck or a century—and a duck did Australia no harm.

Hollies continued to flight the ball well, but Morris was as precise, as wide-batted, as thoroughly over every ball as ever. Hassett stayed with him until the end of play.

England—First Innings

L. Hutton, c Tallon b Lindwall	30
J. G. Dewes, b Miller	1
W. J. Edrich, c Hassett b Johnston	3
D. Compton, c Morris b Lindwall	4
J. C. Crapp, c Tallon b Miller	0
N. W. D. Yardley, b Lindwall	7
A. Watkins, lbw b Johnston	0
T. G. Evans, b Lindwall	1
A. V. Bedser, b Lindwall	0
J. Young, b Lindwall	0
E. Hollies, not out	0
Extras (b 6)	6
Total	**52**

Bowling Analysis

	O	M	R	W
Lindwall . .	16·1	5	20	6
Miller . .	8	5	5	2
Johnston . .	16	4	20	2
Loxton . .	2	1	1	0

Fall of Wickets

1	2	3	4	5	6	7	8	9	10
2	10	17	23	35	42	45	45	47	52

Australia—First Innings

S. G. Barnes, c Evans b Hollies . . .	61
A. R. Morris, not out	77
D. G. Bradman, b Hollies	0
A. L. Hassett, not out	10
Extras (b 3, n–b 2)	5
Total (for 2 wkts) . . .	153

Bowling Analysis

	O	M	R	W
Bedser . .	15	4	35	0
Watkins . .	4	1	19	0
Young . .	19	6	38	0
Hollies . .	32	7	50	2
Compton . .	2	0	6	0

Fall of Wickets

1	2
117	117

Second Day—Monday, 16th August

Monday opened as slowly as only a Monday could. Hassett was in one of his most adamant moods. He sauntered into the line of the ball and allowed it to hit his bat as if the whole thing were an academic exercise. Bedser bowled very sharply for a long time on a typically discouraging Oval wicket: in his support, Edrich could not find the extra yard of pace to make him dangerous to such batsmen. Young was his invariably steady self; but Hollies—Hollies was the bowler England had been lacking all the series. He bowled a length and flighted the ball and spun it. Morris handled him enquiringly, Hassett thoughtfully, and while neither batsmen could get him profitably away, Hollies could not quite break through. Morris came comfortably and inevitably to his century, and the two Australians played through an hour and a half of the morning. It was the five-day-match process of 'making certain'—the process designed to squeeze the heart out of the losing side.

It was Young, coming on for his second spell, who got rid of Hassett—lbw to a ball which straightened—for thirty-seven out of the two-and-a-quarter-hour third-wicket stand of 109. Miller came next, with instantly apparent ideas of enlivening the morning's play—bent on getting at the bowling. Hollies bowled impeccably to him: Miller checked at one ball. He reached too far forward to the next, which was a healthy leg-break, missed by the size of the break, overbalanced, fell forward, and was stumped: 243-4-5. Harvey did not relish the turning ball, but used his quick eye and feet to hit it twice very hard indeed. The attempt at a third hit gave Young a catch at mid-off—and another wicket to Hollies: 265-5-17. Morris continued unmoved, playing handsomely within the bounds of perfect safety—bounds extended by his magnificent footwork. The watchers at the 1948 series became so accustomed to the presence of Morris at the wicket that, after a time, comment on him ceased. His gifts are great, and they had been exhibited over the hours. He lost Loxton to Edrich. Loxton showed little relish for the new ball: several times he played with confidence at the place where the ball would have been if it had not swung, was once disturbed by Bedser's leg-cutter, and then poked in an annoyed fashion at a short ball from Edrich as it went by—and Evans caught him standing back.

Lindwall began as belligerently as he had left off at Leeds. Two fours set him well under way, but he hit too soon at a good-length ball from Young, and was caught by Edrich, fielding, unusually for him, at cover-point. Tallon, too, began to attack the bowling as soon as he came in, and continued to bat well after Morris was out— which seemed like a suspension of the laws of Nature. Tallon played a stroke to third man where Simpson was fielding (he was taking the place of Watkins, whose bruised shoulder had set and stiffened so that he could not field). Morris ran, but Simpson's pick-up and throw were so rapid and so single an action that Morris was clearly run out. To have missed his double century by four runs was disappointing for Morris—and for many who admitted him ready for any of the statistical seals to be placed upon a great batsman.

Then two very good catches at slip by Crapp finished off the Australian first innings, to general surprise, for 389. They had, certainly, a lead of 337, but the early morning play had threatened an even more astronomical advantage. Apart from Morris, *who scored half their runs*, the Australian batsmen had not done well against steady English bowling backed by England's best fielding of the series.

Hutton and Dewes again went in first, and again Miller and Lindwall received them hostilely. Hutton once more displayed what it means to be an utterly skilful batsman, moving with grace and certainty, never out of the heart of the play. Dewes was solid: he is not a graceful batsman, but he is both dogged and thoughtful. He played one remarkable stroke: it was a perfectly executed orthodox hook, to a ball from Lindwall rising over his leg-stump. Everyone looked to square-leg, and then, bewildered, looked back to see that the ball had gone all along the ground, off the middle of the meat of the bat for four—to third man: a most remarkable stroke. It was again the inswinger to the left-hander—Lindwall's natural swing—that beat Dewes, and bowled him by way of bat and pad for ten: 20 for 1 wicket.

With an hour left for play, Edrich came in to bat better than at any time during the series. It is remarkable that he so frequently pulls out superb form and stroke-play when he goes in late in the day. He and Hutton handled the entire Australian bowling so capably that Englishmen began to forget the collapse of Saturday—and to hope. To be sure, no spectator of any country could have hoped to see two of his country's batsmen play better than Edrich and Hutton played on that rather gloomy August evening—so gloomy indeed, that when, with five scheduled minutes remaining, a Lindwall flyer flew by Edrich unseen, the umpires stopped play for bad light.

England—First Innings—52 (Hutton 30; Lindwall 6 for 20, Miller 2 for 5, Johnston 2 for 20)

Australia—First Innings

S. G. Barnes, c Evans b Hollies	.	.	.	61
A. R. Morris, run out .	.	.	.	196
D. G. Bradman, b Hollies	.	.	.	0
A. L. Hassett, lbw b Young .	.	.	.	37
K. R. Miller, st Evans b Hollies	.	.	.	5
R. N. Harvey, c Young b Hollies .	.	.	17
S. J. E. Loxton, c Evans b Edrich .	.	.	15
R. R. Lindwall, c Edrich b Young	.	.	9
D. Tallon, c Crapp b Hollies	.	.	.	31
D. Ring, c Crapp b Bedser .	.	.	.	9
W. A. Johnston, not out	.	.	.	.	0
Extras (b 4, l-b 2, n-b 3) .	.	.	.	9
Total	.	.	.	389

Bowling Analysis

	O	M	R	W
Bedser . .	31·2	9	61	1
Watkins .	4	1	19	0
Young . .	51	16	118	2
Hollies . .	56	14	131	5
Compton .	2	0	6	0
Edrich . .	9	1	38	1
Yardley .	5	1	7	0

Fall of Wickets

1	2	3	4	5	6	7	8	9	10
117	117	226	243	265	304	332	359	389	389

England—Second Innings

L. Hutton, not out	.	.	.	.	19
J. G. Dewes, b Lindwall	.	.	.	10
W. J. Edrich, not out .	.	.	.	23
Extras (b 1, n-b 1) .	.	.	.	2
Total (for 1 wkt)	.	.	.	54

Bowling Analysis

	O	M	R	W
Lindwall	5·5	0	20	1
Miller	4	0	13	0
Loxton	6	1	9	0
Johnston	5	2	10	0
Ring	4	4	0	0

Fall of Wickets

1
20

Third Day—Tuesday, 17th August

Barely had the day's cricket slid into its grooves, barely had the crowd recalled its hope of the night before, than Lindwall burst into the English innings. He let loose his fastest ball of all, pitched it at good length and it moved in off the pitch to bowl Edrich—as it would probably have bowled any batsman in the world.

Hutton was still Hutton: to Hutton the crowd clung for comfort, for it was comfort they needed. Defeat in so relatively even a match as the Leeds Test, or rain preventing a win at Manchester, these were reverses to be accepted as the rub of the green. The battering of the first innings at the Oval, however, was different, the English reaction was to hit back—and Hutton was hitting back. There was more of affection in their attitude to Hutton in this fifth Test of 1948 than when he broke the Test record on the same ground ten years earlier. Then he had been the successful batsman: in this later day he stood as the solid rock without whom the side must collapse.

Hutton and Compton, the two greatest batsmen in English cricket, now came together at the wicket, the major rampart against Lindwall, Miller and Johnston. Hutton was playing his strokes on the off-side with an

imperious follow-through of the bat, punching the ball
into the barrier of four fieldsmen placed around the arc
of the covers for the bowling of Johnston or Ring. All
four were perpetually in action, and their standard of
fielding never flagged under the steady peppering they
received from Hutton. Compton was not himself, his
scoring strokes appeared less natural, more contrived,
than when he is at his best. Still, he and Hutton stayed
until lunch and a total of 121 for 2 wickets.

Just four runs after lunch their stand, and the wildest
English hopes, were broken. Bill Johnston made a ball
float away from Compton and lift slightly off the pitch,
Compton snicked it, and Lindwall held an extremely
sharp catch at slip: 125-3-39.

Crapp, who always has an eye to eternity, began to
take a long look at the Australian bowling. Miller's bowling about this time was a subject for study. He ran the
gamut of pace, both swings, several sorts of active spin,
and one or two which did not redeem a promise to turn.
Then he hit Crapp full in the middle of the skull with
a rising ball. Crapp, remarkably, remained on his feet.
After a few minutes he resumed his innings—under the
handicap of a headache, which was still with him when
he caught the Bristol express on Wednesday afternoon.

At last Hutton faltered and was caught by Tallon,
standing back to Miller, for an historic sixty-four, which
must stand with his record score of 1938. This innings
was full of good strokes and of cool, measured defence
under a horrible burden of anxiety and impending defeat.
It was an innings to make one wonder whether, if Washbrook could have been there with him, all this could have
happened. Now the light began to go. Miller bowled
Crapp; Ring had Watkins as his first Test wicket, and
even Evans was bowled by a ball from Lindwall which

he never saw in the gloom; then the umpires stopped play for bad light. At once rain began to fall and ended the day. England were 159 runs behind the Australian first-innings total, with only three wickets to fall, and there were two days for the weather to clear and the wicket to dry.

England—First Innings—52 (Hutton 30; Lindwall 6 for 20, Miller 2 for 5, Johnston 2 for 20)

Australia—First Innings—389 (Morris 196, Barnes 61; Hollies 5 for 131, Young 2 for 118)

England—Second Innings

L. Hutton, c Tallon b Miller . . .	64
J. G. Dewes, b Lindwall	10
W. J. Edrich, b Lindwall	28
D. Compton, c Lindwall b Johnston . .	39
J. C. Crapp, b Miller	9
N. W. D. Yardley, not out	2
A. Watkins, c Hassett b Ring . . .	2
T. G. Evans, b Lindwall	8
Extras (b 9, l-b 4, n-b 3)	16
Total (for 7 wkts) . . .	178

Bowling Analysis

	O	M	R	W
Lindwall .	22·5	5	43	3
Miller .	15	6	22	2
Loxton .	10	2	16	0
Johnston .	25	11	37	1
Ring .	28	13	44	1

Fall of Wickets

1	2	3	4	5	6	7
20	64	125	153	164	167	178

Fourth Day—Wednesday, 18th August

The players went through the motions required formally to end the game in twenty minutes of Wednesday morning. Australia had won the rubber and the series weightily and beyond all question. Each department of the English team had succeeded at least once in the series —but had more often failed.

There was a large crowd, interested, rather than excited, waiting rather than demanding, about the pavilion when Bradman said good-bye, and the 1948 Australians took leave of their latest victory.

England

L. Hutton, c Tallon b Lindwall	30	c Tallon b Miller	64
J. G. Dewes, b Miller	1	b Lindwall	10
W. J. Edrich, c Hassett b Johnston	3	b Lindwall	28
D. Compton, c Morris b Lindwall	4	c Lindwall b Johnston	39
J. C. Crapp, c Tallon b Miller	0	b Miller	9
N. W. D. Yardley, b Lindwall	7	c Miller b Johnston	9
A. Watkins, lbw b Johnston	0	c Hassett b Ring	2
T. G. Evans, b Lindwall	1	b Lindwall	8
A. V. Bedser, b Lindwall	0	b Johnston	0
J. Young, b Lindwall	0	not out	3
E. Hollies, not out	0	c Morris b Johnston	0
Extras (b 6)	6	Extras (b 9, l-b 4, n-b 3)	16
Total	52	Total	188

Bowling Analysis

	O	M	R	W		O	M	R	W
Lindwall .	16·1	5	20	6	....	25	3	50	3
Miller .	8	5	5	2	....	15	6	22	2
Johnston .	16	4	20	2	....	27·3	12	40	4
Loxton .	2	1	1	0	....	10	2	16	0
Ring .	—	—	—	—	....	28	13	44	1

Fall of Wickets

1	2	3	4	5	6	7	8	9	10
2	10	17	23	35	42	45	45	47	52
20	64	125	153	164	167	178	181	188	188

Australia—First Innings

S. G. Barnes, c Evans b Hollies . . .	61
A. R. Morris, run out	196
D. G. Bradman, b Hollies . . .	0
A. L. Hassett, lbw b Young . . .	37
K. R. Miller, st Evans b Hollies . . .	5
R. N. Harvey, c Young b Hollies . . .	17
S. J. E. Loxton, c Evans b Edrich . . .	15
R. R. Lindwall, c Edrich b Young . .	9
D. Tallon, c Crapp b Hollies . . .	31
D. Ring, c Crapp b Bedser . . .	9
W. A. Johnston, not out . . .	0
Extras (b 4, l-b 2, n-b 3) . . .	9
Total . . .	389

Bowling Analysis

	O	M	R	W
Bedser . .	31·2	9	61	1
Watkins .	4	1	19	0
Young .	51	16	118	2
Hollies .	56	14	131	5
Compton .	2	0	6	0
Edrich . .	9	1	38	1
Yardley .	5	1	7	0

Fall of Wickets

1	2	3	4	5	6	7	8	9	10
117	117	226	243	265	304	332	359	389	389

Australia won by an innings and 149 runs

The Test averages are interesting for several reasons. They reflect the courage of the English tail-end batting of Evans, Bedser and Laker, but they show the mighty Australian batting towering above the figures of ordinary courage. Please to notice, too, my friend Ern Toshack—fifth in the Australian batting figures, despite the fact that he was not fit to add to his aggregate at the Oval. Much of the story of the Tests is in these averages: they do not, however, show any figures of fielding, because none is conceivable—run-saving cannot be tabulated. If fielding figures were available, they would show Australia at least as superior there as in batting and bowling.

AVERAGES, 1948

Test Matches: Australia—won 4; drawn 1

AUSTRALIA
Batting

	Innings	Not Out	Runs	Highest Score	100s	Aver.
A. R. Morris .	9	1	696	196	3	87·00
S. G. Barnes .	6	2	329	141	1	82·25
D. G. Bradman .	9	2	508	173*	2	72·57
R. N. Harvey .	3	1	133	112	1	66·50
E. R. H. Toshack .	4	3	51	20*	—	51·00
S. J. E. Loxton .	3	0	144	93	—	48·00
A. L. Hassett .	8	1	310	137	1	44·28
R. R. Lindwall .	6	0	191	77	—	31·83
D. Tallon .	4	0	112	53	—	28·00
K. R. Miller .	7	0	184	74	—	26·28
W. A. Brown .	3	0	73	32	—	24·33
W. A. Johnston .	5	2	62	29	—	20·66
I. W. Johnson .	6	1	51	21	—	10·20

Also batted: D. Ring 9; R. Saggers 5.

Bowling

	Overs	Maidens	Runs	Wickets	Aver.
R. R. Lindwall .	222·5	57	530	27	19·62
K. R. Miller .	137·5	43	301	13	23·15
W. A. Johnston .	309·5	92	630	27	23·33
E. R. H. Toshack .	173·1	70	364	11	33·09
D. Ring .	28	13	44	1	44·00
S. J. E. Loxton .	63	10	148	3	49·38
I. W. Johnson .	183	60	427	7	61·00

Also bowled: S. G. Barnes 0 for 11; A. R. Morris 0 for 24.

* Signifies not out.

ENGLAND

Batting

	Innings	Not Out	Runs	Highest Score	100s	Aver.
D. Compton	. 10	1	562	184	2	62·44
C. Washbrook	. 8	1	356	143	1	50·85
L. Hutton	. 8	0	342	81	—	42·75
W. J. Edrich	. 10	0	319	111	1	31·90
T. G. Evans	. 9	2	188	50	—	26·85
J. Laker	. 6	1	114	63	—	22·80
A. V. Bedser	. 9	1	176	79	—	22·00
J. C. Crapp	. 6	1	88	37	—	17·60
N. W. D. Yardley	9	0	150	44	—	16·66
T. Dollery	. 3	0	38	37	—	12·66
J. Young	. 5	2	17	9	—	5·66

Also batted: C. J. Barnett 8 and 6; A. Coxon 19 and 0; K. Cranston 10 and 0; J. G. Dewes 1 and 10; G. Emmett 10 and 0; J. Hardstaff 0 and 43; E. Hollies 0* and 0; R. Pollard 3 and 0*; A. Watkins 0 and 2; D. V. P. Wright 13* and 4.

Bowling

	Overs	Maidens	Runs	Wickets	Aver.
N. W. D. Yardley	. 84	22	204	9	22·66
E. Hollies	. 56	14	131	5	26·20
A. V. Bedser	. 274·3	75	688	18	38·22
R. Pollard	. 102	29	214	5	42·80
J. Laker	. 155·2	42	472	9	52·44
A. Coxon	. 63	13	172	3	57·33
J. Young	. 156	64	292	5	58·40
D. V. P. Wright	. 40·3	12	123	2	61·50
K. Cranston	. 21·1	1	79	1	79·00
W. J. Edrich	. 53	4	238	3	79·33
D. Compton	. 37	6	156	1	156·00

Also bowled: C. J. Barnett 0 for 36; L. Hutton 0 for 30; A. Watkins 0 for 19.

* Signifies not out.

SKETCHES OF THE PLAYERS

D. G. BRADMAN
(*South Australia and Australia*)

IT is, so it seems, pleasant to be an Australian and to feel
that you have a stake in Don Bradman. Whether it is as
pleasant to be Don Bradman is doubtful. I do not know a
cricketer who would change places with him.

It is impossible to discuss Bradman the cricketer without first recognizing Bradman the public figure. More
people are interested in Bradman, but not in cricket, than
are interested in Bradman *and* cricket. Because he is Bradman, he is constantly singled out from his team-mates. If
he attempts to step back into the line of the team, the
person who has approached him is offended. If, with
normal courtesy, Bradman accepts the advance as a
gesture of well-meant admiration—then he widens the
gap between himself and his fellow-players. He is news
on the field and potential gossip off it.

Because he is 'a success', because he is a public figure,
because he is Bradman, he has missed much of the best
of cricket. He has never been a temporary failure among
other temporary failures, never shared with ten others,
neither appreciably greater nor appreciably less than
himself, that sympathy and mutual delight in temporary
success which the other cricketer knows. He has never
played a game at Bath or Melton Mowbray or Basing-
stoke where players outnumber spectators, and a batsman
who is out may take off his pads and saunter unmolested,
hands in pockets, round the ground to the marquee for a
quiet drink. Horace Hazell can throw his boots and
flannels into a bag and catch the 'bus to Bristol; may talk

to the man in the next seat unrecognized, or, if he is recognized, is recognized as 'Horace,' a pleasant chap and one of us. But your Bradman must hurry to a car and hide himself from the crowd that pickets his hotel.

Rising forty, which is veteran age for an Australian cricketer, he came to England in 1948 for his last tour. 'Is he still the Bradman of old?' was the question. Of course he damned well wasn't. Any man in possession of all his faculties *must* develop and change in ten years. D. G. Bradman of the 1948 Australian team was a great batsman in his 1948 right. He scored hundreds, brilliant hundreds, hundreds which could hardly have been more appropriate if he had stage-managed them. Because he was an older man, eighteen years older, than the Bradman of 1930, he was less hungry for records. He was concerned to make runs for his side, no doubt he found it pleasant still to make a century. He could still annihilate almost any bowling on a friendly wicket. But some of the old fierce single-mindedness which urged him to go on breaking record after record was gone. The quality of his single-mindedness had not weakened, but the will to that particular single-mindedness was blunted by maturity and a wider consciousness, a different *general* aim. At forty some of the strokes of the early twenties are no longer business cricket: like Hobbs, Bradman, with cricketing maturity, discarded those strokes of youth which had demanded the extremes of the eye and speed of youth. Yet Bradman in 1948, forty years old, was still playing strokes impossible to any other cricketer in the world. He stood at the crease perfectly immobile until the ball was on its way to him, then his steps flowed like quicksilver out of trouble or into position to attack. He could still pull the ball outside the off-stump accurately wide of mid-on's right hand to avoid a packed off-side field. He still played the ball off his back foot past mid-off before that fieldsman could bend to it. He still hit through the covers with the grace of a swooping bird. He could cut and glance, drive, hook and pull, and he could play unbelievably late in defence. He often made a shaky start —the shakiest starts of all before his biggest scores. Those who had never seen Bradman bat until 1948 saw a great batsman: those who knew his batting between 1930 and 1938 saw a new greatness, a greatness owing more to the brain. He could grow tired now—naturally, as any who have spent more than a few minutes 'in the middle' would expect. There were times when, as the ball came slowly to him in the field, with the batsmen not attempting a run, he stooped like a very tired man. But let speed be essential in a stop and throw, and he moved with most of the old dancing alertness—never more than during his last Test at the Oval.

As a captain he did the right thing almost automatically, for the idiom of the game is become his native language. High-shouldered, shirt collar turned up to the chin, cap pulled well on, he walked backwards to his position in the field as the bowler walked to his mark. His eyes moved alertly as a blackbird's, and he would stop the game while, back cautiously turned to the batsman, he passed his latest intelligence to the bowler. He set the defensive field with true Australian mastery. He nursed his bowlers wisely and received magnificent service from his fieldsmen.

From late April until late September 1948, in England, Donald George Bradman played cricket, captained a cricket team, made speeches, was polite to bores, ignored the spite of those who grudged him that he had earned, kept his temper and consolidated a great public reputation.

LEONARD HUTTON
(*Yorkshire and England*)
AND
CYRIL WASHBROOK
(*Lancashire and England*)

Len Hutton and Cyril Washbrook are by no means indistinguishably linked in my mind like the 'William-anmary' of the history books, although they happen currently to open the innings for England. I link them here because together, in the cricket season of 1948, they justified themselves and their kind.

English professional cricket is unique: only Spanish bullfighting, of the sports of the world, approaches it as a life, a study and a craft. English cricket has scientifically evolved on the bowling side, and scientifically overcome on the batting side, all the variations and the varying employments of the spin and swing of a ball and the deployment of fieldsmen. The growth· of the game has been a history, a history with shifting stresses and landmarks, crises as fundamental, within cricket, as the stages of English social history which cricket has so often reflected.

Craftsmanship is becoming almost a curiosity in everyday life in England, and the craftsman an occasional echo of what was once a way of living for an entire social class. Assuming that cricket is solvent as an entertainment, then, the professional cricketer survives as a craftsman because he cannot be replaced by a machine and because he himself desires to practise a craft which is for him the way to a romantic adventure. The young man is attracted to cricket by delight in the clash of his powers against those of another man, by the prospects of glory, by the desire for an active life in the open air. The financial gain is negligible, which ensures that the game is played by enthusiasts. With increasing experience of the game, the young adventurer becomes a man who, on the subject of his game, is profoundly knowledgeable.

Two of the finest examples of the craftsman-cricketer in the game to-day are Hutton and Washbrook; dissimilar in almost every other way, they are so closely akin in this that they cannot be regarded separately in any assessment of the play in England in 1948.

Since the war, only an ageing Alf Gover has remained in English cricket to recall the former glories of English fast-bowling. County opening batsmen have become accustomed, day in, day out, to playing fast-medium swing bowling, usually inswing.

In 1948, for the first time since 1939, the English batsmen had faced to really fast outswing bowling and under English conditions which allow appreciably more swing and for a longer period than in Australia.

Hutton and Washbrook at Nottingham, despite Hutton's 74, and again at Lord's were manifestly uneasy. They were failing to time Miller and Lindwall—they themselves recognized this, and it struck at the very roots of their batting. They could no longer rely upon their trained and seasoned reflexes, but had now to try to superimpose thought upon their normally automatic assessment of the ball bowled and the stroke required. Hutton carried an additional handicap in an injury which had permanently shortened one arm. Here again, thought had to be first substituted for, and then superimposed upon, reflex, to reorientate his strokes to this shortening.

No practice could be found for Hutton and Washbrook anywhere in England against bowling of comparable speed. They took their practice only in matches against

Australia. In the first two Tests it was an inescapable conclusion that Washbrook's involuntary flick at the rising ball outside the off-stump might bankrupt his batting in the Tests. And, despite his good scores, Hutton's manifest physical dislike of the short rising ball was likely not only to lose him his wicket, but also to disturb the morale of the batsmen who followed him.

Hutton and Washbrook are men who live their cricket: each will talk cricket in preference to any other subject under the sun. The problem of adjusting their batting afresh to fast bowling stayed with them over weeks of the season. Characteristically, Hutton was more anxious than Washbrook, and the force of the impact of this new problem was more apparent on his play than on Washbrook's. Each, separately, solved the problem, fundamentally, out of his craft-sense for the game.

Hutton missed the Old Trafford Test when Washbrook played magnificently. At Leeds both Hutton and Washbrook were master-batsmen again, the new problem overcome—it may be that Washbrook's confidence acquired at Manchester was communicated to Hutton. At the Oval, with Washbrook unable to play because of injury, Hutton was the only English batsman to play the Australian fast bowling confidently. This was no mere gathering of runs against Australia, neither should it be interpreted as showing the greatness of two men alone. Washbrook and Hutton are the best type of professional cricketer, and, in overcoming the challenge of Australian fast bowling, they vindicated English professional cricket.

The contrasts between the two are striking as they walk out together. Washbrook, short but high-shouldered, has an air of briskness, he throws his head up and his jaw is firmly set, his cap is at a gay angle. His whole bearing is self-reliant, his eyes move very quickly, and he can be monosyllabic while he concentrates on his batting. Test cricket has rarely seen the Washbrook of county cricket. There, match after match, after playing himself in very quickly, he will whip an attack mercilessly and score at racing speed. Against any bowling short of the very fastest he scores runs in amazing profusion between cover-point and slips, accepting the challenge of the rising ball outside his off-stump and flicking' it away with strokes of exquisite timing. He drives commandingly, particularly past mid-on, and his hooking of the short ball is merciless. The essence of Washbrook as a batsman is in his allowing the inswinger to hit him when it would be dangerous to play it. By quick judgment and artful thigh-padding he takes the ball on the leg, his bat lifted out of danger. See Washbrook's face then, and you see the face of a man who knows what he is doing—and knows he knows.

As the pair go out to the wicket, Hutton is likely to be looking down to the ground. At the crease he is more obviously nervous than Washbrook. He touches his cap to the bowler, turns his bat in his hand, picks at the chest of his shirt and taps the crease in quick nervous pats. Yet between delivery of ball and playing of stroke his degree of cool concentration and thought, as opposed to pure reflex, is striking—it results in his being able to play extremely late and on fuller evidence than most batsmen.

The early Hutton tended to extreme competence in the building of long scores. But in 1948 he was one of the most handsome stroke-players in the game. Hutton, Compton and Miller of modern Test batsmen most tend to exhibit the full glory of off-side play. From the drive through mid-off to the late cut, Hutton excels. The adjustment to his shortened arm has resulted in a slightly abbreviated follow-through, but his strokes are executed with grace and fluency. Such is his judgment of strokes that, in playing a ball from the line of the leg-stump to mid-on, he plays with a perfect pendulum of bat, which passes closer than seems possible to the left pad. Hutton has every stroke in the game, and employs them with such consummate artistry that more than one member of the Australian team has declared that he is the best batsman in England.

For me, Hutton is at his best in playing spin-bowling. Then his extremely deep knowledge and the profundity of his cricket are most apparent. Against the turning ball his footwork carries him perfectly into position for the stroke played close to the pads, and, whether he plays the ball or, at the last possible moment, leaves it to pass outside the stumps, his head is always absolutely over the line of it. He is a master of deflection of the turning ball, playing it late and *with* the spin, his stroke is sympathetic to the break, and the ball seems to be persuaded, rather than hit, away. There are many players who, because their batting is soundly based, their back-play strong and their eye good, play spin-bowling soundly. Hutton is more than sound; he is imaginative in dealing with the spinner, so that his stroke is the perfect, spin-sensitive stroke for each particular delivery.

The Australians regarded Hutton's batting as a major problem of the 1948 series. To the end of solving the problem, Miller and Lindwall, at their freshest, employed the short ball rising along the line of Hutton's body. Now this is a form of attack which no batsman in the world likes. It combines the physical danger of being hit—a very serious matter at such pace—with the cricketing danger of the edged stroke. After a few experiments,

Hutton decided that the cricketing danger of playing these deliveries was too great to be profitably accepted. He therefore, like Edrich, against whom it was employed less often, decided to concentrate on avoiding the kicking ball. In this aim, however, one of Hutton's chief merits as a batsman contributed to his difficulties. He moves automatically into the line of the bowled ball—once there he now had to decide upon the ball to avoid—and this at the great speed of Lindwall or Miller. The same ball, bowled by Miller to Compton when Compton was well set at Trent Bridge, beat him by its speed. A bouncer from Lindwall knocked Compton's bat out of his hand at the Oval and appeared to unsettle him. Every batsman dislikes the bouncer, no English batsman to-day plays it well, if only from lack of practice—and it was bowled to Hutton more than to any other batsman in the English team. By the time he came back into the side at Leeds, he was escaping disaster when it was bowled to him: at the Oval he appeared its master.

Len Hutton is a naturally shrewd Yorkshireman. On the subject of cricket his judgment on play or a player is as near infallible as any of our time, yet about cricket as it is for him he has still the enthusiasm of a boy; because he also is imaginative, this enthusiasm can drive him into over-anxiety.

Something more than a Test Match or a series of Test Matches depended upon Hutton and Washbrook when they went out to bat at Leeds. When they made their two century first-wicket stands, they not only laid a bogy, but they also vindicated the craft in which they stand high.

KEITH MILLER

(*New South Wales and Australia*)

Keith Miller, the finest all-rounder in the world, is the direct opposite of Don Bradman in one important respect —a respect which indicates a fundamental contrast between the two. Don Bradman, as a public figure, has taken seriously his duty to the public. Keith Miller, finding himself a public figure, shrugs his shoulders and continues to be Keith Miller.

The Keith Miller he continues to be is a happy, comradely and often humorous man. He has discovered that the world is his oyster, and he proposes to swallow it without caring a damn what anyone thinks. Before the oyster can be swallowed, however, it has to be opened— Keith Miller likes to open his oysters for himself—and, if he has to do so with his bare hands, then that is exactly the sort of challenge he relishes.

He is the gayest and most stimulating of company— with an ease of manner which puts his companions at ease. He is, too, generous—in a gentler fashion than those might suspect who know him only at long range. As to what the critics say of him, what the crowd thinks of him, or what the averages declare to be his value, he cares nothing at all. He is rather annoyed that his freedom to do anything he wants to do should be complicated by his being a famous cricketer. Of all the members of the Australian party he was the most uncomplicated—if his character was unusual, it was, nevertheless, almost entirely without contradictions. Keith Miller decided long ago how he wanted to live, and everything he does is consistent with that decision. Yet he, of all the team, was least understood by English crowds.

Keith was, and is, potentially the best batsman, the best bowler and the best fieldsman in the world. Consider—when the Australian batting threatened to straggle off, at Leicester, in the second game of the tour, Keith Miller pulled it together with a double century. When, against Yorkshire, his side was in trouble on a turning wicket, Miller converted himself into an off-break bowler to bowl Yorkshire out—and then he made the top score of the innings to save the Australian batting. In the first Test, particularly after Lindwall was injured and unable to bowl, Miller became the match-winning bowler. At Leeds, after Bradman and Hassett had been dismissed in one over, it was Miller who, with one of the greatest innings ever played, pulled the game round and set his side on the way to winning. When Crapp and Hutton threatened a stand at the Oval, Miller came on to break it. If the almost impossible catch came his way, it was a challenge to be accepted—and caught—and he caught it.

Yet, when the Australians were carving a batting record out of Essex bowling at Southend, Miller took his bat out of the course of the first ball bowled to him—refusing even to offer at it—and allowed himself to be bowled. Keith Miller has never been interested in cheap runs or easy wickets—he relishes a strong challenge and will go to meet it. Away from cricket—with a single skittle standing at the end of a long and uneven skittle-alley, then, despite the handicap of rough cider, Keith could say he would hit it—and hit it.

He reacted to admiration as to the buzzing of a mosquito in the ear, but, out of his good nature, he was always considerately courteous to his admirers. The cheering of a crowd is a noise to him and little more—but how he loved it when, as the crowd at Leicester surged forward to see Bradman come out at No. 3—Miller walked out. With the broadest of grins he bowed, in dumb show he apologized for being Miller—and then went to the wicket and scored a double century. He would bowl a bouncer at a batsman for the sheer fun of annoying the crowd. One of his closest friends is Denis Compton, yet, when Denis was the batsman whose challenge Miller's side had to face and overcome if they were to win—he did not hesitate to bowl bumpers to him in real cricket-earnest. Yet the feeling between those two great cricketers was always one of camaraderie.

Let us examine the equipment of Keith Miller as a cricketer. He is of magnificent but carefully proportioned physique, comfortably six feet tall. As a batsman his foot-work often appears as improvised as Denis Compton's, yet it takes him late and with amazing speed to the pitch of the ball. He can hit with immense power but, true to his nature, he is likely to hit the best ball hardest. He will drive Alec Bedser straight for four, but he will probably prefer to score from the leg-spinner by means of a late cut. He hits on the off-side regally and with delight. Bowl him the short ball, and you will see a hook of frightening power, comparable with Bradman's hook—but unlike it, because this is Miller's hook. The characteristic of Bradman's hook is safety and control, of Miller's, fierce power and speed—which achieves the same result of being safe and effective. Often Miller will experiment at the crease, playing the ball impossibly, yet successfully, late—almost as if he were trying to make the whole thing more difficult.

Miller, the bowler, was as dangerous as Lindwall. Miller is a fast bowler when he wants to be. If he prefers, he can be fast-medium, or, again, a medium-pace off-spinner. No doubt, if he wanted, he could be a leg-break bowler—in the first Test he ran up to the wicket in the midst of a spell of fast-bowling and bowled a perfect-length googly. His swing is varied and well controlled, his pace from the pitch is enormous. The point about a bouncer from Keith Miller is that it is not pitched very short. Such is the perfection of his casual but high delivery that it will drop only fractionally short of good length and yet rise as high as a long-hop from a fast bowler of less perfect action. Now watch him bowl the bumper. The batsman hastily ducks and the ball flies viciously past him. The next few balls are of good length, but the batsman is obviously looking for another bumper and is ready to duck under it. Now Miller drops the ball on the same spot as that from which his bumper flew—but it is not the same ball—he has checked his body-swing—and the ball, instead of leaping, goes straight at the stumps. The batsman should be there to play it—if he has ducked he is lbw—with any part of his body. This Miller is the least mechanical of bowlers: he has no normal run. He will measure out a run, certainly, and probably bowl his first ball from that mark but, again and again, he will walk back towards his mark and then, when he is half-way to it, will suddenly swing round on his heel, run-up and bowl. But his run-up does not condition the ball he is about to deliver: some of Miller's fastest balls of the 1948 summer were bowled with a half-length run. Above all, he loves to bowl against good batsmen; as for the rabbits, he would rather give them easy runs than bowl them out.

Miller usually fielded at gully or in the slips for Bradman's team: in either position he was a wonderful catcher, performing a gymnastic miracle to reach the catch at all—and another to retain hold of it without touching it to ground when his body landed. He was brilliant at extra-cover, where he picked up and threw in with a single eager action. He is probably the best cover-point in the world—only Rowan of South Africa compares with him among contemporary players I have watched. Yet Miller rarely fielded at cover in 1948.

Here was a great cricketer—when he was needed to be a great cricketer. Here was that rare cricketer without conceit, without respect for averages, who never cared what the crowd thought of him. Yet he was as human as the man in the next hospital bed; he was as gay as a sparrow; he never dogmatized; he knew cricket inside out and loved the game. Although he could give of his transcendent best only when the moment demanded it, he was desperately keen for Australia to win the Tests; he never relaxed for a single ball; he never failed to appeal for anything. Keith Miller did not care who had a personal success so long as Australia won.

Keith Miller among cricketers reminds us that 'great' is a great word; and, as one facet of *living*, he is a great cricketer.

RAY LINDWALL
(New South Wales and Australia)

An old cricket saying declares that all wicket-keepers and fast bowlers are mad. Certainly some fast bowlers have taken wickets without that concentration on strategy, length and control demanded of those who bowl with less pace—for the obvious reason that sheer speed will often beat the bat. Certainly, too, there have been relatively successful fast bowlers who were poor as batsmen and fieldsmen and who generally lacked cricket-sense. Ray Lindwall is that rare cricketer, the highly intelligent fast bowler. He was one of the greatest

successes of a side which broke records for success.
Before he was even picked for the tour, he gave up football rather than risk injury which might prejudice his
selection or impair his performance. In 1948 he would be
twenty-six—peak age for a fast bowler: in this tour lay
his clearest opportunity of achieving cricketing greatness.
He foresaw his own success, planned it, carried out his
plan with care and thought, and deserved all that he
achieved.

In the opening matches of his first tour Lindwall was
not particularly fast. He ran and bowled well within
himself. In the unaccustomed damp chill of the English
climate his muscles were less supple than in the drier air
of Australia, and he did not propose to risk muscle injury
by bowling at full stretch too soon—particularly since
he had also to become used to softer ground underfoot.
Again, while he tuned up physically, he was also adjusting his technique to fresh conditions. The good-length
ball in England pitches at least a foot nearer the batsman
than on the faster wickets of Australia. Again, his normal
swing, which had been slight in the rarefied atmosphere
where he had developed his bowling, became quite
pronounced in the more humid English air: the ball
which went straight on after pitching on a Bulli soil
wicket, 'moved' off the 'green' in England. Ray Lindwall
studied these phenomena, in relation to his bowling in
detail and at his leisure—taking thought to add cubits to
his bowling stature.

The month of May was a period of training, preparation and building towards peak performance. Then, in
the tenth match of the tour—against Notts at Trent
Bridge—Lindwall 'slipped himself'—a real test on so unhelpful a wicket. He rested the three days of the next
match, and returned to the side against Sussex—on

another plumb batsman's wicket at Hove—and, at full
speed, took 11 wickets for 59 runs. Now he was ready for
the first Test three days away.

In the Trent Bridge Test he injured a groin. A less-
thoughtful man might have indulged heroics and gained
a spurious reputation for 'bravery' by continuing to bowl
and thus aggravating an injury until it became a permanent disability. Keen as he was to bowl in the Test, Lindwall knew that no man can face the strain of bowling fast
unless he is perfectly fit. If a pace bowler feels the slightest
reluctance to place full strain on any part of his body, he
destroys his rhythm, and fast bowling without rhythm
loses its essential pace from the pitch.

Although he batted, he made no attempt even to field.
He began treatment for his injury at once. By the Lord's
Test he was again fit and in form to shoot away
the main strength of the English batting. At Manchester and at Leeds he was sharp in attack, and at the
Oval no English batsman except Hutton could stay
against him.

He is as scientifically relaxed between deliveries as a
veteran boxer between rounds. As he walks back to his
bowling mark he allows his whole frame, so thick as to
belie his height of five feet eleven, to relax completely—
even to the extent of scuffling his feet. His trousers are
wide, and his preliminary arm-swings drag up his shirt to
flap loosely in the breeze: thus not the slightest check is
imposed upon his movement. As he turns to run in he
braces himself and pauses a moment as if for complete
mental and physical stocktaking. Then he starts body-
swing and run in slow tempo.

His run-up is cumulative, he accelerates gradually and
easily over twenty yards, and bowls at the top speed
of his run. He drags his right foot, as many great fast

bowlers have done, but, by careful practice, has made it unnecessary for him to worry about, or be worried by, the possibility of delivering a no-ball. His arm is a little low at the moment of release, which deprives him of an inswing. He commands the more dangerous outswing, however, bringing the ball away from the right-hand bat late and sharply, and, in place of the inswinger, bowls the ball which comes in off the pitch.

The major feature of Lindwall's bowling is its variety and his concealment. He bowls many balls which are appreciably slower than his fastest and, while he can bowl a most precise length and direction—particularly when pitching his outswinger where it must be played—he also employs a most alarming bumper. This bumper took relatively few wickets of itself, but it took many without actually being bowled. Because batsmen were constantly looking for it, when it did not come for one or two consecutive overs, they were half-expecting it every ball, so it constantly took wickets indirectly, by psychological effect.

There was never anything mechanical about Lindwall's bowling—except possibly his strictly uniform action, which gave no indication to the batsman of the type or pace of the ball he was about to bowl. Always, in addition to his pace, he was trying to outwit the batsman. Well-nursed by Bradman, he always had the extra yard of pace at his disposal, and was effective, whether he was employing his full pace or playing upon the batsman's looking for it.

The ball with which he beat Emmett at Manchester was masterly both in itself and in its context. While Lindwall nursed himself up to full speed, Emmett was almost allowed to play himself in against bowling well short of his fastest: Emmett was moving confidently into the line of the ball almost as it left the bowler's hand. Then came the fastest ball, a little, only a little, short of a length, but with the extra yard of pace—its length and speed made it completely different from any earlier ball of the innings. Emmett, with a startled jump, involuntarily and hastily, popped up a simple catch to Barnes at forward short-leg.

Because Lindwall is a fast bowler, there was an automatic tendency to ask just how fast he was. If a comparison must be made, then he was not quite so fast as Larwood. It may be that 'Hopper' Read of Essex and Jack Gregory at times bowled a ball slightly faster than Lindwall at his fastest. Such a question blinks the fact that Lindwall as a fast bowler was not solely a man who bowled *fast*—he did not take wickets by speed alone, but by *strategic* use of his capacity to bowl very fast, in conjunction with thought, control, length and variation. It must be said that he might have been less successful if the English batsmen of 1948 had had opportunities for practice against bowling of comparable speed. Against that argument, Lindwall's gifts were such that even in a good year for fast bowlers as we have known them, he must have been outstandingly successful.

THE PAVILION LIBRARY

All books from the Pavilion Cricket Library are available through your local bookshop or can be ordered direct from Pavilion Books Ltd.

	hardback	paperback
Through the Caribbean Alan Ross	£10.95	£5.95
Hirst and Rhodes A. A. Thomson	£10.95	£5.95
Two Summers at the Tests John Arlott	£10.95	£5.95
Batter's Castle Ian Peebles	£10.95	£5.95
The Ashes Crown the Year Jack Fingleton	£10.95	£5.95
Life Worth Living C. B. Fry	£10.95	£5.95
Cricket Crisis Jack Fingleton	£9.95	£4.95
Brightly Fades the Don Jack Fingleton	£9.95	£4.95
Cricket Country Edmund Blunden	£9.95	£4.95
Odd Men In A. A. Thomson	£9.95	£4.95
Crusoe on Cricket R. C. Robertson-Glasgow	£9.95	£4.95
Benny Green's **Cricket Archive**	£9.95	£4.95

Write to Pavilion Books Ltd.
196 Shaftesbury Avenue
London WC2H 8JL

Please enclose cheque or postal order for the cover price plus postage

UK   55p for first book
24p for each additional book to a maximum of £1.75

Overseas   £1.05 for first book
35p for each additional book to a maximum of £2.80

Pavilion Books reserve the right to show new retail prices on covers which may differ from those previously advertised in the text or elsewhere and to increase postal rates in accordance with the Post Office.